CHINA'S SPIES

CHINA'S SPIES

BEIJING'S ESPIONAGE OFFENSIVE

NIGEL WEST

FRONTLINE
BOOKS

First published in Great Britain in 2025 by
Frontline Books
An imprint of Pen & Sword Books Ltd
Yorkshire – Philadelphia

ISBN: 978-1-39906-571-9

Typeset by Lapiz Digital
Printed and bound by CPI UK

The Publisher's authorised representative in the EU for product safety is
Authorised Rep Compliance Ltd., Ground Floor,
71 Lower Baggot Street, Dublin D02 P593, Ireland.
www.arccompliance.com

For a complete list of Pen & Sword titles please contact:

PEN & SWORD BOOKS LTD
47 Church Street, Barnsley, South Yorkshire, S70 2AS, UK
E-mail: enquiries@pen-and-sword.co.uk
Website: www.pen-and-sword.co.uk

Or

PEN AND SWORD BOOKS,
1950 Lawrence Road, Havertown, PA 19083, USA
E-mail: uspen-and-sword@casematepublishers.com
Website: www.penandswordbooks.com

China can best be described as an intelligence state.

Nigel Inkster
Secret Intelligence Service, 1975–2006

The greatest long-term threat to our nation's information and intellectual property and to our economic vitality, is the counterintelligence and economic espionage threat from China.

Christopher Wray
FBI Director, 7 July 2020
Hudson Institute

The most game-changing challenge we face comes from the Chinese Communist Party. It's covertly applying pressure across the globe.

Ken McCallum
MI5 Director-General, 2020–4
Thames House, 6 July 2022

There are several municipal politicians in British Columbia and in at least two provinces there are ministers of the Crown who we think are under at least the general influence of a foreign government.

Richard Fadden
Director, Canadian Security
Intelligence Service 2009–13
22 June 2020

CONTENTS

BOOKS BY NIGEL WEST

Spy! (with Richard Deacon)
MI5: British Security Service Operations 1909-45
MI6: British Secret Intelligence Service Operations 1909-45
A Matter of Trust: MI5 1945-72
Unreliable Witness: Espionage Myths of World War II
The Branch: A History of the Metropolitan Police Special Branch
GARBO (with Juan Pujol)
GCHQ: The Secret Wireless War
The Friends: Britain's Postwar Secret Intelligence Operations
Molehunt: The Search for the Soviet Spy in MI5
Games of Intelligence
Seven Spies Who Changed the World
Secret War: The Story of Special Operations Executive
The Faber Book of Espionage (Anthology)
The Illegals
The Faber Book of Treachery (Anthology)
The Secret War for the Falklands
Counterfeit Spies
Crown Jewels (with Oleg Tsarev)
VENONA: The Greatest Secret of the Cold War
The Third Secret: Solidarity, the CIA and the KGB's Plot to Assassinate the Pope
MASK: MI5's Penetration of the Communist Party
The Guy Liddell Diaries (Ed. 1939–42; 1942–45)
The Historical Dictionary of British Intelligence
The Historical Dictionary of International Intelligence
At Her Majesty's Secret Service
The Historical Dictionary of Cold War Counterintelligence
The Historical Dictionary of World War II Intelligence
The Historical Dictionary of Sexspionage
TRIPLEX: Secrets from the KGB Archives
The Historical Dictionary of Ian Fleming's James Bond
The Historical Dictionary of Naval Intelligence
SNOW (with Madoc Roberts)

Historical Dictionary of Chinese Intelligence (with I.C. Smith)
Historical Dictionary of Signals Intelligence
MI5 in the Great War
Double Cross in Cairo
Black Ops
Cold War Spymaster
Churchill's Spy Files
Spycraft Secrets
Codeword OVERLORD
Spy Swap
The Historical Dictionary of Cold War Intelligence
Spies Who Changed History
Hitler's Nest of Vipers: The Rise of the Abwehr 1933-42
Hitler's Trojan Horse: The Fall of the Abwehr 1942-45
Classified! The Adventures of a Molehunter

GLOSSARY AND ABBREVIATIONS

AFB	Air Force Base
APT	Advanced Persistent Threat
ASIO	Australian Security Intelligence Organisation
CBP	US Customs & Border Protection
ChIS	Chinese Intelligence Services
CIA	Central Intelligence Agency
CIIE	China International Import Expo
CSIS	Canadian Security Intelligence Service
DARPA	Defense Advanced Research Projects Agency
DIA	Defense Intelligence Agency
DoC	US Department of Commerce
DoD	US Department of Defense
DoJ	US Department of Justice
FBI	Federal Bureau of Investigation
HCSEC	Huawei Cyber Security Evaluation Centre
HPSCI	House Permanent Select Committee on Intelligence
HSI	Homeland Security Investigations
JSSD	Jiangsu Province Ministry of State Security
MI5	British Security Service
MSS	Ministry of State Security
NIH	National Institutes of Health
NKVD	Soviet intelligence service
NSA	National Security Agency
NSB	Taiwan's National Security Bureau
NUDT	National University of Defence Technology
OGPU	Soviet intelligence service
PLA	People's Liberation Army

PLA2   People's Liberation Army Second Department
PLAAF   People's Liberation Army Air Force
PLAN   People's Liberation Army Navy
SIS   Secret Intelligence Service
SSBN   Submarine, Ballistic, Nuclear

INTRODUCTION

While many of Chinese President Xia Jinping's increasingly aggressive foreign policies, manifested by expansion into the South China Sea, trade confrontation with Australia, and political suppression in Hong Kong, have become obvious, there has been a covert dimension to the offensive that has gone largely unreported outside the 'Five Eyes' (the US-UK-Canada-Australia-New Zealand intelligence forum) liaison.

Beijing's Ministry of State Security (MSS) has significantly shifted its priorities to hostile penetration of the US security and intelligence community, as has been demonstrated by the recent cases of Glenn Shriver, Jerry Chun Shing Lee, Ron Rockwell Hansen, Kevin Mallory, Dickson Yeo, and the brothers David and Alexander Yuk Ching Ma.

Hitherto the MSS has concentrated, at the direction of the Chinese Communist Party, on the collection of foreign technology and proprietary information, while also monitoring political dissidents, Tibetan and Taiwanese nationalists, and Uyghur and Falun Gong religious activists. The MSS also tended to recruit ethnic Chinese and was less interested in the collection of political intelligence or mounting influence operations.

The MSS has now undergone a radical change in doctrine and, having consolidated its grip on supposedly independent commercial joint ventures and academic research institutions, is leveraging control over these ostensibly legitimate enterprises to access intelligence agencies now perceived as adversaries, such as the CIA and FBI.

As the rhetoric and tensions between the West and China mount, and with the current US administration calling America's relationship with Beijing 'the biggest geopolitical test of the 21st century', China's unseen espionage offensive is one of the most serious developments in recent times in an increasingly unstable world.

Unlike the world's other intelligence agencies, relatively little is known about the MSS, and only two known MSS have been arrested and convicted of crimes in the United States. The first was 42-year-old Xu Yanjun, the deputy division director of the Sixth Bureau of the Jiangsu provincial MSS who in November 2021 was convicted in Cincinnati of economic espionage and sentenced to 20 years' imprisonment. Xu, alias Qu Hui and Zhang Hui, claimed to represent the Jiangsu Science and Technology Promotion Association, and was accused of having enticed David Zheng, an ethnic Chinese engineer employed since 2012 by General Electric Aviation, to China in March 2017, ostensibly to present an academic paper at the Nanjing University of Aeronautics and Astronomics, but then he cultivated him as a source of sensitive information about composite aircraft gas turbofan engine technology. GE Aviation had invested heavily in the development of ceramic material with the French Safran Group, details of which interested Xu.

During the trial the FBI revealed that Xu had been engaged in industrial espionage since 2013, and claimed there was a direct link between his activities, having thought he had successfully recruited Zheng, and malware that had been downloaded onto the laptop of a Safran project manager, Frederic Hascoet, during a visit to China in January 2014.

Zheng and Xu agreed to meet again, in Belgium, but the engineer reported the episode to the FBI and in January 2018, having been asked for 'system specification, design process' information, was given a two-page document that included a company proprietary information warning. This was passed by Zheng, acting as a double agent, to Xu when they met in April 2018, and Xu was arrested. He was indicted in October 2018, along with eleven others, and extradited to Ohio for trial. Although the FBI was unable to extract any information from Xu's iPhone, it was possible to download his iCloud back-up account which was found to contain incriminating evidence which helped secure his conviction.

One of the prosecution witnesses was a former Boeing employee, Sun Li, who testified that he had been approached by Xu in 2015 with an offer to pay his annual travel expenses to see his father in China. One of Xu's emails read: 'Boeing being an international defence enterprise, it must have sufficient experience for us to reference. I think there is a lot of room for an exchange even in your field of expertise.'[1]

The imprisonment in the United States of an MSS officer arrested in Europe was a major breakthrough for the Western counter-intelligence community and marked a significant milestone in dealing with the challenge of China's spies.

Although there is abundant evidence of Chinese intelligence activity, and not just in the field of technology transfer and the theft of intellectual property, Western agencies know painfully little about the internal structure, personalities, order-of-battle or deployment of Chinese intelligence services (ChIS) beyond the existence of three principal protagonists: the first is the MSS, which is answerable to President Xi's State Council and to the Party's Politburo Standing

Committee. Most of the MSS staff, estimated at 50,000, are based at provincial state security bureaux. In June 2018 a White House policy document assessed the MSS's overseas strength at 40,000. However, playing the numbers game is inherently redundant in a Chinese environment when every individual citizen, every state-managed entity, be it an academic institution, cultural centre, commercial enterprise or private company, can be co-opted to collaborate with the relevant authority. In practical terms this means almost *everyone* and *everything* can become an intelligence asset, thereby giving the security apparatus unlimited resources – a concept hard to grasp in the West.

This 'whole state' approach exists in parallel to two other organisations that routinely provide cover for ChIS clandestine operations: the United Front Work Department exists to maintain a relationship with the worldwide Chinese diaspora, but inevitably this ostensibly benign, culturally-orientated association peddles influence, monitors dissidents and provides a convenient concealment for covert activities. Similarly, the Political Work Department Liaison Bureau seeks to identify and influence (or interfere with) policy-makers, both activities that impinge on MSS responsibilities.

The other ChIS components are the Second Department of the People's Liberation Army (PLA2) which is controlled by the Central Military Commission, chaired by President Xi, and a relatively new agency, the Strategic Support Force, which is responsible for conducting signals intelligence and cyber warfare. In the absence of inside sources, or well-informed defectors, the only way to judge the performance of these organisations is to identify and assemble to pieces of the jigsaw. Certainly there is a need for hard facts, rather than speculation and conjecture, as was expressed by the Parliamentary Intelligence and Security Committee in July 2023, concluding an inquiry conducted over a period of nearly five years.

China almost certainly maintains the largest state intelligence apparatus in the world. The nature and scale of the ChIS are – like many aspects of China's government – hard to grasp for the outsider, due to the size of the bureaucracy, the blurring of lines of accountability between party and state officials, a partially decentralised system, and a lack of verifiable information.[2]

Chapter I

HONEY BADGER

We've now reached the point where the FBI is opening a new China-related counterintelligence case about every 10 hours. Of the nearly 5,000 active FBI counterintelligence cases currently underway across the country, almost half are related to China.

Christopher Wray
FBI Director, 7 July 2020
Hudson Institute

In 1985, at the height of the Cold War, the CIA's Soviet/Eastern Europe Division noted with growing alarm the escalating number of losses that it was experiencing in terms of sources dropping from sight. Not only were individual agents being recalled to Moscow, but the KGB appeared to be taking elaborate measures to conceal the exact nature of the purge, if that indeed was what it was. The institutional reaction to this set of circumstances was the establishment of AM/LACE, a task force to investigate the losses and advise on what had gone wrong. This was the classic counter-intelligence reaction to a very specific challenge, but the prospects were not good. In such circumstances the first step is to establish the nature of the problem and then take the appropriate countermeasures, but the evidence itself was nebulous. The questions to be addressed were themselves vague. Was this a result of some communications compromise, perhaps a failure in tradecraft, a double agent penetration or a combination of different influences? Was there any evidence of a mole? What were the common denominators, if any? Could innocent lapses be a possible explanation? Such inquiries are invariably doomed to failure because a mole is sufficiently skilled to cover his/her tracks professionally, and finding links between the cases from the files was unlikely to provide any useful pointers. Moles do not leave telltale signs of their existence, and know the traps to avoid. Counter-intelligence specialists learn their trade by studying past cases,

1

so they know how to evade detection. Not surprisingly, AM/LACE would drift on for years, making little or no progress. When, after seven years, there was a breakthrough, it was not a lead that emerged through dint of solid research, but rather a lucky chance that was an unexpected and entirely fortuitous consequence of adopting an aggressive strategy. In a law enforcement content, this was the equivalent of a stymied detective concentrating not on the crime itself, but focusing on the personalities capable of committing the offence. As the old hands in the counter-intelligence business are fond of remarking, 'the vigilance of colleagues never caught a spy; nor did study of the files'.

AM/LACE was wound up after the arrest of the FBI's Robert Hanssen in 2001. The first penetration, by Aldrich Ames, was terminated with his exposure in February 1994, following an unexpected tip regarding his overseas travel. Then it was realised there must have been a second mole, and Hanssen was caught when he was betrayed by a venal Soviet retiree. Put simply, the investigators' strategy of old-fashioned bribery would achieve better results than conventional sleuthing.

This was the background to a joint FBI/CIA investigation that lasted nine years, would identify two moles, and involve the deaths of a dozen assets. Faced with not-dissimilar horrors in 2010, when the CIA's Far East Division experienced losses on an equally debilitating scale, the Clandestine Service's management initiated a task force, code-named HONEY BADGER to find out what had gone wrong with up to eighteen potential cases. The joint FBI/CIA operation was run out of a secret facility in northern Virginia and included no more than ten or so individuals, all considered expert in Chinese operations by their respective agencies.

Whereas AM/LACE, headed by the FBI's John Quattrocki, had been handicapped by inter-agency rivalry as the FBI component was convinced from the outset that the leak came from the CIA, whereas the Counterintelligence Centre was less certain and resented the assumption that the culprit could not be in the FBI. Accordingly, there was the inevitable disagreements, with the FBI staff concluding that the compromises was due to simply sloppy tradecraft by CIA personnel.

The challenge for HONEY BADGER was infinitely greater than anything AM/LACE had faced. The KGB was well known to CIA analysts who could rely on a drip-drip of information relating to the organisation, personalities and operations supplied by defectors. This kind of source was unpredictable, in the sense that a 'walk-in' might materialise at any moment without warning, and the key element in handling such material is the analyst's readiness to spot the single item that might be relevant to the investigation. Furthermore, the collapse of the Soviet Bloc had offered unprecedented opportunities to buy insider knowledge from opponents who, five years earlier, would never have contemplated selling secrets. The new Russian Federation was a free-for-all, Wild West environment in which loyalty counted for nothing and pensions had become worthless.

In contrast, Beijing's Ministry of State Security (MSS) remained relatively opaque, rarely suffered defectors and, by Western standards, conducted its business in a very unusual manner. Conventional counter-intelligence techniques that worked so well against the Soviet target, such as intensive physical and technical surveillance on a KGB *rezidentura*, barely concealed in diplomatic premises, simply did not gain any traction against suspected MSS targets who appeared to operate independently, without the support of a station or station chief.

Defectors, the hardy perennials of the counter-intelligence matrix, were few and far between, the best of all having been Yu Qiangsan, code-named PLANESMAN, who had switched sides in Hong Kong in November 1985 and had proved himself to have been exceptionally well-informed about MSS staff, operations and assets. His knowledge had been acquired over many years, for he was the adopted son of Kang Sheng who, until his death in 1975, had headed the Ministry of Public Security. Furthermore, Kang Sheng had been a close family friend of Mao Zedong's wife, Jiang Qing, and was a member of the privileged ruling elite. Although there had been other MSS turncoats, none had accumulated the knowledge possessed by PLANESMAN who had been persuaded to defect by his French mistress. PLANESMAN had been exfiltrated to the United States in an operation code-named JADE POWDER and placed in a resettlement programme. Once in the FBI's hands PLANESMAN identified a long-serving CIA officer, Larry Wu-Tai Chin, as an MSS mole. The information supplied by PLANESMAN led to Chin's arrest and conviction, but he committed suicide in his cell in February 1986 before he could be sentenced. Nevertheless, Chin had given a detailed confession to the FBI in which he acknowledged that he had omitted to mention his retirement from the CIA in January 1981, and had continued thereafter to sell supposedly authentic, up-to-date information to his MSS handlers who appeared not to notice any change in the quality of Chin's reporting.

PLANESMAN died in 2013, having served as a consultant to all the 'Five Eyes' membership, and since then only a couple of intelligence defectors have been declared publicly, among them Wang Liqiang who sought political asylum in Australia in November 2019. The Australian Security Intelligence Organisation later concluded that Wang was a conman who had peddled hair-raising stories about supposed MSS influence operations and corrupt politicians, but was basically a fraud. Another defector, who was taken seriously, was 37-year-old Chen Yonglin who fled the PRC consulate-general in Sydney with his wife and daughter in May 2005 and was granted political asylum. Chen, who had been posted to Sydney in 2001, subsequently described how Falun Gong had been one of his principal intelligence collection targets.

The realisation that the MSS had been preoccupied with what were essentially domestic security issues, such as monitoring Tibetan and Taiwanese nationalists, Uighur activists, democracy campaigners and Falun Gong adherents, had, in one sense, been reassuring to Western observers who concentrated on the growing evidence of MSS participation in technology transfer, an apparent response to the Chinese determination to modernise.

In retrospect, confidant that the MSS was undergoing a discernible metamorphosis, from an opportunistic, ubiquitous bureaucracy seeking to exploit perceived weaknesses in Western business to steal mainly economic secrets, with varying degrees of sophistication, counter-intelligence analysts perceived a developing maturity that suggested a change in direction. Hitherto, the MSS had conformed to a pattern which, characteristically, blurred the boundaries between industrial espionage, which typically involved the theft of intellectual property, patented manufacturing techniques and commercially-sensitive proprietary data, and the 'operational games' more closely associated with the KGB during the Cold War. Put simply, there was some evidence that the MSS was shifting from a relatively primitive agency, with limited objectives, into a serious contender. Thus between March 2008 and July 2010 the US Department of Justice (DoJ) successfully prosecuted twenty-six cases of Chinese espionage and convicted forty-four defendants.

A retrospective review of recent espionage cases appeared to suggest that the MSS transition had been driven in part by opportunities that must have looked too attractive to ignore. One such was Ronald M. Montaperto, a 68-year-old former Defense Intelligence Agency (DIA) analyst who had joined the Agency in 1981 and was promoted head of the China Section, but in 1989 had made an unsuccessful application for a transfer to the CIA. Instead, he took a post at the National Defense University. In 2000 he contributed an article 'China: The Forgotten Nuclear Power' to the journal *Foreign Affairs*.[1]

Reportedly Montaperto had been betrayed by a defector in 1991, and was suspected of having compromised a technical source that had disclosed Chinese involvement in illicit arms sales to Iran, Syria and Pakistan, but an investigation proved inconclusive and no further action was taken. Montaperto subsequently moved to Hawaii where he was appointed dean of the Asia-Pacific Center for Security Studies. Re-interviewed in 2003, Montaperto admitted to having been cultivated by the Chinese embassy's air attaché Colonel Yu Zhenghe and to contact with Colonel Yang Qiming, to whom he had passed classified information verbally. In June 2006 Montaperto pleaded guilty to mishandling classified information and served four months' imprisonment. In his defence, Montaperto averred, quite accurately, that while at the DIA he had been cleared to talk to foreign air staff, and thus his estimated sixty meetings had been entirely legitimate. In such circumstances the polygraph may be regarded as less effective as the routine question 'Have you had any undeclared meetings with hostile foreign nationals?' may be redundant.

What can now be seen as the turning-point in the MSS's growing professionalism was its recruitment of a student, Glenn Shriver, who was an undergraduate at Grand Valley State University, Michigan when he joined a summer study programme in Shanghai, and then spent a year at the East China Normal University, studying languages and international relations. After his graduation Shriver, aged 23, was invited to research an innocuous monograph on US-China relations relating to Taiwan and North Korea, This task completed, Shriver was introduced in 2005 to a pair of MSS officers who paid him $20,000 to sit the US Foreign Service Exam in Shanghai. He failed twice, but in 2007 was paid $20,000 to apply to join the CIA. He subsequently moved to South Korea and in June 2010 underwent a series of interviews with the CIA. However, when he attempted to catch a flight in Detroit to Korea, he was arrested by the FBI and charged with conspiring to collect defence information for the PRC. In October 2010, as part of a plea bargain, Shriver pleaded guilty to one charge and in January 2011 was sentenced to four years' imprisonment. He would be released in late 2013. According to the FBI analysis of the case, Shriver had been paid about $70,000 and had met his MSS contacts who called themselves 'Amanda', 'Mr Wu' and 'Mr Wang', on about forty occasions.

The FBI has not disclosed either how or when Shriver first came under suspicion, but the case was the first of its kind, and demonstrated the MSS's willingness to make a long-term investment through the recruitment of a US national, who was not an ethnic Chinese, and direct him into government employment to act as a mole. This time-honoured 'entryism' technique was as old as espionage itself, but had not been previously detected as being adopted by the MSS. The tradecraft involved was also something of a revelation. Having held monthly meetings with Shriver in China, his handlers had expressed a willingness to rendezvous in Hong Kong, if that was safer for him.[2]

* * *

As HONEY BADGER sifted through the evidence to identify potential clues a consensus developed which suggested that the management of some of the compromised cases had been flawed. In particular, the missteps included a tendency to meet assets in the same restaurants, and to take the same travel routes. There was also a thought that the Agency's communications system had been compromised. Both agencies were initially reluctant to consider that there could be a mole within the Agency, but as time went on and assets were continuing to be exposed, that theory began to have legs. There was considerable resistance within some areas of the Agency before they finally began to zero in on one suspect.

One solid lead for the FBI during the HONEY BADGER investigation was Jerry Chun Shing Lee, a 53-year-old CIA retiree who had resigned in 2007 after a career as a case officer lasting 14 years. Born in Hong Kong, he had been brought up in Hawaii and in 1982 had joined the US Army. He later gained a degree in international business management from Hawaii Pacific University and took a master's course in human resource management in 1993.

After resigning from the clandestine service Lee had moved to Hong Kong to work for Japan Tobacco International, a company that had hired one of Lee's Agency colleagues, David Reynolds, to investigate counterfeiters and smugglers. However, in 2009 he was fired on suspicion of having developed too close a liaison relationship with the MSS, and instead joined a former Hong Kong police officer, Barry Cheung Kam-lun, to form their own 'brand integrity' agency, FTM International, to combat the fraudsters.

In mid-August 2012 he was lured to Honolulu with the offer of a lucrative contract. While Lee attended meetings to discuss the plausible project, the FBI searched his hotel room for evidence of espionage, and found plenty, including two small books containing handwritten notes that contained classified information including, but not limited to, true names and phone numbers of assets and covert CIA employees, operational notes from asset meetings, operational meeting locations and locations of covert facilities.[3]

Lee was not arrested when the two incriminating booklets were found, and they were still in his possession when his hotel room in Reston, Virginia was searched later on the same trip when he talked to the CIA about a new job. Indeed, over the next year Lee was interviewed five times but eventually, after the fifth meeting which was held in June 2013, he took his family back to Hong Kong where in 2016 he found a job with the Christie's auction house, working in a small physical security unit protecting the staff and customers.

Born Zhen Cheng Li, he had joined the Agency in 1994, having previously served in the US Army, Lee amounted to the kind of low-hanging fruit, recent retirees, perhaps harbouring a grudge, who might either approach the MSS directly, or might be susceptible to a pitch. During his five meetings in Hawaii he was asked specifically about any foreign contacts, and he had denied there had been any.

Lee was arrested at Kennedy Airport in January 2018 and charged with unlawful retention of national defence information and, having pleaded guilty, was sentenced in November to 19 years' imprisonment. In his confession he admitted to having received hundreds of dollars after he was contacted by the MSS in May 2010. Subsequently he had stayed in contact with his handlers until December 2013.

Another HONEY BADGER suspect was 61-year-old Kevin Mallory, a CIA retiree who had worked for the Agency for six years from 1990, and then again as a contractor from 2010 to 2012. Prior to his role as a case officer he had served in the DIA and then joined the State Department's Diplomatic Security Service for three years from 1987, but had lost his security clearances in October 2012 after he had been found to have 'improperly disclosed classified information'. He had also been employed by the American Institute in Taiwan.

A 1981 graduate of Brigham Young University and fluent in Mandarin, Mallory was $230,000 in debt when he was taken into custody in June 2017 at Chicago's O'Hare Airport upon his return from China. When searched he was found to be carrying $16,000 in cash and a Samsung Galaxy smartphone which had been adapted to include a covert communications channel. Scrutiny of the text memory included a highly incriminating message addressed to an MSS officer named Michael Yang 'Your object is to gain information, and my object is to be paid for . . . I will destroy all electronic records after you confirm receipt. I already destroyed the paper records. I cannot keep these around, too dangerous.'

Mallory admitted having been paid $25,000 in March and April 2017 while on visits to Shanghai by Yang who had posed on LinkedIn as a researcher for a think tank, the Shanghai Academy of Social Sciences. During his trial the prosecution showed CCTV footage of a FedEx store in Leesburg when Mallory scanned classified documents onto a SD memory card, and then shredded the original paper.

Reportedly Mallory, who was employed as a consultant by GlobalEx, behind in his mortgage payments on his home in Raspberry Falls in Leesburg, Virginia, had attracted attention to himself by trying to pump former colleagues for information. A search of his home revealed the digital device containing eight secret and top secret documents which included details of a couple who had travelled to China on a DIA mission in 2017, and an assessment of an unnamed country's intelligence capabilities. Found guilty by a jury, he was sentenced to 20 years' imprisonment in May 2019.[4]

A third case pursued by the HONEY BADGER task force was Ron Rockwell Hansen, a 60-year-old former DIA officer who was arrested at Seattle–Tacoma Airport in June 2018 as he tried to board a connecting flight to Shanghai. Fluent in Mandarin and Russian, Hansen lived in Syracuse, Utah, and had served in a US Army signals intelligence unit with the rank of warrant officer before joining the DIA in 2006. He had more than $200,000 in personal debt and his company, Nuvestack, which provided a cloud storage service, had registered a loss of $1 million in 2014.

Hansen also worked part-time for H-11 Digital Forensics Services which provided him with an apartment and office in China where a partner, identified in his indictment only as 'Robert', liaised with the MSS. This relationship would become ambiguous, and when in 2012 Hansen tried to rejoin the DIA, he was interviewed by the FBI, an occasion on which he revealed that an MSS officer named Max Tong had offered him a private consultancy fee of $100,000 for non-existent computer repair work.

Found guilty of a lesser charge of attempting to sell classified information, Hansen, a father of six, was sentenced in September 2019 to ten years' imprisonment. At his trial Hansen admitted, as part of a plea agreement, that he had been paid a total of at least $800,000 at numerous meetings held between May 2016 and his arrest. Allegedly Hansen had asked a colleague, a DIA officer, for information to pass to the Chinese, and he had reported the approach to the DIA and then become a confidential informant for the FBI. Shortly before Hansen's arrest at the airport this DIA officer passed him documents concerned with military readiness in Korea, marked SECRET/NOFORN, for delivery to the Chinese.

In his confession Hansen described how the MSS routinely evaded money-laundering obstacles on international bank transfers by exploiting the worldwide Visa credit card settlement system. Put simply, the MSS credited a company controlled by its payee, thus allowing that individual to transfer the surplus amount into their own bank account. The only paper trail to be followed displayed all the hallmarks of a legitimate card transaction.[5]

In yet another contemporaneous case, a 63-year-old Mandarin-speaking US State Department staffer, Candace Marie Claiborne, was convicted in July 2019 of selling internal documents to Chinese contacts for $550,000 over a period of five years. She had joined the State Department in 1999 and served in Baghdad, Khartoum and Shanghai. She was given top secret clearances, and one of her brothers was an FBI special agent.

During Claiborne's posting to Beijing in November 2009, as the single mother of four grown-up children, she complained of being short of money and gave the impression that she recognised that the MSS was manipulating her son, who was never charged, and doubtless this tactic applied pressure on her to comply with MSS requirements.

At her trial it was disclosed that in January 2017 she had been approached in the street in Washington, D.C. by an FBI special agent pretending to be a Chinese spy, who had thanked her for 'helping the ministry'. She had been arrested two months later, and sentenced to 40 months' imprisonment and a fine of $40,000.[6]

There was one further case involving penetration which emerged in August 2020 when a 67-year-old Hong Kong-born retiree, Alexander Yuk Ching Ma, was arrested. A naturalised US citizen, he had moved to Honolulu in 1968 and graduated from the University of Hawaii at Manoa. Aged 30, he joined the CIA which had employed his older brother David from 1961 until 1983 when he had been fired for abusing his position to help Chinese nationals enter the United States. In that same year Alex Ma underwent training as a Clandestine Service case officer prior to being posted to the Far East. Alex resigned in 1989 and in 1995 moved to Shanghai. Meanwhile, David was living in Los Angeles where he was convicted of defrauding a lending institution of $145,623 and sentenced to five months' imprisonment and five years' probation.

Ma's espionage for the MSS allegedly began with a three-day interrogation conducted In a Hong Kong hotel in March 2001. The following year he moved back to Hawaii and two years later was employed by the FBI's Field Office as an interpreter, translating Chinese-language documents. He and his Hong Kong-born wife Amy also purchased a condominium on Hawaii Kai Drive in Oahu for $600,000. However, in 2000 Alex had been stopped by US Customs as he returned from China, and was found to be in possession of an undeclared $9,000.[7]

In January 2019 Ma was trapped by an undercover FBI special agent pretending to be an MSS representative who in March paid him $2,000. At both meetings Ma acknowledged his past espionage and his willingness to resume passing information. After a third rendezvous in August, Ma was arrested and charged with conspiracy with an unindicted co-defendant, his older brother David, who was deemed to suffering from dementia. The prosecution of Alex was set for 2014, and the published indictment claimed that he had sold secrets to the MSS for about $50,000. The document noted that in March 2006 Alex Ma asked his brother, now established as an immigration adviser in Los Angeles, to help him identify five suspected FBI confidential informants.

The extent to which these six cases (Mallory, Lee, Hansen, Claiborne and the Ma brothers) explained or at least dealt with all the losses investigated by HONEY BADGER is unknown, but there were several common threads running through them. All six had money problems which made them potentially susceptible to cultivation. All had sufficient past experience to adopt the appropriate tradecraft required to avoid detection. None were ideologically motivated and all were managed from within the PRC by handlers who conducted personal meetings, usually in hotels.

In terms of investigative techniques, Claiborne and Alex Ma were the subject of entrapment ploys, a high-risk strategy in which the target is invited to make self-incriminating remarks to an undercover FBI special agent in front of a concealed video camera. This is a last-resort tactic that may be relied upon in the absence of any evidence that could be adduced in a criminal trial, For example, during the period when 'Five Eyes' agencies were in pursuit of leads supplied by the defector Vasili Mitrokhin some very cold cases were resurrected, including that of Colonel George Trofimoff who was convicted in Florida in June 2000, largely on the testimony of FBI Special Agent Dmitri Droujinsky. He was also deployed against David Boone, arrested in October 1998, and Robert Lipka, arrested in February 1996. Thus in the example of Claiborne and Ma it may have been impossible for the FBI to reveal how the suspects first came to its attention, the classic 'sources and methods' dilemma.

In order to assess the MSS's role in active penetration, which is a sophisticated and dangerous policy usually associated with very mature, well-resourced agencies, there are other essential data that would have been available to the HONEY BADGER analysts. During the 1980s the MSS acquired a reputation bordering on the reckless in which very large numbers of potential targets were 'pitched' almost spontaneously, devoid of the careful planning associated with its Western counterparts. This was the 'scattergun' methodology in contrast to the 'sniper' preference. The result was a large number of reports of apparently ill-judged pitches, with another unknown number of individuals who presumably accepted recruitment. One of the disadvantages of the MSS tactic was that it exposed and compromised the recruiter, but this did not seem to deter the MSS, which enjoyed a limitless budget supporting vast human resources. The contrast between the MSS and its Western opponents, focusing laser-like on a single individual, could not have been starker, but which achieved the best results? This conundrum would have left the HONEY BADGER analyst wondering if the six cases were aberrations, or merely the tip of a counter-intelligence iceberg.

Although there was a view, immediately following the arrest of Jerry Lee in January 2018, that the losses had ceased, there was continuing evidence that in terms of penetration, the MSS remained committed whenever the opportunity arose. That happened in March 2016 when an FBI technician working at the New York Field Office, Kun Shan Chun, was arrested and charged with espionage. Chun had been employed by the FBI since 1997, but for four years from 2006 he undertook assignments for his MSS contacts to whom he had been introduced through an American company, Kolion Technology. Chun had been cultivated skilfully by his handlers who paid for plenty of overseas trips, including some to destinations in France and Italy. The information required by the MSS was typical counter-intelligence building-blocks, such as the FBI's internal order-of-battle, its operational priorities, methods to identify FBI personnel traveling abroad, and details of FBI surveillance equipment. A naturalised US citizen, Chun was convicted and sentenced in August 2016 to 24 months' imprisonment and fined $50,000.[8]

In terms of relative value to the MSS, three of the penetration agents had accumulated a collective experience of 42 years in the Clandestine Service's Far East Division, with Lee's 14 years (1994–2007), David Ma with 22 (1961–83) and Allex Ma's 6 (1983–9), These figures will have been interpreted as showing that the organisation was likely the subject of hostile (but maybe retrospective) reporting across the period 1961 to 2007, and might easily account for subsequent losses in the 2010–12 period studied by HONEY BADGER.

By any standards, with even the most rigorous internal security and compartmentalisation, this coverage, while not comprehensive, is very impressive, and the additional leaks from the DIA and FBI may also have contributed to it. Even Candace Claiborne, though not herself an intelligence officer, would have had knowledge of use to the MSS, such as personality profiles, security procedures, use of diplomatic and consular cover, classified spaces, and patterns of behaviour. All these items would be of intense interest to a counter-intelligence organisation seeking to concentrate its resources on the highest value targets.

The implications of penetration on such a scale are myriad: it will be assumed that Lee and the Ma brothers were quizzed about their colleagues and acted as talent-spotters to identify other potential sources for the MSS, or other individuals susceptible to corruption.

Overall, as a counter-intelligence disaster, the penetration of the Far East Division over some 50 years paints a bleak picture of the CIA's ability to keep secrets, to recruit assets who were not double agents, and to mount operations that would not be compromised from the outset.

Only the CIA's Counterintelligence Staff will know how many of its current or former officers have reported suspicious approaches by Chinese-affiliated entities, such as academic institutions, think tanks and consultancies, or have been invited to submit their resumes over social media, but the egregious data loss that occurred when the US Office of Personnel Management was hacked in April 2015 resulted in the compromise of an estimated 22.1 million security clearance records. The files contained personal details of government employees and contractors who had undergone the screening process, and detailed social security numbers, current addresses, dates and places of birth, together with health and pension data. Each file consisted of the 127-page questionnaire designated Standard Form 86, completion of which was required by most past, current and prospective US government employees, but excluded the CIA, which managed its own bespoke system of security clearances.

The subsequent investigation suggested that the perpetrator was the Jiangsu State Security Department, an organisation assessed as a MSS subordinate, that had broken into a mainframe run by a subcontractor. The PlugX tool was used to gain access to the central database.

Perhaps coincidentally, in November 2019 a 38-year-old Singaporean, Jun Wei Yeo, known as Dickson Yeo, was arrested when he arrived at Dulles Airport and charged with assisting the PRC to spy on the United States. According to his indictment, Yeo had been recruited by the MSS in 2015 while visiting Beijing as a doctorate student to give a lecture on the political situation in South-East Asia. A graduate of Singapore's National University and the Lee Kuan Yew School of Public Policy, Yeo accepted an offer to undertake ostensibly innocent research projects for four different Chinese think tanks, and over the next four years made more than forty visits to China to report to his handlers. By 2018 he had created a dummy consultancy business in the United States and selected targets from LinkedIn who were invited to submit their resumés for consideration as future contributors to various unspecified academic journals. Meanwhile, he attended George Washington University as a visiting scholar and cultivated dozens of casual acquaintances, concentrating on those working for the US government. At least two of his contacts reported his behaviour to the FBI and he was taken into custody. In October 2020 he pleaded guilty to one charge and was sentenced to 14 months' imprisonment. Taking time served into account, Yeo was released in December 2020 and flown back to Singapore where he was detained by the Internal Security Department for a year.[9]

Counter-intelligence analysts noted that Yeo had initially been directed towards his own region, South-East Asia, for collection through the academic community, but was switched in 2017 to Washington, D.C. where he tried, and failed, to gain government employment. Although he made regular visits to the PRC for instruction and payment, he was given complete independence in selecting his recruitment prospects, and had not received details of specific individuals, as might have been expected to happen if the Office of Personnel Management database was being exploited by the MSS. On the contrary, Yeo was expected to harvest the resumes and pass them on to the MSS.

Chapter II

POLITICAL INFLUENCE

We see the Chinese authorities playing the long game in cultivating contacts to manipulate opinion in China's favour – seeking to co-opt and influence not just prominent Parliamentarians from across the political landscape, but people much earlier in their careers in public life, gradually building a debt of obligation.

Ken McCallum
MI5 Director-General
Thames House, 16 November 2022

The MSS's role as a recruiter, facilitator and conduit for the Chinese Communist Party to gain influence in the West, particularly the United States and Australia, is well documented and these operations attracted considerable controversy when details emerged of the FBI's flawed investigations in 1996 of illegal campaign donations, code-named CAMPCON, and then PARLOUR MAID, centred on the political consultant Katrina Leung.

Although twenty-two suspects were convicted of various crimes during CAMPCON, the charges against Leung were dismissed for prosecutorial misconduct and her FBI handler J.J. Smith was allowed to retire in May 2004 without the loss of his pension. Nevertheless, the episode illustrated a toxic mix of political influence, atomic espionage and the collapse of the Leung investigation code-named POETIC FIT, which amounted to a massive counter-intelligence failure.

The common denominator throughout CAMPCON and POETIC FIT was the MSS which was also engaged in espionage at Los Alamos where the main suspect was an ethnic Chinese physicist, Dr Peter Lee, code-named ROYALTOURIST. Among the documents acquired by Leung from her lover in 2002 were reports pertaining to the then live FBI investigation into the theft of nuclear secrets from the National Laboratory.[1]

Evidently the MSS experienced minimal disruption or embarrassment by the Leung case as similar tactics were apparent in the cultivation from 2012 of a Democratic member of the House Permanent Select Committee on Intelligence, Eric Swalwell, by Christina Fang. Formerly a student at California State University East Bay, where Fang had enrolled in 2011, she was elected president of the Chinese Student Association and then the Asian Pacific Islander American Public Affairs, and became engaged in political fundraising and Chinese cultural events.[2]

Fang was also active in California politics and worked in 2004 as a volunteer for the campaign run by a Democrat, Ro Khanna, for a Congressional seat, which he eventually won in 2016. Coincidentally, FBI surveillance on a regular visitor to the Chinese consulate-general in San Francisco led investigators to Fang, but she left the country unexpectedly in mid-2015, prompting speculation that she had become aware of the FBI's interest in her. After her sudden departure the FBI warned several of the aspiring politicians with whom she had come into contact, and learned that she had arranged for an internship in Swalwell's Congressional staff.

In another, similar case, Senator Dianne Feinstein was warned in 2013 that a driver employed by her San Francisco office was under investigation as an MSS asset run by the consulate-general. He was promptly invited to retire.

In May 2009 the FBI established an investigative unit within the National Security Division dedicated to the problem of Chinese influence operations, and this would become an arm of the DoJ's much vaunted China initiative.

* * *

The MSS's attempts to peddle influence in Australia became controversial when in January 2018 the Labor Party senator Sam Dastyari resigned, and a ban was imposed on political contributions made by foreigners. Born in Iran, Dastyari had moved to Australia with his family in January 1988 at the age of 4. He gained a law degree from Sydney University and became a Labor Party activist, and was then in August 2013 appointed to the Senate. Subsequently he declared various foreign donations, in 2014 and 2015, and then opposed his government's position regarding Chinese territorial claims in the South China Sea. This led to his removal in 2017 from his Senate post as Deputy Opposition Whip and accusations that he had received money from Chinese businessmen allied to Beijing.

There were more claims of political corruption in June 2020 when the Sydney home of a Labor Party member of the New South Wales Legislative Council, Shaoquett Moselmane, was raided by the police as part of an Australian Security Intelligence Organisation (ASIO) investigation into the controversial Lebanese-born politician whose outspoken public support for President Xi had created controversy. Moselmane was cleared by the Parliamentary Privileges Committee and resumed his seat in October 2020, although one of his advisers, John Zhang, was the subject of a further enquiry into money-laundering.

In April 2023 a 55-year-old communications infrastructure consultant, Alexander Csergo, was arrested after a period under surveillance by ASIO. He was accused of passing information to two Chinese intelligence officers, calling themselves 'Ken' and 'Evelyn', whom he had known in Shanghai for the past two years and had given him an envelope of cash. The couple, whom he met regularly in quiet cafes, had tasked him to collect information about the AUKUS and QUAD alliances, lithium mining and 'iron ore risk'.

* * *

In Canada there has been widespread suspicion about the extent of MSS influence operations, and in January 2021 report the Canadian Security Intelligence Service (CSIS) described how the MSS uses three colour-coded 'political-interference tactics' to gain influence over Canadians at home and those travelling to China. BLUE refers to sophisticated cyber-attacks on targets' computers, smartphones and hotel rooms for possible blackmail. GOLD refers to bribes, while YELLOW involves sexual entrapment.

In February 2022 CSIS circulated another report, apparently acquired from a consular source, on attempts to recruit or compromise politicians, officials and businessmen, and cited instructions described as circulars sent to consulates to alert Beijing to the travel plans of potential targets. Specifically, the Bank of China was directed to divulge the details of attendees at any conferences for foreigners organised by the Bank. According to CSIS, the MSS targets were corporate executives, academics and vulnerable Chinese-Canadians and objective was to obtain political, economic, scientific and military intelligence and neutralise or co-opt Canadian critics of Chinese policies, including repression of Uyghurs and Tibetans, the crackdown on free speech and democracy in Hong Kong and its designs on Taiwan, with Beijing reserving the right to use force to annex Taiwan, a self-ruled island it considers a breakaway province.

In terms of political interference, CSIS assessed that Beijing sought the return of a minority Liberal government, so the MSS had been directed during the 2021 federal elections to undermine Conservative politicians considered unfriendly. The project would include disinformation campaigns, cash donations to friendly candidates and arranging for business owners to hire Chinese students studying in Canada to campaign in support of preferred Liberal candidates. To cover these activities, Beijing deployed Chinese diplomats in early 2022 to warn 'friendly' influential Canadians to reduce their contact with federal politicians so as to distance themselves from any subsequent investigations into foreign interference. In one specific example, it was alleged by CSIS that the Chinese consulate in Montreal tracks visa applications of influential and prominent Canadians travelling to China. Reportedly the Bank of China's visa section was required to submit details of Canadians planning to attend major exhibits such as the China International Import Expo (CIIE) trade fair. Furthermore, in December 2021 Zhang Heng, the acting consul-general in Montreal, was directed to share the names of government officials, Members of Parliament and business executives who had made visa applications. Specifically, Beijing wanted the names of presidents and vice-presidents of large Canadian corporations and the presidents of small and medium-sized companies. These individuals were to be considered 'work targets', according to the Montreal consulate visa office in an explanation sent to the Bank of China in early December 2021. Zhang also complained to consulate colleagues that he had only learned about 'certain unspecified Canadians' who were to attend the November 2021 CIIE trade fair from the WeChat Chinese social-media platform. Regarding campaign finance, CSIS alleged that Beijing intended to donate money to the Pierre Elliott Trudeau Foundation, which promptly undertook to reject any such payments.[3]

* * *

In January 2022 MI5 made an unprecedented public statement by issuing a 'security alert' to MPs which named a north London solicitor, Christine Lee, as 'an agent of influence who was engaged in political interference activities on behalf of the Chinese Communist Party'. Specifically, she was identified as acting on behalf of the CPC's United Front Workers' Department, a well-known MSS front organisation.[4]

Lee arrived in Northern Ireland from Hong Kong in 1974 at the age of 11, and went to a boarding school in Belfast where her parents ran a Chinese takeaway. She moved to the West Midlands in 1985 and in 1989 married her second husband, Martin Wilkes, also a solicitor, and had two children.

She founded her own solicitor's practice in 1990, dealing mainly with immigration clients, a business that brought her into regular contact with the embassy which in 2008 appointed her its legal adviser. In 2018 her role was expanded and she acted for the Overseas Chinese Affairs office in Beijing, a department closely associated with the MSS. She was also active in the British-Chinese Project, which promoted the Chinese diaspora and organised trips to China, and with the help of Barry Gardner MP created the Chinese in Britain All-Party Parliamentary Group. During this period Lee's firm prospered, accumulating declared assets of £1.6 million, and she opened an office in Birmingham and in London moved to Tintagel House on the Albert Embankment, directly opposite MI5's riverside headquarters. Her home in Solihull's affluent Shirley district was in a private, gated cul-de-sac estate.

In July 2022, MI5's Director-General, Ken McCallum shared a platform at Thames House with FBI Director Christopher Wray, to denounce the Chinese for 'mounting patient, well-funded deceptive campaigns to buy and exert influence'.[5]

The mechanism for distributing the alert was Alison Giles, Parliament's director of security, who acts as a liaison between the Security Service and Parliamentarians. The MP directly affected by the disclosure was Barry Gardner, who had been elected to represent Brent North in 1997, and had served as a junior minister in Tony Blair's administration before being sacked by Gordon Brown in 2008. Over a period of six years he received £584,177 from Lee, ostensibly to support his office. He also employed Lee's son, Daniel Wilkes, as his diary manager, and his local party had also been given cash donations.

Although Christine Lee had not been convicted of any crime, MI5's security alert effectively terminated her lobbying activities and Gardner's political career. Thereafter MI5 turned its attention to a curious phenomenon of the establishment of an international network of an estimated 100 informal Chinese 'secret police' premises in cities with large expatriate populations. These 'police stations' had no official or consular status, but anti-regime campaigners complained that these sites were being developed to collect information about dissidents and pro-democracy activists. According to reports from the FBI, Swedish SAPO and German BfV dating back to 2018, the bases were staffed by MSS agents posing as volunteers who routinely monitored, and occasionally harassed students. Located in Croydon, Hendon, Glasgow and Belfast, usually in existing premises such as restaurants and real estate offices, the bureaux were described as 'police service stations' by Beijing spokesmen who claimed that their activities were limited to assisting Chinese nations with official paperwork, such as the renewal of driving licences. Nevertheless, all the sites were closed down, including the Loon Fung Cantonese seafood restaurant in Glasgow's Sauchiehall Street.

The crackdown on 'transnational repression' followed a raid on two sites in New York, one in a Fujianese community centre in Manhattan's Chinatown, in October 2022 when two men were arrested, Similar action was taken against nine sites in Spain and four in Italy. According to the Spanish-based pressure group Safeguard Defenders, the '110 Overseas' programme was maintained by the Public Security Ministry in Fuzhou and Qingtian to intimidate political protestors and engage in 'persuasion operations'. Following publication in September 2022 of the Safeguard Defenders 20-page report *110 Overseas: Chinese Transnational Policing Gone Wild*, the address in Capel Street, Dublin, and Hunter Realty in Hendon, removed their signage,

Strikes against Chinese overseas suspects are not limited to the nine forbidden countries as the Fujian pilot origins demonstrate. While many of the publicly-reported operations appear to have been conducted mainly through online means, on 22 January 2022, Liu Rongyan, Director of the Overseas Chinese Police Office of the Public Security Bureau in Fuzhou City, Fujian Province, announced that the Fuzhou Public Security Bureau had opened its 'first batch' of thirty overseas police service stations in twenty-five cities in twenty-one countries. The combination of the overseas stations and an online platform used for services such as receiving reporting is together called '110 Overseas'.[6]

According to the report, Beijing has created a list of high-value targets, code-named FOX HUNT, who were to be regarded as priorities for repatriation and prosecution. The method of persuading these individuals to return home was brutally simple: the threat to apply pressure to the person's family. If that failed, straightforward abduction was considered justified:

A further Safeguard Defenders report, released in January 2022, *Involuntary Returns: China's Covert Operation to Force 'Fugitives' Overseas Back Home* set out the scale of FOX HUNT, which was introduced in mid-2014 and netted 10,000 targets.

When China launched its much-touted Operation Fox Hunt (猎狐) in 2014, a programme to forcibly return fugitives overseas accused of corruption back home, the government had already claimed that some 18,000 officials had fled abroad. Fox Hunt, which seeks to extend the reach of China's transnational repression, is intricately linked to General Secretary Xi Jinping's domestic 'anti-corruption' drive (反腐败斗争), a campaign that is seen as key to the CCP's survival. With the Chinese diaspora growing at an ever faster rate as more people seek to leave China, and with the CCP keen to keep control of them also, Beijing has never been more motivated to expand the powers of its security forces overseas. Even before Xi Jinping took power in 2012, China faced resistance in securing foreign governments' cooperation in repatriating its citizens. Many countries were hesitant to enter into extradition agreements with China, and even when deals were struck, the agreements often limited the kinds of people it covered to specific target groups, and even then, extradition requests were sometimes denied. Against this backdrop, China launched multiple campaigns, some using alternative means, to force the return of target individuals. The scale of these operations, even according to official statistics, has been growing, and there is little to indicate that this will change.[7]

The report detailed three techniques adopted by the PRC in pursuit of FOX HUNT targets:

China employs, outside of bilateral agreements (extradition and deportations), to forcibly secure the return of Chinese fugitives and other targets abroad. This report calls these 'involuntary returns' in contrast to the CCP's portrayal of these as 'voluntary returns.' We have found that the vast majority of the 10,000 cases are handled in one of these three ways. A combination of persuasion, intimidation and harassment is used, either via the target's family, relatives and loved ones still in China (type 1) or by agents approaching the target overseas (type 2). Threats centre on warnings that family members will be arrested or worse, unless the fugitive returns. For type 2, agents may include Chinese police officers working illegally in the target country, as well as locally hired individuals. China describes both types as 'persuasion'. Almost all of the claimed 10,000 people returned to China since Operation FOX HUNT began have been through non-judicial procedures, including illegal operations on foreign soil.

Involuntary returns: The use of non-traditional, often illegal, means of forcing someone to return to China against their will, most often to face certain imprisonment. Methods range from threatening family back in China, sending agents to intimidate target in host country, to direct kidnappings. or 'negotiated returns'. Type 3 is the use of state-sanctioned kidnapping, called 'irregular methods, which also includes covert cooperation with host country forces to trick the target into heading to a third country where they can be extradited or simply handed over to Chinese agents for deportation without due process.[8]

Chapter III

COMPROMISE

An unwillingness to name China as our chief espionage adversary – and to prioritise our CI efforts and resources accordingly – is itself a threat to our national security.

Mark Kelton
CIA Counterintelligence Chief
The Cipher Brief, 7 April 2022

For reasons that are unclear, the MSS has gained a reputation as being rather prudish in the recruitment and management of sources involving sexual exploitation, but these is some evidence that the Chinese are as willing as anyone else to prey on weakness and persuade women to manipulate vulnerable men. As we shall see, the MSS is not averse to taking advantage of a same-sex relationship if the opportunity arises.

In March 2013 a 57-year-old US Army Reserve officer, Lieutenant-Colonel Benjamin Pierce Bishop, based at the US Indo-Pacific Command (USPACOM) at Camp H.M. Smith on Oahu as a contract employee for the defence contractor Referentia Systems Inc. was arrested and charged with passing classified information to a 27-year-old Chinese national over an 11-month period from May 2011. Bishop, with 29 years' service in the army as a logistics expert, had worked for Referentia since May 2012 and had held a Top Secret security clearance since July 2002, and Secure Compartmented Information access from November 2002 to April 2012. Between May 2010 and May 2012 he had worked as a planner in 'extended deterrence' before a move to cyber security duties.

Referentia was a small computer security business, based in Hawaii and employing less than 100 staff, but specialising in software development for the defence of 'mission-critical computer networks from advanced persistent threats and enable secure inoperability of the power grid'. Categorised as a 'disadvantaged business' and therefore controlled by socially and economically disadvantaged owners, Referentia Systems had been eligible to bid for government contracts on preferential terms as part of a federal scheme to promote entrepreneurs in deprived districts.

According to the Naval Criminal Investigative Service, and the FBI's Special Agent Scott Freeman, Bishop's girlfriend was a graduate student studying in the United States on a J-1 visa at a university in the Washington, D.C., area. The couple had met in Hawaii during a conference relating to international military defence issues and in June 2011 had begun an affair, though he did not declare the relationship to his employer, as required. Bishop and his Thai wife, Sisiporn Amornsuwan, had divorced in 2012, when she had returned to Ogdon, Utah, with their daughter.

The FBI suggested that the Chinese woman 'may have been at the conference in order to target individuals such as Bishop who work with and have access to US classified information'. When the FBI's physical and electronic surveillance revealed their intimacy, Bishop received several security briefings to reminding him of his contractual obligation to report relationships with foreign nationals. Nevertheless, in February 2012 Bishop submitted a leave request to travel to Great Britain to visit the woman but, according to the FBI, he changed her name slightly altering her given name to a masculine form of the same name and by adding a letter to her surname, thereby obscuring her gender and identity.[1]

Interception of Bishop's emails showed that on 14 May 2012 he had transmitted information about current war plans, nuclear weapons, and relations with international partners to the woman, all at the Secret level. Then, on 2 September, he had telephoned her to tell her of a planned deployment of US strategic nuclear weapons and to explain the ability of the United States to detect short- and medium-range missiles. On 12 September he called her again twice and disclosed information about the deployment of US early-warning radar systems in the Pacific Rim. She was also heard several times to tell Bishop that she did not want him to disclose classified information to her, and he would reply that he would not; but he did anyway, and she continued to ask him about his work.

In November 2012 the FBI searched Bishop's home in Kapolei, and twelve secret documents were discovered, including *Defense Planning Guide 2014–2018*. Others were *Optimizing US Force Posture in the Asia-Pacific, US Department of Defense China Strategy*, and a classified photograph of a Chinese naval asset his lover had asked for. Other papers were titled *Initiative Summary Sheet Reaper UAV; Extended*

Deterrence and Force Employment Planning; and a USPACOM Joint Intelligence Operations Center special report dated January 2013.[2]

On 5 February 2013 the woman asked Bishop to find out what Western nations knew about the operation of a particular Chinese naval asset, and although this was rather outside his usual sphere, he researched open and classified sources for the information. In doing so, he misrepresented himself to other US government personnel as an active-duty army officer in order to gain access to the classified information.

Bishop's release pending trial was short-lived as he breached one of the conditions under which he was allowed to live in a halfway house, a ban on him contacting his girlfriend. However, he did so by email, so his bail conditions were rescinded in December 2013 and he was remanded to the Federal Detention Center in Honolulu. His defence attorney remarked, 'it's a case about love, not espionage, and I think this just goes to show the extent of that love'. In March 2014 Bishop pleaded guilty to various charges, and on 18 September he was sentenced to 87 months' imprisonment and three years of supervised release.[3]

Bishop's prosecution was quite unusual as his girlfriend's name was never disclosed by the FBI, and she was never prosecuted for receiving or eliciting classified information, let alone abusing her visa. In May 2016 Bishop was back in the news when he was attacked by his cellmate, Michael Tanouye, who had been diagnosed with paranoid schizophrenia.

Some Allied counter-intelligence analysts take the view that in the past the MSS sometimes manifested what approaches a degree of prudery in its involvement in honeytraps, and in particular the exploitation of same-sex honeytraps. While that may have been true in the 1980s, SIS learned the hard way in 1999 that a high-flying Foreign Office diplomat had been honey-trapped while on an official delegation to Beijing. The official, who probably had been targeted because of his fluency in Mandarin, had joined the Foreign Office a decade earlier, and had turned down an SIS post. However, while on a free evening in Beijing 'Simon' returned after dinner to his hotel room accompanied by a young man. During the course of the evening Simon detected the sounds of technical surveillance in his bedroom, and realised too late that there was a concealed camera recording the scene. As soon as the delegation returned to Hong Kong Simon declared the incident to the local SIS station commander, and six months later, by mutual agreement, he quietly resigned his post and took up another highly successful career in London.

Chapter IV

THE PEOPLE'S LIBERATION ARMY

Adapting to a world affected by the rise of China is the single greatest priority for MI6. We are deepening our understanding of China across the UK intelligence community, and widening the options available to the government in managing the systemic challenges that it poses. This is not just about being able to understand China and Chinese decision making. We need to be able to operate undetected as a secret intelligence agency everywhere within the worldwide surveillance web.

Sir Richard Moore
Chief, SIS 20 November 2021
International Institute for Strategic Studies

The principal intelligence branch of the People's Liberation Army (PLA) is the Second Bureau, or 2PLA. The organisation, like its conventional foreign counterparts, deploys defence attachés overseas, but is distinguished from its competitors by indulging in cyber warfare on a massive scale, to the point that *in absentia* four senior officers, named as Wang Qian, Wu Zhiyong, Xu Ke and Liu Lei, were indicted in the United States in February 2020 on charges planning and executing a massive hack of the Equifax credit agency to acquire information about 170 million consumers, through Unit 61398, a 2PLA department originally publicly identified in 2003.

According to the US Attorney-General William P. Barr, this was the largest data theft in history and involved compromising 10 million American driving licences, and he claimed that:

the hackers broke into Equifax's network through a vulnerability in the company's dispute resolution website. Once in the network, the hackers spent weeks conducting reconnaissance, uploading malicious software, and stealing login credentials, all to set the stage to steal vast amounts of data from Equifax's systems. While doing this, the hackers also stole Equifax's trade secrets, embodied by the compiled data and complex database designs used to store the personal information. Those trade secrets were the product of decades of investment and hard work by the company.[1]

Barr went on assert that this particular attack, which had taken place in the summer of 2017, was not an isolated incident, and had been conducted with MSS support which revealed:

> a pattern of state-sponsored computer intrusions and thefts by China targeting trade secrets and confidential business information: hacks by a group known as APT 10, which worked in association with the Chinese Ministry of State Security, or MSS, to target managed service providers and their clients worldwide across industries; hacks by MSS intelligence officers who sought to steal intellectual property related to turbofan engines by using both insiders and computer operations, and hacks by PLA officers who targeted victims in the nuclear power, metals, and solar products industries for the economic benefit of Chinese companies. Indeed, about 80 per cent of our economic espionage prosecutions have implicated the Chinese government, and about 60 per cent of all trade secret theft cases in recent years involved some connection to China.[2]

Unit 61398 had been operating since at least 2011 and in February 2013 the US Department of Homeland Security declared that it had been responsible for 115 cases of unauthorised intrusion. In May 2014, 61398 was also blamed for breaches made in US companies dealing with power, metals, and solar production.

Initially, little was known about 61398 in the West until it attracted attention to itself, apparently by acting on its own initiative and engaging in disruption schemes that had no obvious strategic purpose. Originally located in a nondescript 12-storey building near 208 Datong Road in a public, mixed use area of Pudong in Shanghai, the Unit possesses considerable resources and is considered a component of the PLA's signals intelligence structure.

The Unit's preferred methodology is to access and compromise a target's internal software on legitimate web pages so as to infiltrate target computers. Using a wide range of techniques, such as 'spear-phishing' (an email scam that targets businesses, individuals or organisations by sending what appears to be innocuous emails from trusted sources), 'malware' (malicious codes), 'beacons' (a technique that notifies the unit of the successful penetration of the targeted computers), 'hop points' (to access other victims computers and research other potential victims), and domain names (to conceal malicious communications) etc. By some estimates, the Unit has attacked more than 1,000 organisations.

In November 2018 the DoJ established the China Initiative as part of a campaign to restrict China's illicit access to US technology and to investigate the theft of trade secrets, espionage, foreign influence activities, and supply chain subversion. The foundation of the Initiative was a total of 77 existing criminal cases already underway against more than 150 defendants. Some of the cases, such as the indictments charged Huawei and its chief financial officer, Meng Wanzhou, with theft of trade secrets and fraud. Also included were examples of third-country nationals and companies alleged to have breached export controls, engaged in hacking, economic and national security espionage, and failures to register as a foreign agent. Unsurprisingly, many of these cases did not have any obvious links to Beijing, and the numbers were boosted by the inclusion of 'nontraditional collectors' based at American universities. Additionally, suspecting illicit transfer of technology and intellectual property, the DoJ charged about twenty US-based Chinese and American researchers with hiding their Chinese connections. Indeed, several of the cases involved researchers who had applied for federal grants without disclosing their participation in Beijing's Thousand Talents plan.

Although controversial, because of a perceived adverse impact on Chinese students studying in America, the China Initiative was officially terminated in February 2022, and the last major prosecution resulted in the conviction of a 60-year-old Harvard academic, Dr Charles Lieber, who headed the University's Department of Chemistry and Chemical Biology at Harvard University, who was arrested in January 2020 and charged with making a materially false, fictitious and fraudulent statement.

Also involved was Zaosong Zheng, a 30-year-old Chinese national, who was arrested in December 2019 at Boston's Logan International Airport and charged with attempting to smuggle twenty-one vials of biological research to China. The FBI file on Zaosong Zheng showed that he had entered the United States in August 2018 on a J-1 visa and conducted cancer-cell research at Beth Israel Deaconess Medical Center in Boston until December 2019 when he stole the twenty-one vials which were discovered hidden in a sock inside one of Zheng's bags. He started to lie, but then admitted he had stolen the vials from the Beth Israel laboratory, explaining that he had intended to take the vials to China, conduct research in his own laboratory, and publish the results under his own name. In January 2021 Zaosong was sentenced to time served (approximately 87 days), three years of supervised release and deportation.[3]

Also charged, in a connected case, was Lieutenant Yanqing Ye. A 29-year-old PLA officer, she was accused of visa fraud, making false statements, and acting as an agent of a foreign government and conspiracy while posing as a Boston University student. However, she fled the country after being interviewed by the FBI. The DoJ's last prosecution of the China Initiative, Yanqing had falsely identified herself as a 'student' who on her J-1 visa application had lied about her military service at the National University of Defense Technology (NUDT). She was also charged with offences relating to her studies at Boston University's Department of Physics, Chemistry and Biomedical Engineering from October 2017 to April 2019.

According to the FBI, Ye's mission to the US was to conduct research, assess US military websites and send US documents and information to China. In April 2019 Ye had been questioned at Boston's Logan International Airport when she had falsely claimed that she had minimal contact with two NUDT professors who were high-ranking PLA officers. Her claim was contradicted by a search of her electronic devices which revealed that she had accessed various US military websites, researched US military projects and compiled information for the PLA on two US scientists with expertise in robotics and computer science. Furthermore, a review of a WeChat conversation revealed that Ye and another more senior PLA officer from NUDT were collaborating on a research paper about a risk assessment model designed to decipher data for military applications.[4]

Chapter V

MILITARY UNIT COVER DESIGNATOR 61398

I'm not saying China's an enemy of the United States of America. I'm just simply saying that if we do not handle the emergence of the People's Republic well, it will be catastrophic for the world.

General Michael Hayden
8 March 2016
Director, CIA 2006–2009

The first disclosures relating to the PLA's Unit 63198 were made in November 2011 by a Taiwanese policy research organisation, the Project 2049 Institute, based in Arlington, just outside Washington D.C. The 30-page report, *The Chinese People's Liberation Army Signals Intelligence and Cyber Reconnaissance Infrastructure*, provided a detailed analysis of the PLA's investment in signals intelligence, and described 61398's role:

> Second Bureau (61398). The Second Bureau appears to function as the Third Department's premier entity targeting the United States and Canada, and likely focusing on political, economic and military-related intelligence. Subordinate offices are concentrated in Shanghai, although one may be in the Kunming vicinity. More specifically, the Bureau's Second Office is in Dachangzhen, and Third Office is based in Shanghai's Changning District. The Fourth Office has a presence in the northern Shanghai suburb of Gucunzhen as well as Chongning Island. It appears to have a mobility mission. The Seventh Office is in Huohangzhen. Another office is in Changnin District on Yan'an Zhong Road.[1]

Within a few years 61398 had established a reputation within the Western intelligence community as an aggressive cyber warfare facility that demonstrated both collection and offensive capabilities. Western analysts watching Chinese networks assessed that an anonymous military computer facility in Shanghai was actively recruiting personnel with distinctive skills, such as fluency in English, cyber security and network operations. In February 2013 the private cyber security firm Mandiant released *APT1: Exposing One of China's Cyber Espionage Units*, a 74-page forensic study which described the company's years of monitoring twenty advanced persistent threat perpetrators that had been identified as having links to 61398.

Mandiant spent seven years logging attacks against 150 targets and, concentrating on twenty aggressors, tracked them back to Shanghai and, more specifically, to a location in the Pudong New Area which was consistent with 61398's known street address, a walled compound containing a 12-storey, 130,663ft^2 block built in 2007 by the Jiangsu Longhai Construction Engineering Group to accommodate up to 2,000 personnel at 208 Datong Road, Gaoqiaoznen, and assessed that various characteristics manifested by APT1 suggested it was a state-sponsored actor.

Physical inspection of the neighbourhood revealed the existence of the support infrastructure, such as a medical clinic, guest accommodation and kindergarten, often associated with major PLA sites. All the suspected associated real estate was photographed discreetly from the street, and overhead imagery was captured by commercial satellite services (and doubtless interested state actors).

Other evidence included a provision by China Telecom of high-volume fibre-optic cables which were categorised 'national defence'. APT1's collection activity was prodigious, focusing on 141 different companies with much of the work undertaken by three individuals who operated under nicknames. In terms of quantities, an estimated several hundred terabytes of data had been downloaded, often over a period of months. In many examples, the *modus operandi* followed a pattern, using GETMAIL and MAPIGET to access emails, GETMAIL was designed to extract attachments and folders from Microsoft Outlook, while MAPIGET stole emails from the Microsoft exchange server.

Apparently active 365 days a year in Shanghai's time-zone, using Microsoft operating systems and keypads adapted to Simplified Chinese fonts, a review of the APT1 victims showed that 87 per cent were in English-speaking countries.

In the last two years we have observed APT1 establish a minimum of 937 Command and Control (C2) servers hosted on 849 distinct IP addresses in 13 countries. The majority of these 849 unique IP addresses were registered to organisations in China (709), followed by the US (109).[2]

The Mandiant study estimated that a typical APT1 attack involved the coordination of 1,000 servers, a huge investment that was quite beyond the capability or needs of an actor in the private sector. Similarly, once APY1 had gained access to a Western victim, it did not behave like other cyber criminals and download proprietary information for future extortion, or even insert malware into the system, but rather maintained the access, usually for an average of 356 days. The longest access continued for 60 months. By most standards, this was bizarre behaviour unless the perpetrators were completely confident that their own installation was fully protected against interference by local law enforcement. Furthermore, APT1 often attacked dozens of victims simultaneously, rather than one-by-one, as might be expected. This kind of parallel exploitation, conducted against industries or entities that were not necessarily commercially obvious targets for conventional criminals, such as banks and vulnerable financial institutions, inferred that APT1 was very unusual and enjoyed vast resources, especially in data storage, a characteristic than in many jurisdictions would attract the attention of administrators. It was also noted, by a review of the targets sector-by-sector, that APT1 prioritised information technology, aerospace, public administration, communications and scientific research. Once again, the indicators suggested a state actor. Analysis of the data stolen showed a similar bias towards manufacturing processes, system designs, and proprietary information, which was by way of long-term investment, rather than short-term monetization. Put simply, no independent hacker would take the risk of such a brazen methodology. Why farm for the future when the same criminality could reap instant results?

Over a period of years the cyber counter-intelligence researchers developed a profile of APT1 and suggested that the theft of entire archives was explained by the need for future constant access, rather than a demand for ransom. The techniques adopted were often intended to conceal the attack, whereas the conventional, independent criminal gangs preferred to give their crimes high visibility, so as to terrorise the victims, ensure quick ransom payment, and spread fear across that particular sector. Furthermore, some of the major APT1 intrusions appeared more like industrial espionage, intended to manipulate markets, rather than seek quick returns. The Russian gangs demanded cash payments, whereas APT1 simply looted the back office, but silently.

As for the individual personalities who were monitored as active participants in APT1, they included the self-styled 'UglyGorilla' who had designed malware; DOTA who had registered dozens of email addresses, all with the same telephone number in Shanghai; and 'SuperHard' who specialised in AURIGA and BANGAT, also based in the Pudong New Area.

Although there was very little open-source material on Chinese networks relating to 61398, on the rare occasions Western researchers found an item, Chinese censors would quickly intervene and remove the indiscretion. Other potential sources of information were the resumés of former staff members circulated online. One such graduate student, Li Bingbing, boasted in 2010 that he had worked at 61398 and circulated a monograph in the *Journal of Sichuan University (Natural Science Edition)* about a steganographic variant that allowed covert messages to be concealed in a Microsoft Word7 program. Clandestine communication techniques of this kind are commonplace in the intelligence community, but have little or no relevance to legitimate businesses. One of Li's former colleagues, Wang Weizhong, mentioned that his English-language skills had been acquired at 61398. Another, Yu Yunxiang, wrote an academic paper for the *Journal of Information Engineering University* on computer operating systems, and credited 61398 as the place where he had acquired his expertise, while Peng Fei authored an article published in a scholarly periodical, the *Journal of Military Communications Technology*, mentioning 61398 as the source of his knowledge of digital signal processing. Similarly, Chen Yiqun wrote about network security, citing his experience at 61398. This kind of exploitation of open-source research is classic intelligence elicitation and amounted to a further piece of the 61398 jigsaw puzzle that, when seen altogether, provided a *prima-facie* case for justifying further research, and devoting more resources to the target.

Another insight into 61398 was study of the unit's employment requirements made available by the science and engineering departments at technical colleges such as the Harbin Institute of Technology and the Zhejiang University School of Computer Science and Technology which held recruitment events and were canvassed for graduates with skills in maths, English, signal and digital circuits, communications engineering and politics.

The first challenge in the investigation of APT1 was to identify the specific incidents that could be associated with the group, which meant categorising all reports of major cyber-attacks, an immense task as many commercial entities were reluctant to make any public admissions about their experiences for fear of undermining market confidence. However, the Japanese division of the Symantec security software company disclosed in 2006 that Ugly Gorilla had sought to penetrate its systems. Other early victims were assessed as Digital Bond in June 2012; Telvent Canada Ltd in September 2012; in November 2012 Ugly Gorilla malware was reported as having been used by 'Comment Group'. Early on, APT1 was thought to masqueraded as 'Comment crew'.

In retrospect it occurred to researchers that Symantec was an odd choice for the target of a cyber-attack, unless one of the objectives was to learn the secrets of a potential adversary and thereby neutralise an opponent in a pre-emptive, surprise knock-out strike. The implication was that APT1 may have had a clearly defined, long-term strategy, as opposed to the smash-and-grab tactics associated with opportunistic criminals eager to move on to their next victim.

Ugly Gorilla would play a major role in the development of APT1, and he has been identified as Professor Zhang Zhaoxhong, a member of the faculty at the National Defence University where he headed the Military Technology and Equipment Department. The author of *Network Warfare* and *Winning the Information War*, Professor Zhang was thought to be the designer of the ManitsMe family of malware, and often declared that his true name was 'Jack Wang'. Born in 1952 in Hebei, Zhang read Arabic at university and, having joined the PLA Navy, was posted as an observer during the Iran-Iraq War, and retired with the rank of rear admiral.

Inevitably there was a common denominator in the way APT1 approached its victims, usually heralded by an aggressive phishing attack on emails in the expectation that several recipients will not recognise a phoney email for what it really is, and inadvertently download malware. The code which these ingenious programs are based will contain telltale characteristics and algorithms that act as fingerprints and will be designed to fulfil various tasks, such as access to remote servers. Once contaminated, the target system is manipulated to evade detection, neutralise countermeasures and take the necessary steps to perpetuate and deepen the breach.

The initial email offers two opportunities for investigators: the originator's email account, if indeed there is one, or the compressed ZIP file containing the malware that may, for instance, open a backdoor into a particular program, or harvest keystrokes for passwords and other related security obstacles. As the ZIP files are visible on the victim's system, they have been given innocuous titles, or mimic legitimate protocols, of which APT1 routinely deployed a dozen or so, thus assisting the categorisation process. However, some variants manipulate the security algorithms to generate an authentic password, thereby enabling access without the risk of tripping an alert. Having acquired ostensibly legitimate credentials, the APT1 intruder can reconnoitre the network and penetrate web portals into connected systems.

The fact that APT1 typically took elaborate technical measures to conceal its origins, paradoxically meant that it stood out from the organised crime gangs who would simply move on to another Eastern European base once a particular target had been attacked. In contrast, APT1 used programs such as Remote Desktop to control intermediary servers and support IP addresses that suggested a location in, for example, the United States. Of the 817 suspect IP addresses researched by Mandiant for two years from January 2011, 98.2 per cent turned out to be Chinese from the Shanghai area.

Having marshalled and weighed the evidence, the 2013 Mandiant report concluded:

> In a State that rigorously monitors Internet use, it is highly unlikely that the Chinese Government is unaware of an attack group that operates from the Pudong New Area of Shanghai. The detection and awareness of APT1 is made even more probable by the sheer scale and sustainment of attacks that we have observed and documented in this report. Therefore the most probable conclusion is that APT1 is able to wage such a long-running and extensive cyber espionage campaign because it is acting with the full knowledge and cooperation of the government. Given the mission, resourcing, and location of PLA Unit 61398, we conclude that PLA Unit 61398 is APT1.[3]

As a commercial organisation, Mandiant's motives for collating the wealth of evidence relating to 61398 may not have been entirely philanthropic, but publication did not appear to have much impact on the PLA which continued its hacking operations. Indeed, seven months after the report's release there was a massive attack on the US defence infrastructure with 'Sykipot' malware. The targets included government contractors and key industry computer hardware which was infected with the virus that infiltrated attachments to exploit vulnerabilities in Adobe Reader, Microsoft Excel and Internet Explorer. By May the following year federal prosecutors were satisfied by the accumulated evidence against 61398 and indictments were issued by the DoJ in Pennsylvania against five named officers, being Wang Dong, Sun Kailiang, Wen Xinyu, Huang Zhenyu, and Gu Chunhui, all identified as 'officers in Unit 61398 of the Third Department of the

Chinese People's Liberation Army'. The indictment alleged that Wang, Sun and Wen, among others known and unknown to the grand jury, hacked or attempted to hack into US entities named in the indictment, while Huang and Gu supported their conspiracy by, among other things, managing infrastructure (e.g., domain accounts) used for hacking. Their victims were named as Alcoa Inc, Westinghouse Electric Co., US subsidiaries of SolarWorld AG, United States Steel Corp, Allegheny Technologies Inc;, and a trade union, the United Steel, Paper and Forestry, Rubber, Manufacturing, Energy, Allied Industrial and Service Workers International Union.

The tactics adopted by the DoJ, proceeding on complaints of industrial espionage, were to have only a limited impact on Chinese government policy, which appeared to endorse the continued sponsorship of cyber-attacks, more of which appeared to have a political and nuisance value, but little else, apart from being a good indicator of Beijing's displeasure. A case in point is GhostNet, which emerged in March 2009 as a concerted attack on computer targets in the West identified as having originated in the PRC. The Trojan Horse virus was an attempt to download illicit software containing a remote access tool (RAT) known as 'Gh0st RAT' and concealed behind innocent-looking email attachments sent to systems run by Tibetan refugees on behalf of the Dalai Lama at Dharamsala in India. Pentagon analysts identified GhostNet as Chinese in origin, asserting that the PLA 'often cites the need in modern warfare to control information, sometimes termed "information dominance"' and suggested that 'China has made steady progress in recent years in developing offensive nuclear, space and cyber-warfare capabilities, the only aspects of the PRC's armed forces that, today, have the potential to be truly global'. This view conformed to a policy announced at the 10th National People's Congress in 2003 concerning the creation of 'information warfare units' when General Dai Qingmin was reported as having predicted that internet attacks would be mounted in advance of military operations to cripple enemies. Since then the PLA has been linked by Western investigators to the Red Hacker Alliance, an ostensibly independent group of cyber saboteurs responsible for numerous attempts to overwhelm target commercial and government websites and systems in the United States.

Between 2007 and 2009, GhostNet was assessed to have been responsible for numerous coordinated 'denial-of-service' attacks, and some 1,395 computers in 103 countries had been found to contain covert programs, including some located in embassies that remotely activated recording systems. A Cambridge University study, *The Snooping Dragon: Social Mailware Surveillance of the Tibetan Movement*, published in March 2009, concluded that GhostNet had been officially sponsored by Beijing.

The GhostNet attack aimed at Google was especially sophisticated and was discovered to have compromised the search engine's source codes for the Gaia password management system and to have accessed the legal discovery portals used by the company's management to cooperate with information requests from law enforcement agencies.

In 2008 ExxonMobil, ConocoPhillips, and Marathon Oil all sustained similar attacks, although the damage did not become apparent until the following year. An estimated 20 per cent of Fortune 100 companies had endured similar attacks, such as the notorious Aurora incident in January 2010, which had varied in severity from the siphoning off of proprietary data to the deliberate sabotage of card payment encryption systems.

Chapter VI

ONE THOUSAND TALENTS

We think your information is compatible with the need of Chinese technology . . .
we would like to invite you for an exchange the next time you return to China.
MSS officer Xu Yanjun to Boeing
engineer Sun Li, 2016

In 2008 Beijing announced the Thousand Talents Program, an initiative intended to attract primarily ethnic Chinese, educated or employed in the United States, to return to the motherland and share their knowledge. The scheme was conceived as a reverse brain-drain by the CCP's Central Committee which sought to bridge a perceived technology gap by persuading suitably qualified personnel to do their duty and assist the state. Underlying the plan was the unspoken acknowledgment that the 1966 Cultural Revolution, which lasted a decade, had denuded the country of its intellectuals, leaving the education system at a severe disadvantage, incapable of teaching subsequent generations.

The project, which was to be administered by the MSS, was to target successful professionals for recruitment, with the net drawn widely to include researchers and business entrepreneurs. Many of the best Chinese students who travelled abroad for advanced studies had opted to remain overseas, and the Thousand Talents plan focused on a substantial number of the group who had stayed abroad and gained technical skills that would be valued in China. The objective was to signal a liberalisation of government policies so as to remove any fears the candidates might harbour about the kind of reception they could expect. Instead of being regarded as potential enemies of the state, they were to be welcomed as heroes of the revolution, undertaking their patriotic duty. Participants were to be tempted by paying Western-scale high salaries and given prestigious awards from leading Chinese academic institutions.

An analysis of the scheme produced by the US National Intelligence Council in June 2008 described the Thousand Talents as 'China's flagship talent program and probably the largest in terms of funding'. The NIC assessment calculated the number of recruits at 2,629, of whom 44 per cent were engaged in medicine and healthcare, 22 per cent in applied industrial technologies, 8 per cent in computer sciences and 6 per cent each in aviation/aerospace and astronomy. The remainder were in such areas as economics, finance and mathematics. The concentration of targets in the bio-medical research sector was a reflection of the Chinese priorities, and by November 2019 about 71 institutions, including some of the more prestigious medical schools, were investigating 180 cases involving the theft of intellectual property. The apparently unrelated upsurge in the compromise of sensitive research was noted by the FBI, which issued a public warning, and was manifested most obviously by the US National Institutes of Health which referred twenty-four suspected cases to its Inspector-General's office. The consequent investigations released a pattern of behaviour in which researchers were granted patents in China for work performed in American institutions, often funded by US government grants. In some egregious examples, entire laboratories had been established in China based on stolen research, and more ten individual scientists implicated were dismissed or made to resign.

The FBI described the risks of the Thousand Talents programme in stark terms in a counter-intelligence briefing:

Foreign governments sponsor talent recruitment programs, or talent plans, to bring outside knowledge and innovation back to their countries – and sometimes that means stealing trade secrets, breaking export control laws, or violating conflict-of-interest policies to do so.

While various countries use talent plans, the Chinese government is the most prolific sponsor of these programs – and the United States is one of China's main targets.

The US welcomes international collaboration in academic and scientific research and business development. But American businesses, universities, and laboratories should understand the potential risks and illegal conduct incentivized by Chinese talent plans and take steps to safeguard their trade secrets and intellectual property.

How Chinese Talent Plans Work

China oversees hundreds of talent plans. All incentivize its members to steal foreign technologies needed to advance China's national, military, and economic goals.

China recruits science and technology professors, researchers, students, and others – regardless of citizenship or national origin – to apply for talent plans. Individuals with expertise in or access to a technology that China doesn't have are preferred.

Participants enter into a contract with a Chinese university or company – often affiliated with the Chinese government – that usually requires them to:

- Subject themselves to Chinese laws
- Share new technology developments or breakthroughs only with China (they can't share this information with their US employer or host without special authorisation from China)
- Recruit other experts into the program – often their own colleagues

China will let people with existing jobs in the United States participate in talent plans part-time so they can maintain their access to intellectual property, trade secrets, pre-publication data and methods, and US funding for their research.

Talent plan participants are offered multiple financial, personal, and professional benefits in exchange for their efforts.

China's talent plans have successfully recruited participants around the world to work on key programs like military technologies, nuclear energy, wind tunnel design, and advanced lasers.

Risks and Information for US Businesses, Universities, and Laboratories

Talent plans can sometimes foster legitimate sharing and collaboration as part of an appropriate business arrangement or research exchange, but this is not the norm.

Instead, talent plans usually involve undisclosed and illegal transfers of information, technology, or intellectual property that are one-way and detrimental to US institutions.

Your students and/or employees could be talent plan participants. Many people who participate in these programs work at prominent US laboratories, businesses, and universities, including places where government research is conducted for sensitive military and scientific projects.

Transparency and disclosure regarding an individual's participation in a talent plan are essential. This is the only way US institutions can assess the risks to their intellectual property, prevent abuse of the open access offered by the US research environment, and ensure grant-funding programs are fair and equitable. Unfortunately, many participants do not disclose their involvement in these programs.

An individual's undisclosed participation in a talent plan may:

- Pose risks to national security because of the participant's obligation to the Chinese government
- Result in inappropriate use of taxpayer funds if the participant is awarded a US government grant
- Harm other researchers and scientists by jeopardizing their professional credibility and their ability to obtain future research funding – and denying them the professional and financial benefits of their efforts – if their work is stolen and transferred to China
- Result in the recruiting of colleagues by the participant
- Result in lasting financial damages to your institution due to stolen information or the inability to obtain federal research funding in the future

Even if talent plan participants who steal information are eventually caught and prosecuted, the damage done to your organisation by intellectual property theft may be irreversible.

Risks and Information for Chinese Talent Plan Participants

Although participating in talent plans is not inherently illegal, you may violate US law, especially if you don't properly disclose your affiliation.

You should familiarize yourself with and abide by disclosure and conflict-of-interest rules required by your US employer and the US government. Transparency and full disclosure of talent plan membership and foreign contracts or agreements are essential for institutions to assess risk.

You risk criminal prosecution when you steal intellectual property or misuse grant funds. Talent plan participants have pleaded guilty or been convicted of offences including:

- Export-control law violations
- Economic espionage and theft of trade secrets
- Grant and tax fraud[1]

In June 2008 a Pentagon official testified to the House Armed Services Committee that the Pentagon was 'facing an unprecedented threat to its technological and industrial base,' while noting the US's 'open society' has 'offered China access to the same technology and information that is crucial to the success of our future war-fighting capabilities. We have seen the Chinese target top talent in American universities and research labs of the private sector, including defence contractors and the US government.'[2]

The warnings were effective, and numerous investigations and prosecutions were pursued. Among them was Song Gou Zheng, an immunologist employed at Ohio State University. He was arrested by the FBI in Alaska in May 2020 and charged with grant fraud and making false statements for failing to disclose to his employer and to the US National Institutes of Health (NIH) that he was a Thousand Talents participant while in receipt $4.1 million in NIH grants. Professor Zheng was accused of having transferred scientific knowledge developed under his NIH grant to Sun Yat-sen University in Guangzhou

Zheng was placed on administrative leave without pay and, having been deemed a flight risk, remanded in custody. In November 2020, he pleaded guilty to making false statements to federal authorities and in May 2021 was sentenced to 37 months in prison for making false statements to federal authorities; he was also ordered to pay more than $3.4 million in restitution to the NIH and $413,000 to the Ohio State University.[3]

Another similar case demonstrated that the Thousand Talents scheme was not limited to ethnic Chinese. In 2008 Dr Charles Lieber had been appointed the principal investigator of the Lieber Research Group at Harvard University, which specialised in the area of nanoscience, and received more than $15,000,000 in grant funding from the NIH and Department of Defense. Applicants for this kind of government funding requires full disclosure of significant foreign financial conflicts of interest, and in 2011 Lieber had become a 'Strategic Scientist' at Wuhan University of Technology and for five years had been a contractual participant in China's Thousand Talents Plan, Beijing's much-publicised scheme to attract high-level scientific talent in furtherance of China's scientific development, economic prosperity and national security.[4]

Past experience had shown that the programme was often used as a cover to conceal Beijing's real purpose, to lure Chinese overseas talent and foreign experts to bring their knowledge and experience to China and reward individuals for stealing proprietary information. Under the terms of Lieber's three-year Thousand Talents contract, he was paid a monthly stipend of $50,000, living expenses of up to $158,000 and awarded more than $1.5 million to establish a research laboratory at Wuhan.

When challenged about his Chinese links, in 2018 and 2019, Lieber lied about his involvement in the Thousand Talents and affiliation with Wuhan. Indeed, when interviewed, Lieber stated that he was never asked to participate in the Thousand Talents Program, but he 'wasn't sure' how China had categorised him. Lieber was convicted in April

2023 and sentenced to time served (two days) in prison; two years of supervised release with six months of home confinement; a fine of $50,000; and $33,600 in restitution to the Internal Revenue Service.

In August 2020 Professor Zhengong Cheng, a chemical engineer at Texas A & M University since May 2004, was charged with concealing his Thousand Talents affiliation while working on sensitive NASA projects. He pleaded guilty in September 2022 and was sentenced to time served (19 months imprisonment) and fined $20,000.[5]

Although internally the FBI's China Initiative was handled as individual cases of espionage, the DoJ prosecutions often concentrated on the contractual issues of non-disclosure, as being an easier prosecutorial route to conviction and a plea bargain. This strategy was apparent in several cases, such as that of Haito Xiang, an imaging scientist who worked for the Climate Corporation, a Monsanto subsidiary. Xiang was intercepted at an airport in 2017 while boarding a plane to China with a one-way ticket. He was found to be carrying proprietary Monsanto information about farming software that aims to improve agricultural productivity. Xiang pleaded guilty in January 2022 and was sentenced in April to 29 months' imprisonment, three years of supervised release and a fine of $150,000.[6] An example of the non-disclosure prosecutions was the professor of biological systems and engineering at Virginia Tech, Yiheng Percival Zhang, who falsified a National Science Foundation grant application to fund research he had already done at a Chinese institute, and used US grant money for other projects in his own US biotech company.[7]

Xiao-Jiang Li, a neuroscientist at Emory University, pleaded guilty to making false statements to federal authorities and in May 2020 was sentenced to a year of probation and restitution of $35,000.[8]

There were also at least four other nondisclosure cases which resulted in resignations or firing where no charges were filed. These include three unnamed scientists who were fired from the University of Texas' MD Anderson Cancer Center, six other scientists fired from the Moffit Cancer Center in Florida, one scientist fired from the University of San Diego's Shiley Eye Institute, and three others who were forced to resign from the University of Florida College of Medicine. All had either failed to report foreign income, or failed to declare a Thousand Talents affiliation. In a single case, the Van Andel Institute in Michigan failed to disclose that two of its own researchers had received Thousand Talents income and an NIH government grant of $3.5 million was repaid.

In 2020, Qing Wang, a heart disease expert who had worked at the Cleveland Clinic for over 20 years, was charged with making false claims and wire fraud related to funds he and his team had received from the NIH. Wang failed to disclose that he had been named dean of the College of Life Sciences and Technology at Huazhong University of Science and Technology through the Thousand Talents and received $480,000 in grants from the Chinese government, including funds from the Chinese National Natural Science Foundation. However, the charges were dropped in July 2021.[9]

For every example of technology transfer with national security implications, the FBI probably handled a further five thefts of proprietary information, trade secrets that had a significant commercial vale. From a counter-intelligence perspective, it was often what appeared initially to be a relatively straightforward case of industrial espionage revealed some state component, usually because of the ubiquitous nature of the MSS, which had tentacles everywhere.

Chapter VII

HUAWEI

Former and current Huawei employees provided evidence of a pattern and practice of potentially illegal behaviour by Huawei officials.

HPSCI Report, October 2012

Created in 1987 with an investment of $5,000 from a former PLA officer, Ren Zhengfei, Huawei is one of the world's largest telecommunications companies with annual billings of $38.6 billion and is based in Shenzhen, Guangdong. Initially manufacturing electronic switches for industry, Huawei expanded into the consumer market to produce smartphones and computers. The key to its success was its apparent ability to significantly undercut its competition.

The company's founder was estimated in March 2019 to have a net worth of $2.1 billion. He was born in Guizhou in 1944, but during the Japanese occupation he moved to Guangzhou where his father worked in a Kuomintang munitions factory. In 1958 Ren's father became a member of the Communist Party and Ren himself attended Chongqing University. He then joined the PLA to work in the information technology research unit. Despite his father's Party membership, Ren's application to join the Party was turned down for most of his military career because of his family's past association with the nationalist Kuomintang. In 1978 he was selected to represent the PLA at a National Science Conference, but four years later he left the PLA as a result of cuts in military expenditure. He then moved to Shenzhen and began his own electronics business, which initially sold telephone exchange equipment from Hong Kong, before developing a manufacturing capability. He was also accepted as a Party member, and reportedly has been married three times. His first wife was Meng Jun, with whom he had two children, a son, Meng Ping, and a daughter, Meng Wanzhou, both of whom took their mother's surname, Meng

Wanzhou is Huawei's chief financial officer. Ren's second wife was Yao Ling, with whom he had a daughter, Annabel Yao, who is 25 years younger than her half-sister. She studied computer science at Harvard University and is an accomplished ballerina who made her debut at the prestigious Le Bal des Débutantes in Paris in 2018. His third wife is Su Wei, said to be a former secretary. Although Ren acknowledges his Party affiliation, he has not admitted having had substantial state support at crucial times during Huawei's expansion. 'When I started out thirty years ago, we really didn't have any telephones. The only phones we had were those hand-cranked phones that you see in old World War II films. We were pretty undeveloped then.'

The company became controversial in June 2017 when the National Intelligence Law was enacted in Beijing, requiring all businesses registered or operating in China to cooperate with the state's security apparatus and, specifically, Article 7 mandated the companies to conceal the collaboration. This situation was exacerbated in November 2021 when a Personal Information Protection Law came into effect to exercise state power over *all* data held by Chinese or foreign companies if *any* of it involves a Chinese citizen.

Supposedly a private company, although the corporate structure is somewhat opaque by Western standards, Huawei employs more than 190,000 staff and is the world's largest provider of Fifth Generation (5G) broadband cell phone technology. It is also deemed to be a threat to national security by the United States, Australia and Japan, on the basis that Huawei's business practices are reprehensible, and that there will always be a suspicion that the company's products may contain backdoors in their codes so as to allow remote access or even control over its performance.

Huawei has been associated with industrial espionage on several occasions. For example, in 2010 Motorola sued Huawei for trade secret theft after an employee, Jin Hanjuan, was arrested while in possession of a large quantity of electronic and paper documents, $30,000 in cash, and a one-way airline ticket to China. Evidently she (and others) had intended to sell the stolen information in China, and an investigation determined that a co-defendant and former Motorola employee, Pan Shaowei, had established a Chinese company, Lemko, after meeting Huawei's founder, Ren Zhengfei, to discuss building wireless technology for Huawei based on Motorola technology. Jin was convicted and sentenced to four years' imprisonment.[1]

Huawei's business standards came under scrutiny in 2003 when Cisco sued the company in Texas for unauthorised use of its own source code which was found in Huawei Quidway routers. The claim, detailing the infringement of copyrights and the misappropriation of IOS software, was settled, but in a similar case brought in 2010 federal prosecutors alleged that Huawei's Santa Clara subsidiary Futurewei had stolen code from the company's San Jose offices. According to the indictment, Huawei had settled the original Cisco claim by recalling the offending products and sending them back to China where the memories were erased, thus destroying the evidence. The issue was subsequently investigated by the House Permanent Select Committee on Intelligence (HPSCI) which initially instructed the committee's staff to 'conduct a preliminary review of the national security threats posed by Chinese telecom companies doing business in the United States. The preliminary review suggested that the threat to the supply chain constitutes a rising national security concern of the highest priority.' Thus, on 17 November 2011, the Committee launched a full investigation, focusing on the two main Chinese telecommunication companies doing business in the United States, Huawei and ZTE. Unlike Huawei, ZTE is partly state-owned and has a record of exporting to sanctioned countries such as Iran and North Korea, in violation of UN restrictions.

In February and April 2012 HPSCI investigators travelled to China to interview officials at Huawei and ZTE headquarters. Then, in May 2012, several members of the committee flew to Hong Kong to meet senior staff from both Huawei and ZTE, and in September 2012 the HPSCI held a rare open hearing, where officials of both Huawei and ZTE testified before Congress, the first time that Chinese executives have done so. In its report entitled *Investigative Report on the US National Security Issues Posed by Chinese Telecommunications Companies Huawei and ZTE* and released in October 2012 the HPSCI advised American firms to avoid Huawei and ZTE. The HPSCI investigation was 'to review the history, management, and operations of key Chinese companies seeking to expand into US infrastructure. The investigation reviewed the extent to which these companies have ties to the Chinese government and Chinese Communist Party, or otherwise provide the Chinese government greater opportunities for foreign and economic espionage.' The report duly noted:

> that modern critical infrastructure is incredibly connected, everything from electric power grids to banking and finance systems to natural gas, oil, and water systems to rail and shipping channels. All of these entities depend on computerized control systems. The risk is high that a failure or disruption in one system could have a devastating ripple effect throughout many aspects of modern American living.[2]

The report complained that 'Huawei and ZTE provided incomplete, contradictory, and evasive responses to the Committee's core concerns' and recommended:

1. US government systems and US government contractors, particularly those working on sensitive systems, should exclude any Huawei or ZTE equipment or component parts. Additionally, the Committee on Foreign Investments in the United States (CFIUS) must block acquisitions, takeovers, or mergers involving Huawei and ZTE given the threat to US national security interests.
2. US network providers and systems developers are strongly encouraged to seek other vendors for their projects.
3. Unfair trade practices of the Chinese telecommunications sector should be investigated by committees of jurisdiction in US Congress and enforcement agencies in the Executive Branch. Particular attention should be paid to China's continued financial support of key companies.
4. Chinese companies should quickly become more open and transparent. Huawei, in particular, must become more transparent and responsive to US legal obligations.[3]

The Committee Chairman Mike Rogers concluded:

Any bug, beacon, or backdoor put into our critical systems could allow for a catastrophic and devastating domino effect of failures throughout our networks. As this report shows, we have serious concerns about Huawei and ZTE, and their connection to the communist government of China. China is known to be the major perpetrator of cyber espionage, and Huawei and ZTE failed to alleviate serious concerns throughout this important investigation. American businesses should use other vendors.

It is our responsibility on the Intelligence Committee to protect our country's national security. That is why we launched this investigation in the first place. We depend on our nation's networks for so much of what we do every day. As this report shows, we have serious concerns about Huawei and ZTE, two Chinese telecommunications companies looking to gain market share in the United States, and their connection to the communist government of China. We warn US government agencies and companies considering using Huawei and ZTE equipment in their networks to take into account the affect if could have on our national security.[4]

Following the release of the HPSCI report Huawei attracted more regulatory attention, and further evidence emerged of the company's misconduct. In June 2018 a German company, SolarEdge Technologies, filed a lawsuit for patent infringement against Huawei involving

SolarEdge's significant investment in its innovative DC-optimised inverter technology, claiming Huawei had used patented technology without authorisation. In another instance, T-Mobile accused Huawei in September 2014 of several attempts to steal information about the company's robotics designs. Two Huawei employees had entered the T-Mobile laboratory in Bellevue, Washington, to steal details of 'Tappy', a smartphone-testing robot, and removed some of its components.

Unease about Huawei had been building for years, and certainly since the unexpected collapse in 2009 of the Canadian telecommunications giant Nortel. The company operated internationally, with a European manufacturing plant in Paignton, Devon, as part of Standard Telephone & Cables, but there had been numerous complaints that the business had been thoroughly compromised in around 2000 when it began building systems for Huawei, which had routinely cut corners by copying Nortel products and manuals, thereby undermining the company and eventually forcing it into bankruptcy. Another venerable company in Huawei's sights was Marconi which was the subject of a takeover in March 2005. Marconi's board thought the deal would allow the company to expand into China, but Huawei was only interested in establishing itself in Europe where, in December 2004, it had beaten Ericsson to a $186 million contract to provide Holland with a 3G mobile network. By the end of April 2005 Marconi was on the brink of disaster when its biggest customer, British Telecom, chose Huawei instead as a participant in a £10 billion five-year investment programme.

Once again, a familiar pattern emerged, with a company going into partnership of a contractual relationship with Huawei, and then finding its own products undermined or compromised. By November 2010 Huawei's predatory tactics in strategically important sectors had been noted by the intelligence community, to the point that in 2009 the Chairman of the Joint Intelligence Committee, Sir Alex Allan, circulated a paper warning of the possible dangers associated with Huawei.

In July 2018, the Australian government announced plans to ban Huawei from its 5G project over security fears and noted, 'It's a Chinese company and under Communist law, they have to work for their intelligence agencies'. In August 2018 Huawei was found guilty of infringing on LTE technology patents with some smartphones and must pay the Texas-based company PanOptis $10.5 million. The patents involved technology that decoded picture and audio data, and Huawei used the patents without paying the requisite licence.

On 16 November 2018 the district court in Dusseldorf, Germany, ruled that Huawei (and ZTE) infringed patents of two patent holders of MPEG LA's AVC patent portfolio licence by using their technologies in mobile phones that implement the AVC/H.264 standard.

Huawei suffered another body-blow in December 2018 when Ren's daughter Cathy Meng, who was also Huawei's Chief Financial Officer and a Canadian citizen, was arrested at Vancouver Airport on American charges alleging bank and wire fraud in connection with Huawei's Iranian subsidiary, Skycom. The allegations were contained in a US DoJ sealed indictment which was not published until the end of January 2019. According to the complaint, Huawei had required a US bank to clear more than $100 million for Skycom between 2010 and 2014, in breach of American sanctions. At the DoJ FBI Director Christopher Wray observed, 'As you can tell from the number and magnitude of charges, Huawei and its senior executives repeatedly refused to respect the laws of the United States and standard international business practices'.

The charges referred to by Wray concerned the earlier incident involving T-Mobile's Tappy. At the time Huawei had argued in court that the employees responsible for taking Tappy's arms home were 'rogue actors' who had been operating independently and fired, but the DoJ claimed obstruction of justice and revealed that some Huawei emails suggested that the company had encouraged miscreants to steal its rivals' secrets, and had even provided an encrypted method of communication for the thieves. Although T-Mobile's civil lawsuit had ended in federal court in May 2017 with the financial damages, the DoJ was still in pursuit.

All these charges were later dropped, and Meng returned to China in September 2021. Meng's arrest continued to have political and trade ramifications for Canada, including long prison sentences for two Canadians, Michael Kovrig and Michael Spavor, arrested in China on espionage charges. Observers interpreted this development as pressure on Canada to release Meng. China also blocked imports of Canadian shipments of canola and pork worth billions of dollars. Both men were released on the day Meng flew to Beijing. Christopher Wray later commented 'as a country, we must consider carefully the risk that companies like Huawei pose if we allow them into our telecommunications infrastructure'.[5]

Commentators were quick to point out that for a company devoid of any official government links, Huawei received instant support from Beijing when Cathy Meng was detained, and some aspects of the incident were troubling. Quite apart from the two Canadian hostages, there was an unusual incident in the East China Sea in June 2019 when two Chinese Army Air Force Sukhoi-30 jet fighters aggressively buzzed HMCS *Regina*. This episode, as the frigate transited the Straits of Taiwan with the supply ship *Asterix*, was interpreted by analysts as a none-too-subtle exercise of military power to underpin a political position.

In January 2019 the Chinese manager at Huawei's local office in Warsaw, Wang Weijing, alias Stansilaw Wang, was arrested, together with a former Polish intelligence officer and cyber security expert, Piotr Durbajlo, and charged with spying for China. A former Chinese diplomat who had graduated from the Beijing University of Foreign Studies, Wang had been a language student in Łódź before being appointed a cultural attaché at the Chinese consulate in Gdańsk. He then joined Huawei's Enterprise Business Group in 2017 His accomplice, Durbajlo, formerly worked for the Agencia Bezpiecznenstwa Wewnetznego (ABW) as the deputy director in the Department of Informational Security. At the time of his detention, he was employed by the French firm Orange Polska, Poland's leading communications provider. Huawei fired Wang after the arrest, and both Wang and Durbajlo faced 15 years' imprisonment if convicted at their trial, which opened *in camera* in June 2021 and ended soon afterwards with Wang's deportation.

In 2017 the African Union discovered that the computer system at its plush $200 million (Chinese-built) headquarters in Addis Ababa had been operating at high volume between midnight and 0200 for the past five years. When monitored, the activity turned out to be the transfer of huge quantities of data to a server located in Shanghai. Furthermore, an electronic security sweep of the building revealed dozens of hidden microphones and illicit recording equipment.

On 19 May 2019, President Trump added Huawei to a trade blacklist of companies that makes it difficult for them to conduct business with their US counterparts, prompting Google to cease providing Huawei with access, technical support and collaboration involving its proprietary applications and services, a move bound to damage Huawei's smartphone business outside of China.

In November 2019 the Australian Strategic Policy Institutes International Cyber Policy Centre concluded that many Chinese high-tech companies, including Huawei, were directly supporting China's surveillance of Xinjiang Province and the mass indoctrination campaign, especially against the Uighurs.

* * *

The British reaction to these events was a series of briefings by the security and intelligence agencies, MI5, GCHQ and the Secret

Intelligence Service, identifying China as a major global cyber threat. This was reflected by the Parliamentary Intelligence and Security Committee which addressed the issue in the 2012–2013 annual report:

> Whilst state actors continue to pose the greatest threat (China and Russia, for example, are alleged to be involved in cyber-attacks), we have been told that a number of countries are also using private groups to carry out state-sponsored attacks. [XXXX] These state-affiliated groups consist of skilled cyber professionals, undertaking attacks on diverse targets such as financial institutions and energy companies. These groups pose a threat in their own right, but it is the combination of their capability and the objectives of their state backers which makes them of particular concern.[6]

The Committee then set out the scale of the current challenge:

> Given the potential for the loss of sensitive information, protecting the Government's own IT systems is of crucial importance. In recent years, many government departments have come under cyber-attack: often, this has involved websites being disrupted by 'denial of service' attacks, and last summer over 200 email accounts across 30 government departments were targeted in an attempt to steal confidential information. It appears that the Government systems' defences are reasonably well developed, although evidence we have taken suggests that it is a constant challenge to ensure that cyber 'hygiene' is maintained (e.g. updating anti-virus software), and to ensure that cyber defences develop quickly in response to the changing nature of the attacks.
>
> Government departments are also targeted via attacks on industry suppliers which may hold government information on their own systems. We have been told that cyber espionage '[has] resulted in MOD data being stolen, [XXXX] This has both security and financial consequences for the UK.[7]

The creation in 2010 of the Huawei Cyber Security Evaluation Centre (HCSEC), was an early recognition of the British government's central dilemma, that is was committed to developing broadband and interconnectivity, but was plainly vulnerable to Chinese attacks. The expedient was an agreement between the company and HM Government about mitigating any perceived risks to UK national security arising from the involvement of Huawei in parts of the UK's critical national infrastructure. HCSEC provides security evaluation for a range of products and services used in the UK market. Through HCSEC, the UK Government is provided with insight into Huawei UK's strategies and product ranges. GCHQ, as the national technical authority for information assurance and the lead Government operational agency on cyber security, leads for the Government in dealing with HCSEC and with Huawei more generally.[8]

According to HCSEC's first annual report, dated March 2015:

> The HCSEC Oversight Board was established in early 2014 on the recommendation of the UK National Security Adviser [Kim Darroch]. The Board is chaired by Ciaran Martin, DG for Cyber Security at GCHQ. It comprises senior executives from Huawei, including in the role of Deputy Chair, as well as senior representatives from across Government and the UK telecommunications sector. The role of the Oversight Board is to oversee and ensure the independence, competence and overall effectiveness of HCSEC. By doing so it is then able to advise the National Security Adviser (to whom this report is formally submitted), allowing him to provide assurance to Ministers, Parliament and ultimately the general public that the risks are being well managed. The Oversight Board's role relates only to products that are relevant to UK national security risk.[9]

The HCSEC set out the background to the evolving relationship with Huawei, based on its sudden and overwhelming appearance in the British market, as a supplier of key components to virtually every part of the telecommunications industry:

> Huawei UK came to prominence in the UK in 2004, after successfully bidding for BT's major network upgrade. Over recent years, Huawei has significantly increased its access into the UK communications market including securing contracts with Vodafone, EE, O2, Talk Talk, Virgin Media and Sky.
>
> The modern reality is that virtually every telecommunications network worldwide incorporates foreign technology. Most manufacturers have some of their equipment built in China and use technical components from a global supply chain, regardless of the location of their headquarters. That said, as Huawei's customer base in the UK expanded, the UK Government has sought to put in place a mitigation strategy to manage any potential security risks associated with the prevalence of Huawei equipment in UK networks. Towards the end of the last decade, the Government embarked on a series of discussions with Huawei aimed at reaching a mutually acceptable framework for providing assurance that any such risks to UK national security were being mitigated. This culminated in the company and the Government agreeing to a set of arrangements for the governance of Huawei's involvement in the UK in 2010.[10]

Having accepted the need to cooperate with GCHQ in order to maintain its grip on the British market, and having already won the contract to expand British Telecom's network, Huawei's management must have considered that paying for twenty-five staff and accommodating them in an HCSEC office Banbury a small price to pay Daniel while he supped with the lion. As the HCSEC reported:

> Although outside the formal work of the Board, in the interests transparency, this report includes a summary of the discussions between senior Government representatives and the company in January 2015. At the invitation of Huawei HQ, the Chairman of the Oversight Board, Ciaran Martin of GCHQ, together with the then Director of the Cabinet Office's Office of Cyber Security and Information Assurance, James Quinault, and GCHQ's Technical Director, Dr Ian Levy, visited Huawei Headquarters in Shenzhen, China. They met with company leaders and held extensive discussions with Ken Hu, rotating Chief Executive Officer, Ryan Ding, Executive Director and Deputy Chair of the Oversight Board and Chen Lifang, Huawei's Board member for public affairs. They also met with a variety of cyber security specialists working for the company.
>
> During the visit Huawei presented the delegation with an overview of the Huawei Cyber Security Strategy and a summary of progress made on the implementation of the strategy over the last four years. The Government representatives received continued assurance from Huawei about their commitments to HCSEC and the broader arrangements, and were informed during the visit that the company had agreed to a funding request to move HCSEC to a larger building to facilitate any further expansion. Subsequently the Managing Director of HCSEC is developing appropriate business plans and budget proposals in order to implement an enhanced operational model, agreed with GCHQ Technical Authority, to help overcome current recruitment, operational and accommodation related issues.[11]

The HCSEC concluded that Huawei's cooperation with GCHQ had been 'exemplary', but the honeymoon was not to last.

On 8 January 2019, Oxford University suspended donations from Huawei due to 'public concerns raised in recent months surrounding UK partnerships with Huawei'. This announcement followed Defence Secretary Gavin Williamson's remark that he had 'very deep concerns' about Huawei's involvement in the UK's rollout of 5G. Apparently the British government had received advice from GCHQ expressing doubts over the quality of Huawei's engineering and the company's commitment to security. The next HCSEC annual report, published in September 2020, set out the problems:

Product version management
Huawei continues to maintain multiple product versions for the same product, and continues to provide large patches which modify a significant proportion of the product. Correspondingly, it continues to be necessary for HCSEC to analyse a different codebase for each operator, despite them using the same product. In 2019, HCSEC was required to analyse five different versions of Huawei's 5G base station across the UK's four operators. Huawei claim that these are from a global product line, but we have no evidence to support this, meaning that HCSEC cannot derive any benefit from international analysis of Huawei products.

Configuration management
For specific products used in the UK, Huawei have simplified and made significant improvements to the build process, although issues remain. While a positive outcome, we do not yet have evidence that this is a holistic shift in Huawei's approach, rather than a point-fix for these products. Correspondingly, we do not yet have confidence that this improvement will be sustained.

Binary equivalence
HCSEC has now verified binary equivalence across eight product builds. This provides confidence that the specific products deployed in UK networks have been inspected by HCSEC. Huawei have committed to delivery of binary equivalence across officially released versions of all carrier products sold into UK from Dec 2020. Unfortunately, binary equivalence remains a bespoke project, rather than a consistent output of Huawei's build process, as has been recommended by NCSC. Consequently, the NCSC does not have confidence that binary equivalence will be sustainable.

Product Quality
Major quality deficiencies still exist in the products analysed by HCSEC. Sustained evidence of poor coding practices was found, including evidence that Huawei continues to fail to follow its own internal secure coding guidelines. This is despite some minor improvements over previous years. Huawei has made improvements against certain metrics, and most point-issues identified in previous quality reports have been remediated.

During 2019, HCSEC identified critical, user-facing vulnerabilities in fixed access products. The vulnerabilities were caused by particularly poor code quality in user-facing protocol handlers and the use of an old operating system. The vulnerabilities were a serious example of the issues that are more likely to occur given the deficiencies in Huawei's engineering practices, and during 2019 UK operators needed to take extraordinary action to mitigate the risk. Huawei have since fixed the specific vulnerabilities in the UK, but in doing so, introduced an additional major issue into the product, adding further evidence that deficiencies in Huawei's engineering processes remain today.

In this example, the code quality in these user-facing protocol handlers was sufficiently poor that NCSC has required Huawei to fully rewrite the code, and rearchitect the product's security. Huawei have committed to doing so by June 2020.

Component management

The major component management issues identified in previous reports remain. Huawei continues to include a wide range of old and duplicate components in products deployed in the UK, and fails to properly manage these components.

As discussed at length in previous reports, Huawei continues to use an old and now out-of-mainstream support version of a well-known and widely used real time operating system supplied by a third party. During 2019, Huawei have created a remediation plan and have proactively worked with UK operators to move products onto an internally maintained operating system (Huawei RTOS, based on an externally maintained Linux distribution) or to replace the boards. Of the very large number of boards impacted in the UK, 17% had been updated or replaced by December 2019 in line with the remediation plan agreed between Huawei and the operators. Hence despite efforts by both Huawei and UK operators, there remains a significant number of boards containing critical out-of-mainstream support components in UK networks, and Huawei's access to support for this component is likely inhibited by the US Entity Listing. This leaves the UK exposed to risk.

The causes of the on-going risk are as follows:

1. Huawei had inadequate component management and did not align end-of-life dates of components with the end-of-life date of products. Furthermore, Huawei did not identify the issue themselves.
2. Once identified by NCSC, Huawei did not remediate the issue promptly. It took 18 months for network remediation to begin.
3. Remediation of nationally distributed access networks, including product replacement where necessary, takes time and is resource intensive.

The issue has been compounded by Huawei being placed on the US Entity List.

The success of the remediation programme is dependent on Huawei actively maintaining Huawei's replacement operating system (Huawei RTOS). NCSC investigated Huawei's plans to manage and maintain

Huawei RTOS during 2019 and found that the plans for RTOS were not practically sustainable.

During 2019, further component management issues were identified with Huawei's use of open-source components and its vertical integration of components. Some improvements were made by Huawei to rationalise components and reduce the number of duplicated components, demonstrating the company is fixing specific point-issues when directed to do so.

NCSC continues to have no confidence that Huawei will effectively maintain components within its products. It is likely that further issues will occur in the future which will require remediation and potentially product replacement, as is on-going today.

Transformation

In 2018, Huawei presented to the Oversight Board its intent to transform its software engineering process through the investment of $2 billion over 5 years (completing in 2023). The NCSC reported last year that it has no evidence that this is more than a proposed initial budget for as yet unspecified activities. This year, HCSEC has evaluated individual products, which show some limited improvements in certain metrics. However, the set of significant vulnerabilities in a product that had gone through the transformation programme means that we still cannot have any confidence that these represent a systematic change in Huawei's approach. The Board will require sustained evidence of better software engineering and cyber security quality verified by HCSEC and NCSC.

As set out in last year's report, formal oversight of Huawei's global transformation plan does not fall within the scope of Oversight Board activities. However, it is important that the Board see details of the transformation plan and evidence of its impact on products being used in UK networks before it can be confident it will drive the change needed to address the risks identified. Unless and until a detailed and satisfactory plan has been provided, it is not possible to offer any degree of confidence that the identified problems can be addressed by Huawei.

Conclusion

NCSC continues to believe that the UK mitigation strategy, which includes HCSEC performing technical work and the Oversight Board providing assurance as two components, is the best way to manage the risk of Huawei's involvement in the UK telecommunications sector. The discovery of the issues in this report are an indication of the model working properly. Huawei continues to engage with this process.

The work of HCSEC summarised above continues to reveal serious and systematic defects in Huawei's software engineering and cyber security competence. While there have been limited improvements in 2019, the significant deficiencies and associated risks detailed in the

2018 report remain. There is not yet evidence that Huawei is undergoing a significant transformation to sustainably fix these deficiencies. For this reason, NCSC continues to advise the Oversight Board that it is only appropriate to provide limited technical assurance in the security risk management possible for equipment currently deployed in the UK, since the NCSC has not seen evidence that Huawei software engineering and cyber security will sustainably improve. Even this limited assurance is possible only on the basis that, thanks largely to the work of HCSEC, the defects in Huawei equipment are fairly well understood in the UK. Given that knowledge, in extremis, the NCSC could direct Huawei on remediation for equipment currently in the UK, as happened in one case this year. This should not be taken to minimise the difficulty in doing so or to suggest that this would be a sustainable approach. In some cases, remediation will also require hardware replacement (due to CPU and memory constraints) which may or may not be part of natural operator asset management and upgrade cycles. Given both the shortfalls in good software engineering and cyber security practice, the lack of visibility of the trajectory of Huawei's R&D processes through their announced transformation plan, and the product modifications being made as a result of the US Entity Listing, it is highly likely that security risk management for new products will be more difficult.[12]

Although the report was written in what Whitehall denizens call 'Mandarin', the HCSEC revealed that it had discovered flaws in Huawei's software which had not been admitted, and that the issues arising had not been addressed for 18 months. Worse, the HCSEC had little or no confidence the situation would improve, thereby creating a risk for Britain's national security. Obviously the restrained language was intended to keep Huawei cooperative, but not necessarily compliant.

The question of Huawei's role in Britain's 5G network became a political time-bomb and on 23 April 2019 when the *Daily Telegraph* published a leak from the National Security Council, attended by intelligence chiefs and senior members of Prime Minister Teresa May's Cabinet. The report claimed, with considerable accuracy, that the prime minister had agreed to allow Huawei to play a major role in building the UK's 5G internet system, despite continued pressure from the United States. Williamson was accused of being the source of the leak and fired. The investigation had been conducted by the Cabinet Secretary, Sir Mark Sedwell, who produced 'compelling evidence' that Williamson had been responsible for the unauthorised disclosure.

Huawei's reaction to the growing controversy about Britain's dependence, especially in the construction of a new generation of nuclear power plants and 5G, was a case study in the purchase of influence inside Whitehall. Although often considered a model for independent administration, the British civil service had evolved into a body that relied on trust rather than a rule-book, and the ease with which senior civil servants were able to retire and take up lucrative roles in commerce and industry often attracted adverse comment. In Huawei's case, there were several examples of the 'revolving door' into lucrative appointments in the private sector. In January 2011 John Suffolk flew to China with a team from GCHQ to confront the firm with the latest security breaches, acting at the Cabinet Office's chief information officer. A month later, Suffolk announced his intention to accept Huawei's offer of a job as the company's global head of cyber security. In March 2015 Sir Andrew Cahn, the former head of UK Trade and Investment, became a non-executive director of Huawei's British subsidiary. Similarly, Lord Browne, preciously the Chairman of British Petroleum, also joined Huawei UK as non-executive chairman.

Almost inevitably, as the evidence against Huawei mounted, the US government imposed sanctions on Huawei in May and two months later London followed suit, declaring a ban on any purchase of Huawei 5G equipment after 31 December 2020, and the removal of all Huawei equipment from the 5G network by the end of 2027.

The global fallout of the Huawei ban would be immense. For instance, in February 2019, New Zealand's prime minister, Jacinda Arden, had announced an independent assessment of the risk of using Huawei technologies in her country's 5G networks after it had been suggested that British precautions could be used by other nations. In November 2018, New Zealand's signals intelligence agency, the Government Communications Security Bureau, rejected an initial request from the telecommunications service Spark to use Huawei's 5G equipment. Soon afterward, in April 2019, current and former Pentagon officials warned of the risks to future military operations posed by allies using Chinese technology in their 5G wireless networks, suggesting that allies allowing Chinese firms, including Huawei, to equip their networks posed an unacceptable risk of espionage and disruptive cyber-attacks on military operations due to the firms' ties with the Chinese government. In other words, Huawei's participation in any art of the 'Five Eyes' communications architecture might compromise the other partners in the alliance. In fact the Australian government had banned Huawei and ZTE from its own network in August 2018.

Paradoxically, the blacklisting of Huawei, which had led to a dramatic deterioration of relations between Canberra and Beijing, would be the catalyst in May 2023 for a new military agreement, designated

AUKUS, in which Australia, the US and the Royal Navy would design and build a new class of nuclear-powered bur conventionally-armed submarines in British and Australian shipyards. Under the terms of the agreement Australia will buy five *Virginia* class attack submarines from the US. In addition, the Royal Australian Navy's shore base near Perth in Western Australia, HMAS *Stirling*, will host a British *Astute* class hunter-killer and four US Navy *Virginia* class submarines from 2027.

Although it would be simplistic to detect a common thread running through Huawei's aggressive tactics and corporate misconduct through to the West's reaction to the deteriorating relationship with Beijing, the company's exclusion from its target markets will have a lasting impact on the company, and indeed the whole Chinese economy.

Chapter VIII

SIGNALS INTELLIGENCE

We are not thinking long-term enough about the threat that China poses, given its aspirations are out to 2049, 2039, 2025, depending on which of their documents you read and of course all of those are way beyond traditional government planning cycles.

Jeremy Fleming, July 2019
Director GCHQ 2017–23

Within the intelligence spectrum, signals intelligence (SIGINT) is often regarded as the most sensitive of sources as it is so easily compromised and terminated. One hint that a particular channel is being exploited is likely to ensure its demise. Western knowledge of Chinese SIGINT must have greatly increased in 1979 when, following the overthrow of the Shah, the National Security Agency was obliged to evacuate the ground-stations at Astara, Behshahr, Kabkan, Khorramabad, and Shirabad. To restore coverage of Soviet communications traffic across Afghanistan, then a priority because of the unexpected occupation of Kabul at Christmas, and missile test telemetry traffic, the CIA's Ted Price reportedly negotiated with Vice Premier Deng Xiaoping in January 1980 for the construction of two sites, at Korla and Qitai in central Xinjiang province.[1] With the approval of the Central Committee's International Liaison Department, these facilities would operate for some two decades without a leak, and in 1996 a further listening post was established at Ruili in Yunnan province, allegedly to monitor the movement of illicit drug shipments from Burma, following talks conducted between President Jiang and Bill Clinton in October 1997. Altogether the joint monitoring programme established thirty-four sites on PRC territory, all run by PLA3.

The most dramatic expansion of China's intelligence-collection capability has been the huge investment made in SIGINT and the dramatic rise in the number of purpose-built surface vessels deployed to monitor an adversary's communications traffic. Hitherto, Chinese involvement in SIGINT appeared to be limited to small-scale interception based on primitive equipment suites placed in the PLA's huge militarised offshore fishing fleet. The PLA's Third Department, responsible for SIGINT, is known to operate a network of intercept stations close to its foreign borders, with a large installation on Lake Kinghathu, at Jilemutu, and at Jixi monitoring Russian traffic in the north-east. Others at Erli and Hamian cover Mongolia. Indian communications are intercepted at Chengdu and Dayi, with Vietnam monitored from Kunming. In addition, there are large intercept facilities at Shenyang, near Jinan, and in Shanghai and Nanjing. Surveillance on Taiwan is maintained by a chain of sites in the Fujian and Guangdong military districts.

The Third Department, which is estimated to employ a staff of 20,000, is closely associated with the Fourth Department, the PLA organisation responsible for electronic warfare, and incorporates an Electronic Countermeasures and Radar Department that also conducts cryptographic operations from numerous ground stations. The Third Department's headquarters is located close to the GSD First (Operations) Department complex in the hills north-west of the Summer Palace and is staffed by a large number of linguists trained at the PLA's Foreign Language Institute.

SIGINT collection operations are controlled centrally from Beijing, with subordinate satellite sites spread across the country. A large station in Lanzhou monitors Russian traffic and also functions as a strategic early-warning facility, while the Shenyang station covers Russia, Japan, and Korea. The Chengdu facility monitors India, Pakistan, and Southeast Asia, while Nanjing concentrates on Taiwan. Guangzhou covers Southeast Asia and the South China Sea, and smaller stations undertake a tactical role.

The PLA Navy's (PLAN) interest in maritime interception did not become apparent until October 1982 when the Type 812 was launched and began to experience severe engineering problems. Based on the design of a survey ship, work had started on the blueprints in 1977, and the construction contract was given to the Shanghai Hudong Shipyard. When the *Xiangyanghong 21* was completed she was assigned to the South Sea Fleet and effectively was the PLA Navy's first generation ship to receive the NATO designation 'AGI' for 'Auxiliary General, Intelligence' and displayed the antenna arrays on masts so familiar to NATO analysts who had studied the Soviet AGI fleet. This was quickly followed by the Type 814A *Bei-Diao* which entered service in September 1986 and received the NATO designation DADIE ('Big Spy' in Mandarin). Reportedly the PLAN's SIGINT activities were coordinated by an analytical centre integrated into the South Sea Fleet headquarters at Zhanjiang.[2]

A year later, in 1987, the Type 856 *Xing Fengshan* underwent sea trials. Based on the design of a submarine rescue vessel, the *Xing Fengshan* was unusual in that she was armed with machine guns. The PLAN would probably have continued with this rather relaxed development programme if Beijing had not been left aghast by the 1991 'shock and awe' campaign that marked DESERT STORM, the Coalition's assault on Saddam Hussein's regime which had been distinguished by the total elimination of Iraq's air defences. As a demonstration of precision bombing by stealth aircraft, and the war-winning significance of electronic warfare in general, the offensive was hugely impressive, and the impact was felt and understood in China where a third generation of SIGINT, represented by the *Beijixing*, entered service in 1999 and boasted a helicopter hangar and flight-deck. Study of the three parabolic antennae suggested that the ship's role had been extended to the interception of telemetry during missile tests, another major milestone in the development of a modern SIGINT capability, combined with a surface presence to support a growing submarine fleet that would include up to five *Jin* class ballistic missile (SSBN) boats. The first of these was spotted by a satellite at the Xiaopingdao base in July 2007, and two others were photographed at the Bohai shipyard in October 2007.

Thus far, the PLAN's operational experience of SSBNs has been limited to the Type 092 *Xia* which never completed a mission and for years was moored in Jianggezhuang, near Qingdao, constantly undergoing repairs and refits. Intended to be armed with twelve JL-1 missiles, it never ventured outside Chinese territorial waters and was beset with radiation leaks from the reactor.

By 2023 the PLAN's maritime SIGINT platforms consisted of nine ships, masquerading as oceanographic research vessels, of which five display acoustic detection apparatus, including towed arrays, equipment that is usually associated with advanced anti-submarine warfare techniques.[3]

Although the cover for many of the AGIs was hydrographic research, that discipline had become a necessity as the PLAN tentatively entered the field of submarine operations with a fleet of some fifty conventional coastal boats, and six *Shang* class nuclear-powered hunter-killers. The Chinese authorities expressed their sensitivity about their progress in submarine technology when in March 2009 an American vessel, the USNA *Impeccable*, was the subject of aggressive harassment as it conducted acoustic research in the Yellow Sea, 75 miles outside the PLAN's base at Yulin on Hainan Island. The *Impeccable*, one of a class of five purpose-built twin-hulled support ships, was surrounded by five Chinese vessels and forced to abandon her mission and depart the scene. Naturally, the exact nature of *Impeccable*'s mission was not disclosed, but the class's striking design and configuration is intended for the deployment and servicing of acoustic arrays which are planted on the ocean floor and are capable of detecting the sound of target submarines over vast distances, or are sensors towed from the stern of a submarine or surface vessel. Doubtless the PLAN's intemperate reaction to the *Impeccable* reflected a degree of frustration at the American strategy of brazenly conducting anti-submarine tactics in China's backyard, a strategy that would be interpreted in Beijing as provocative, even in international waters.

Understandably, heavy secrecy surrounds the PLAN's submarine assets but satellite launches and the insertion of low-orbit space vehicles are harder to conceal. Similarly, the construction of tracking stations at Neuquen, in Argentina's Patagonia; Ungwana Bay, Kenya; Karachi and Kaka Shah Kaku near Lahore in Pakistan; and Swakopmund in Namibia; and a new facility in Bejucal, Cuba, reflects Beijing's determination to catch up with its competitors and currently is estimated to manage some 207 satellites with varying missions. Other sites, with the potential for dual use, have been identified at Santiago, Chile; Chancay in Peru; Mexico, Brazil and Venezuela. Although this does not amount to a truly global coverage, as boasted by the 'Five Eyes' alliance, the construction of four huge Type 718 *Yuan Wang* class satellite tracking ships allows the PLAN to take advantage of newly-built port facilities at Djibouti, Panama and El Salvador.[4]

By its nature, much about SIGINT is invisible in that intercept facilities are easily disguised, either concealed in diplomatic premises or contained in a portable suite that can be aboard an ostensibly harmless ship. It is the festoons of antenna arrays that give the game away but even these can be places in radomes or similar structures to camouflage their purpose, or the range of frequencies being targeted. Similarly, airborne collection was limited to a small group of PLA Air Force (PLAAF) intelligence collection aircraft include Antonov-12 CUBs.

A reverse-engineered version of the Soviet-designed An-12 went into production by the Xi'an Aircraft Company in 1981, renamed the Y-8 (with the NATO designation MOTH). This is the turboprop workhorse of the PLAAF and up to thirty Y-9JZ variants are deployed regularly in a maritime patrol role in the East China Sea, causing political consternation in Japan where the flights were interpreted as deliberate provocations. Most recently, as part of a modernisation programme, a dozen Canadian-built Bombardier Challenger 850 jets have been purchased to join ten Antonov-30 and four Tupolev-154 electronic intelligence platforms.

Another highly visible manifestation of airborne collection has been the so-called weather balloons launched from Hainan Island which have drifted at high altitude over Japan and the United States and, in February 2023, excited considerable media attention, leading to the destruction of one large 30ft platform weighing an estimated 2,000lbs, suspended under a balloon which was shot down at 60,000ft off the coast of South Carolina by a Sidewinder missile fired by an F-22 Raptor. The wreckage was retrieved from the sea and examined at the FBI forensic laboratory at Quantico which declared that the equipment was inconsistent with apparatus employed to collect meteorological data, and possessed some manoeuvrability which enabled it to be directed over, and loiter above, specific targets. Another unusual characteristic was the large solar panels which generated sufficient power to operate a small propeller and relay intercepted signals traffic.

The balloon's flight-path was examined by analysts and was shown to have included several sensitive sites, such as Mamstrom AFB in Montana, Minot AFB in North Dakota, Francis E. Warren AFB in Wyoming and Whiteman AFB in Missouri. All these four bases were equipped with nuclear-capable missiles or aircraft, so were particularly preoccupied with security and conscious of potentially hostile reconnaissance, and this led to speculation that the balloon's sensors were designed to collect imagery and electronic intelligence, and relay it to China via preprogrammed satellites, although the US Air Force escort doubtless took electronic countermeasures to jam any offending transmissions.

On 10 February 2023, six days after the recovered equipment had been delivered to Quantico, the US Department of Commerce announced export restrictions on five Chinese companies that had been assessed as having supplied some of the balloon's (largely American-manufactured) payload. They were the Beijing Nanjiang Aerospace Technology; China Electronics Technology Group Corporation 48th Research Institute; Dongguan Lingkong Remote Sensing Technology Company; Eagles Men Aviation Science 7 Technology Group Company; Guangzhou Tian-Hai-Xiang Aviation Technology Company; and Shanxi Eagles Men Aviation Science & Technology Group.

Confirmation that the balloon's launch site had been on Hainan Island served to attract yet more attention to China's smallest province which accommodates the Lingahui base, the PLA's Third Technical Department, an organisation linked in 2009 to cyberwarfare and, more specifically, the GhostNet group of computer hackers.

Chinese sensitivity about Hainan Island had become obvious in March 2001 when an US Air Force EP-3 Orion flying a routine SIGINT collection mission off China's coast was intercepted by a pair of J-8 jet fighters, one of which accidentally collided with the US plane. The pilot succeeded in landing the badly damaged aircraft on Hainan Island where Chinese troops arrested the crew of twenty-four and examined the sophisticated intercept equipment. After 11 days of tense diplomatic negotiations, the crew was released and the plane was dismantled, packed into two huge cargo planes, and flown back to the United States.

Chapter IX

COMMERCIAL ESPIONAGE

Espionage offers a relatively cheap, quick and easy method to obtain information that can help Chinese companies remain competitive. Many of China's biggest companies are state owned, or have close links to the state. They may receive intelligence collected by the Chinese intelligence services, and are also able to undertake commercial espionage for their own benefit.

The Threat from Chinese Espionage
British Security Service, 2000

In the 1930s, as the Soviet Union attempted to modernise its antiquated industries, Stalin turned to his intelligence apparatus to acquire the skills and techniques necessary to fulfil the over-ambitious objectives of a series of disastrous five-year plans which served only to undermine the country's economy. Stalin's ingenious solution was to direct the NKVD, which already had a well-established presence in the capitalist countries, to develop its contacts with local Communist Parties and their contacts in the socialist-dominated trade union movement to prioritise the collection of intellectual property, industrial techniques, patented chemical formulae and other commercial and protected processes that would benefit and support the Kremlin's vision of a modern industrial base that was not dependent on foreign licences and expensive contracts with Western competitors. One of Stalin's first infrastructure schemes, to create a power grid of electricity-generating plants which could provide energy to an imagined chain of manufacturing centres, would end in paranoia when the Metropolitan Vickers project collapsed with the arrest of a group of British engineers engaged in the construction of electricity power stations and overhead high-tension power cables. One of the engineers was Allan Monkhouse, who had lived in the Soviet Union for nine years and devoted more than 22 years of his life to developing trade between London and Moscow. All his efforts were nullified when, in March 1933, he was arrested and accused of being part of a massive conspiracy to undermine Communism and sabotage Stalin's plans for economic reform and recovery. Monkhouse's detention by the notorious OGPU secret police. together with that of forty-two others, among whom were six British engineers, would cast a long-lasting shadow over relations with Moscow and the role of foreigners in socialist industrialisation.

After some hours of interrogation at the Lubyanka, during which he was accused of espionage on behalf of the British Secret Service, sabotage and bribery, Monkhouse and a colleague, Charles Nordwall, were released on condition they did not leave Moscow. The eventual indictment, handed to the defendants on 9 April, which ran to 85 pages, revealed that Monkhouse's secretary had made an incriminating statement to the OGPU about the activities of Monkhouse's chief engineer, Leslie C. Thornton. At the subsequent trial, in which there were seventeen defendants, Monkhouse's lawyer pleaded his client guilty to a charge of bribery and Thornton made what was purported to be a signed confession in which he admitted having worked for the British Secret Intelligence Service, and named Monkhouse as the organiser of a network of twenty-six engineers, all his agents.

> All our spying operations on USSR territory are directed by the British Intelligence Service, through their agent, C.S. Richards, who occupied the position of Managing Director of the Metropolitan-Vickers Electrical Export Company Limited. Spying operations on USSR territory were directed by myself and Monkhouse, representatives of the above-mentioned firm, who are contractors, by official agreement, to the Soviet Government, for the supply of turbines and electrical equipment and the furnishing of technical aid agreements. On the instructions of C.S. Richards given to me to this end, British personnel were gradually drawn into the spying organisation after their arrival on USSR territory and instructed as to the information required. During the whole period of our presence on USSR territory, from the total of British staff employed, 27 men were engaged in spying operations. Of the above, fifteen men which included Monkhouse were engaged in economic and political spying, also in the investigation of the defence and offence possibilities of the Soviet Union. The remaining 12 were engaged in political and economic spying.[1]

Similarly, a construction engineer, William MacDonald, conceded that he had collected and reported information for SIS from the Zlatoust Armament Works. Monkhouse, who was the senior Vickers representative and identified as the ringleader, pleaded innocent to all the remaining charges and protested that the bribery incident concerned a loan that had been written off as a bad debt. Under interrogation he also made a deposition regarding his predecessor, Anton Simon, who had worked for Metro-Vickers until his death in 1928:

> I knew that Simon had a special fund which he used for bribes. I firmly believe that he was interested in certain counter-revolutionary movements, but I did not enjoy his confidence. He did not trust me for certain personal and political reasons. I cannot give exact information about his activity in this direction. Upon Simon's death I was, immediately afterwards, appointed Metro-Vickers' manager in the USSR.[2]

At his short trial in Moscow Monkhouse was acquitted on the charge of espionage but convicted of having known of Thornton's sabotage, and of complicity in bribery. Thornton was sentenced to three years' imprisonment, Macdonald two years. Together with his South African-born engineer John Cushny and his colleague, Charles Nordwall, Monkhouse was deported to London. Only William Gregory was acquitted on all charges.

The British government expressed indignation at the treatment of the six prisoners from the moment of their arrest but Monkhouse's account of the episode, *Moscow 1911-33*, was not entirely candid.[3] He omitted to mention his own experience as an intelligence officer in Russia during the 1918 Allied intervention in Archangel, service that he had shared with C.S. Richards, the export manager of Metropolitan Vickers. At his trial the Soviet prosecutor emphasised Monkhouse's intelligence connections but in his own version Monkhouse ignored the issue entirely.

The Metropolitan Vickers incident served to exacerbate Stalin's paranoia and demonstrate the value of stealing technology abroad, a strategy that obviated the need to accommodate foreign spies on Soviet territory. As it happens, there was some justification for Stalin's suspicions. The entire Metropolitan Vickers contract had been supervised by SIS which learned a valuable lesson about the vulnerability of employing amateurs to engage in espionage in the Soviet Union.

Stalin's principal foreign intelligence service, the NKVD, maintained a large *rezidentura* at the Soviet consulate-general in New York which managed a network of agents who had access to various industrial processes that were of interest to Moscow. One such source was Harry Gold, a Swiss-born biochemist who had been brought to the United States as a child by his Russian refugee parents, and had engaged in industrial espionage for the Soviets in and around Philadelphia, where he lived alone since 1935 when he had been recruited by his friend Thomas L. Black, who was a chemist and an experienced NKVD courier for another scientist, Earl Flosdork, who taught chemistry at the University of Pennsylvania.

From 1935 Gold had a business partner, Abraham Brothman, a graduate of Columbia University who was engaged in biological research, and from 1938 had run his own firm, the Republic Chemical Machinery Company, in New York. All three men had been members of the Young Communist League, although their involvement in large-scale industrial espionage was motivated by money, not political ideology.

In June 1950 Gold, who was identified as a spy by the atomic physicist Klaus Fuchs, told his FBI interrogator, T. Scott Miller, that as well as holding regular meetings with Brothman, in August 1941 he had been assigned another highly motivated Communist chemist, Alfred D. Slack, following the arrest of his regular handler, Gaik Ovakimyan. Slack had worked at Eastman Kodak at Rochester, New York, and had been collecting industrial secrets of film proprietary film manufacturing processes since 1938, but in October 1944 had obtained a job in the Manhattan Project, the atomic weapons development facility at Oak Ridge, Tennessee. Thus the network which had acquired industrial secrets for Moscow before the war morphed into a spy-ring that penetrated the Anglo-American scientists working on the atom bomb.

Gold had spent much of his adult life engaged in espionage, and even his two years at Xavier University in Cincinnati had been paid for by the NKVD. Of all his Soviet controllers, he had been especially close to 'Sam', an MIT graduate whom he identified from photos as Semyon Semyonov, and his various statements to the FBI, including a 123-page autobiographical account entitled *The Circumstances Surrounding My Work As A Soviet Agent*, led to dozens of investigative leads.[4] Among those implicated by Gold were Joseph Katz and his friends and fellow chemists Ferdinand Heller and Tom Black, who also confessed to having been recruited by Ovakimyan and to supplying industrial secrets to the Soviets. According to their statements, both men had approached the Soviet trading company Amtorg in 1935, volunteering to take their skills to Russia, and had encountered Ovakimyan who had persuaded them to remain in the United States and collect industrial intelligence. In addition, Gold named Ben Smilg, a MIT graduate and aeronautical engineer at the National Aeronautics Center, Dayton, Ohio, and Al Slack.

In retrospect it is hard to assess the impact these industrial spies had on the industrialisation of the Soviet Union, but the model certainly existed both before and during the war, and it is probably not a coincidence that the Chinese followed the Soviet example and directed its agents abroad to focus on commercial rather than political intelligence.

The extent to which the Chinese government participated, or sponsored any of the very large number of incidents of 21st-century commercial espionage is hard to assess. On the one hand, the MSS is presumed to have had some kind of a relationship with all the Chinese nationals involved, but the veracity of any defendants in the relevant law suits is likely to be low, not least because deportation back to China will be the predictable consequence of any adverse judgment. If a Chinese national, caught up in a technology transfer case or the theft of intellectual property, is interviewed by the FBI, the culprit is strongly motivated to deny any official connections, as the entire episode may be revisited by the MSS after a deportation and the slightest hint of cooperation with the American authorities could prove unfortunate.

Nevertheless, any counter-intelligence analysis of the most recent examples of commercial espionage with demonstrable Chinese links, involving trade targets that generally are not government or defence-orientated, reveals a common pattern of behaviour.

* * *

In July 2013 Tung Pham, a senior scientist working for Heraeus, pleaded guilty to charges of having stolen trade secrets between September 2008 and May 2011 from a multi-crystal solar technology company in Pennsylvania for a competing firm in China. Specifically, in November 2010 he had downloaded and copied 1,000 pages of technical data onto his home computer in Conshohocken. He had been recruited as a partner in the Chinese firm during a visit to China in October 2010, when he had met investors. His area of expertise was lead-free glass and aluminium paste, and he had made several important technical advances of considerable commercial value.[5]

* * *

On 3 May 2011 a field manager for the Pioneer Hi-Bred Corporation was driving near Tama, Iowa, when he observed someone kneeling amid the crops in a field. He stopped to investigate, noticing a second man sitting in a car nearby. The manager confronted the person in the field, later identified as Mo Hailong, alias Robert Mo, who said he was attending a nearby conference and that he worked for the University of Iowa. Mo and his companion, later identified as Wang Lei, then fled the scene, driving erratically. Sometime later the FBI heard of the incident, and the local sheriff was alerted to reports of 'Asian men' acting suspiciously near a farm close to Bondurant, Iowa. Further inquiries revealed that the crop grown locally was genetically-modified corn developed by Monsanto for cultivation by Hi-Bred. FBI inquiries showed that in September 2011 Mo had shipped fifteen packages, weighing almost 350lbs, to his home in Boca Raton, Florida, and it was suspected that the material involved was probably stolen crop samples. Accordingly, in early 2012, Mo and his accomplices were placed under surveillance, and on 15 February 2012, using the alias 'Hougang Wu', he toured a Pioneer's Carver Campus facility in Johnston, Iowa, and later was observed touring a Monsanto research facility in Ankeny, Iowa. That evening, Mo attended a state dinner, hosted by Iowa's governor, for a visitor from China. In April 2012 Mo was seen at a farm at Monee, Illinois, owned by a Chinese firm, Kings Nower Seed, which had been purchased the previous month for $600,000. Mo had been employed by Kings Nower Seed's parent company, Beijing Dabeinong Technology Group (DBN). Over a period of months, Mo and his accomplices were watched in an FBI operation code-named PURPLE MAZE as they made large cash purchases of seed corn containing small amounts of the valuable inbred corn mixed in among the hybrid seeds and then kept the bags of corn seed and corn stalks in storage lockers. In September 2012 the FBI fitted an electronic surveillance device to a car rented by Mo's accomplices Ye Jian and Lin Yong, and they were heard to comment that their actions, if detected, could have serious consequences for them. 'They would treat us like spies.' Ye noted that, if caught, 'you can forget about ever coming to the US again, assuming things go wrong'. Lin stated at one point, 'These are actually very serious offences'.[6]

Later that same month, when Ye Jian and Li Shaoming were flying back to China from Chicago's O'Hare International Airport, they were found to be carrying two 'bulk sized microwave popcorn boxes, each appearing to be factory sealed'.[7] When opened, the boxes were found to contain popcorn on top, but underneath were 100 small envelopes with seeds inside. Other seeds were wrapped in Subway sandwich napkins, hidden among packed clothing. On 17 December 2013, the US attorney for the Southern District of Iowa announced the indictment of Hailong, described as the director of international business for DBN. He was married with two children, both of whom were US citizens; Li Shaoming was the chief operating officer of Beijing Kings Nower Seeds S & T. Ltd., a subsidiary of DBN, headquartered in Beijing; Wang Lei was the vice chairman of Kings Nower Seed; Wang Hongwei, a resident of Quebec, Canada, was a dual national who had been seen moving boxes from the farm purchased by the Kings Nower Seed Company and was caught at the US-Canada border with forty-four bags containing corn kernels hidden in a vehicle, as well as a digital camera with photographs of Monsanto and Pioneer production facilities; Ye Jian, a research manager for Kings Nower Seed; and Lin Yong, a Kings Nower Seed employee. The indictment described how the defendants conspired to steal genetically-modified corn seed from DuPont Pioneer, Monsanto, and LG Seeds, said to constitute valuable intellectual property. After stealing the corn seed, the conspirators had attempted to covertly transfer the seed to China, and Mo had shipped more than 1,000lbs of US corn seed to China, where it had been counterfeited by DBN scientists. The indictment included an estimated loss of between five and eight years of research and development, with an estimated loss of $30 to $40 million sustained by US companies. Mo was a Chinese national who had become a permanent resident, having arrived in the United States in 1998. He was arrested on 12 December 2012, but his accomplices escaped to China where there is no extradition treaty. On 2 July 2014, Mo's sister Mo Yun was arrested when she visited the United States with her two children, after she had been indicted for conspiracy to steal trade secrets. She had been employed by DBN from August 2001 to March 2009 and had been in charge of the company's research project management, and her husband was the founder and chairman of DBN, Dr Shao Genhuo. Her charges were later dropped after a federal judge disallowed evidence from electronic surveillance. Mo Yun's husband, Shao Genhuo, had been born in 1965 in Zhejiang Province and had received his doctorate in agriculture from China Agricultural University, and after working as an educator for a couple of years, he started DBN in 1994. His net worth was estimated to be $1 billion.

On 27 January 2016, Mo pleaded guilty to conspiracy to steal trade secrets from DuPont Pioneer and Monsanto and on 5 October was sentenced to three years' imprisonment with an additional three years of supervised release. In addition, two farms located in Iowa and Illinois that were purchased and used by Mo and others in their conspiracy were forfeited. Mo, who had been experiencing medical problems, tearfully told the judge that it had been his dream to spend the rest of his life in the United States and declared, 'I have destroyed everything that I worked for'.[8]

* * *

On 12 December 2013 Zhang Weiqiang, aged 50, and Yan Wengui, aged 58, were charged with a scheme to provide a delegation from China with rice seeds from Ventria Bioscience in Junction City, Kansas. During an investigation it was learned that in 2012 Zhang and Yan had travelled to China where they had visited a research institute. When they returned to the US they arranged for a delegation from that research institute to arrive in December 2013. Both Zhang and Yan were legal permanent resident aliens from China. Wang had graduated from Shenyang Agricultural University and later had obtained his doctorate from Louisiana State University. He lived in Manhattan, Kansas, and was employed by Ventria Bioscience where he was one of six scientists who had access to rice seeds that had health research applications and were developed to produce human serum albumin contained in blood or lactoferrin, an iron-binding protein found in human milk. The trade secret was estimated to be valued at $75 million. Yan was employed as a geneticist for the Department of Agriculture at the Dale Bumpers National Research Center in Stuttgart, Arkansas. When the delegation arrived from China, it first travelled to Stuttgart and then was taken to the Dale Bumpers Research Center.

On 26 October 2016, Yan pleaded guilty to lying to the FBI. He admitted that he knew of the scheme for the delegation to obtain the rice seeds, but he claimed he had refused their request to obtain them from where he was employed. However, he did take them to a rice farm where he knew they would have an opportunity to steal seeds. The delegation toured several facilities that dealt with rice research. Zhang had taken seeds, without authorisation, from his employer and stored them at his home, but when the delegation was catching their return flight to China, US Customs and Border Protection found the seeds in the luggage of the delegation members. In February 2017 Zhang was found guilty of one count of conspiracy to steal trade secrets, one count of conspiracy to commit interstate transportation of stolen property, and one count of transportation of stolen property, offences for which he was sentenced to 121 months' imprisonment.[9]

* * *

In September 2016, Amin Yu was sentenced to 21 months' imprisonment on federal charges of being an illegal, unregistered agent of a foreign government, and for conspiring to commit international money laundering. According to her plea agreement dated June 2016, from at least 2002 until February 2014, at the direction of co-conspirators working for Harbin Engineering University, Yu obtained systems and components for marine submersible vehicles from companies in the United States and then illegally exported them to China to assist in the development of unmanned underwater vehicles, remotely-operated vehicles and autonomous underwater vehicles. Yu had failed to obtain the required export information and she had provided false details.[10]

* * *

In June 2014 GE Healthcare (GEHC) charged a former engineer in federal court with criminal theft of trade secrets for allegedly copying millions of proprietary files and sending them to relatives in China. Jun Xie, a 41-year-old engineer, was charged with having stolen 2.4 million computer files of information, including engineering designs, product testing information, and business strategy, from GE Healthcare. When questioned, admitted to the FBI that he then sent the files in separate storage devices to his wife and brother in China.

A Chinese citizen, in 2008 Xie joined a subsidiary of GE Healthcare in Waukesha, Wisconsin, writing code for the company's magnetic resonance imaging IMRI) systems. GE discovered the theft between March and June 2014, and when questioned by the FBI, Xie said that he planned to follow his wife to China, who had moved there in early 2013, and to work for an unnamed Chinese imaging company starting in July 2014.

Xie claimed that he 'was unaware of the specific content of what he was downloading' from GE's computer network, but admitted that he sent the files on four separate removable electronic storage devices to China. He 'acknowledged that he could use the GE-owned information in a future MRI job', but claimed that he never provided the documents to the Chinese company when he was interviewing for his new job. Xie agreed to return all data that he stole and cooperate with the authorities. In a civil lawsuit, GE charged Xie for 'conversion, breach of contract, state and federal computer fraud, and violations of the trade secrets act'.[11]

* * *

In December 2016 Yu Long, a citizen of China permanently resident in the US, pleaded guilty to charges related to his theft of numerous sensitive military program documents from United Technologies, and taking them to China. Long pleaded guilty to one count of conspiracy to engage in the theft of trade secrets knowing that the offence would benefit a foreign government. He also pleaded guilty to one count of unlawful export and attempted export of defence articles from the

US. In June 2017 Yu Long was sentenced to time served and a special assessment of $200.

In November 2014 Long was arrested in Ithaca, New York, and charged with attempting to travel to China with sensitive proprietary documents that set forth detailed equations and test results used in the development of technologically advanced titanium for US military aircraft. The documents were taken from a Connecticut defence contractor where Long had been employed. Two days earlier, Long had attempted to fly to China from Newark Liberty International Airport in New Jersey. From approximately August 2008 to May 2014, Long worked as a Senior Engineer/Scientist at a research and development centre for a major defence contractor in Connecticut. Both during and after his employment there, Long travelled to China. In August 2014 Long returned to the US from China through John F. Kennedy International Airport and during a secondary Customs inspection was found in the possession of $10,000 in undeclared US cash, registration documents for a new corporation being set up in China, and a largely completed application for work with a state-controlled aviation and aerospace research centre in China. The application materials highlighted certain of Long's work history and experiences that he claimed to have obtained while employed, which had included work on F-119 and F-135 engines. The F-119 powers the F-22 Raptor fighter while the F-135 engine powers the F-35 Lightning II fighter.

On 5 November 2014 Long had boarded a flight from Ithaca to Newark Liberty International Airport, with a final destination of China. During Long's layover in Newark, Customs officers inspected Long's checked baggage and discovered that it contained, among other things, sensitive, proprietary and export-controlled documents from another major defence contractor located outside Connecticut ('Company B'). Further investigation determined that the US Air Force had convened a consortium of major defence contractors, including Company A and Company B, to work together to see whether they could collectively lower the costs of certain metals used. As part of those efforts, members of the consortium shared technical data, subject to stringent restrictions on further dissemination. Company B reviewed the Company B documents found in Long's possession at Newark Liberty Airport and confirmed that it provided the documents to Company A as part of the consortium. Company B further confirmed that Long was never an employee of Company B. A review of Company A's computer records indicated that Long had printed the documents while employed at Company A. The documents bore warnings that they contained sensitive, proprietary and export-controlled material, which could not be copied or communicated to a third party. This investigation was conducted by the FBI, HSI, and CBP.[12]

* * *

In January 2015 a federal grand jury returned an indictment unsealed in Indianapolis, Indiana, charging Fujie Wang, a 52-year-old Chinese national, as part of 'an extremely sophisticated hacking group operating in China and targeting large businesses in the United States, including a computer intrusion and data breach of Indianapolis-based health insurer Anthem Inc.'.[13]

The indictment alleged that Fujie and other members of the group, including an unidentified individual charged only as John Doe, conducted a campaign of hacking into US-based computer systems and had accessed Anthem and three other US businesses named as Victim Business 1, Victim Business 2 and Victim Business 3. As part of this international computer hacking scheme, the FBI claimed that from February 2014, the defendants had employed sophisticated techniques and installed malware and tools on the compromised systems to contaminate others. An analysis of their targets suggested the hackers were interested in personal data and confidential business information. From Anthem they stole material relating to some 78.8 million people, including names, health identification numbers, dates of birth, Social Security numbers, addresses, telephone numbers, email addresses, employment information and income details.

Wang and Doe were charged with one count of conspiracy to commit fraud and related activity in relation to computers and identity theft, one count of conspiracy to commit wire fraud, and two substantive counts of intentional damage to a protected computer. Evidently the group specialised in sending carefully-tailored 'spear-phishing' emails with embedded hyperlinks to employees of the victim businesses. After a user accessed the hyperlink, a file was downloaded covertly which, when executed, deployed malware that would compromise the user's entire computer system by installing a tool known as a backdoor to give remote access to the target system.

The FBI's investigation revealed that the Chinese hackers exercised great caution and patience, and sometimes waited months before executing an attack. During this period they undertook reconnaissance missions to access the data. When the rehearsed infiltration was eventually launched, the stolen data was moved to encrypted archive files and then sent through multiple computers to destinations in China. In the Anthem example the network was accessed on several occasions in January 2015, when the loot was transferred encrypted archive to a data warehouse to China. Having completed the transaction, the hackers then deleted all Anthem's encrypted archive files so as render detection more difficult. By the time the indictment was issued, Fujie, Wang and their accomplices had returned to China.[14]

* * *

A software engineer at a suburban Chicago locomotive manufacturer stole proprietary information from the company and took it to China, according to an indictment unsealed in July 2019 in Chicago. Xudong Yao, also known as 'William Yao,' 57, was charged with nine counts of theft of trade secrets, although he was never apprehended. He had working for the suburban Chicago manufacturer in August 2014 but within two weeks of being hired had downloaded more than 3,000 unique electronic files containing trade secrets. During the next six months Yao downloaded numerous other electronic files of proprietary data, including technical documents and software source code. During this period of this illicit download Yao had sought, negotiated, and accepted employment with a business in China that provided automotive telematics service systems.

Yao was fired in February 2015 for reasons unrelated to the alleged theft, which at that time had not been discovered, and soon afterwards made copies of the stolen material and in July 2015 took it to China where he began working for the Chinese company. Three months later, in November 2015, Yao travelled from China to O'Hare International Airport in Chicago where he was searched and found to be carrying the stolen information, including nine complete copies of the suburban Chicago company's control system source code and the systems specifications that explained how the code worked. Yao was not arrested, but quickly returned to China.[15]

* * *

In May 2015 a 55-year-old Chinese businessman, Xiwen Huang, of Charlotte, North Carolina, was charged with one count of theft of trade secrets, and in October 2015 he pleaded guilty.

After an education in the US, Xiwen had become a naturalised citizen and having worked for companies developing technology for the US government and the private sector. He then stole secret information and took it to China. According to his indictment, from about 2006 to May 2015 Xiwen had stolen trade secrets from several American companies, and intellectual property from the United

States government, with the intention of exploiting the data with own company in China.

Prior to coming to the United States to obtain a doctorate in chemical engineering, Xiwen wrote that he 'had a dream of learning more advanced technology to serve [his] homeland' of China and decided that to 'fulfil [his] wish' he needed to go abroad and then 'return to China with [his] newly acquired methodology and research skills to teach in China'.[16]

According to the FBI, Xiwen had come to the United States in 1998 to study and work, and from about December 2004 until he was fired by his employer in approximately March 2014, he stole proprietary and confidential information, including trade secrets and other intellectual property belonging to a government research facility and two US companies, with the intent to use the stolen information for his own benefit and that of a Chinese company. The material included government-owned technology relating to military vehicle fuel cells, and he also stole from one US company more than 500 documents containing data about 30 different products with research and associated development costs associated of more than $65 million. Xiwen was also alleged to have stolen from a second US company, more than 100 documents containing research and development costs amounting to more than $25 million.

Having been fired from the second US company in 2014, Xiwen returned to China and began working for a local business in a managerial role, to exploit the intellectual property for himself. After returning to China, Xiwen boasted of his thefts in a document entitled *Trip of Dream Realization*:

> Throughout these 16 years, I always have a dream of returning to China to develop my ambition. In order to realize this dream, I have worked in US national research academies [laboratories], largest chemical companies in the world. I have also worked in small companies in the US My goal was to learn, digest, accumulate, and make preparations for realizing the dream . . . Consequently, I started scheming, planning that last for close to 2 years, and returned to China formally in this year, and initiated my own 'Trip of Dream Realization'. . . As the main thrust during the country's development, it is necessary an obligatory for our generation to fulfil our share of responsibility in contributing towards the societal progress of China.[17]

Xiwen had been in federal custody since May 2015, when he was arrested following his return from China. He pleaded guilty to stealing trade secrets from multiple US companies.

* * *

Thomas Rukavina, aged 62, of Plum Borough, Pennsylvania, a former employee of PPG Industries, was charged in May 2015 with the theft of trade secrets. The indictment alleged that Rukavina retired from PPG in July 2012, and as early as June 2014, had passed proprietary and confidential information to JTMG, a glass company based in Jiangsu, China, that specialises in automotive and other specialty glass. The stolen material included PPG's manufacturing specifications for windows, which are made of synthetic plastics for high-speed vehicles, such as aircraft. While at home on bail in June 2015 Rukavina committed suicide.[18]

* * *

In May 2015 Professor Hao Zhang of Tianjin University was arrested as he arrived in the United States from China based on a 32-count indictment issued in San Francisco which charged him and six accomplices with economic espionage and theft of trade secrets for the benefit of universities and companies in China. The defendants were alleged to have illegally obtained and shared US trade secrets with China. Sensitive technology developed by US companies in California had been stolen by two Chinese nationals, Wei Pang and Hao Zhang, who had met at a university in Southern California during their doctoral studies in electrical engineering. While there, Pang and Zhang conducted research and development on thin-film bulk acoustic resonator (FBAR) technology under funding from US Defense Advanced Research Projects Agency (DARPA). After earning a doctorate in approximately 2005, Pang was employed as an FBAR engineer with Avago Technologies in Colorado, and Zhang worked as an FBAR engineer with Skyworks Solutions in Massachusetts.

Avago was described as a designer, developer and global supplier of FBAR technology, which is a specific type of radio frequency filter. Throughout Zhang's employment, Skyworks was also a designer and developer of FBAR technology. FBAR technology is primarily used in mobile devices such as cellular telephones, tablets and GPS devices. FBAR technology filters incoming and outgoing wireless signals so that a user only receives and transmits the specific communications intended by the user. Apart from consumer applications, FBAR technology is a vital component of a variety of military and defence communications systems.

According to the indictment, in 2006 and 2007, Pang, Zhang and other co-conspirators prepared a business plan and canvassed Chinese universities and others, offering to manufacture FBAR technology in

China. Pang, Zhang and others established relationships with officials from Tianjin University.

In 2008, officials from Tianjin University flew to San Jose, California, to meet Pang, Zhang and other co-conspirators. Shortly thereafter, Tianjin University agreed to support Pang, Zhang and others in establishing an FBAR fabrication facility in the PRC. Pang and Zhang continued to work for Avago and Skyworks in close coordination with Tianjin University. In mid-2009, both Pang and Zhang simultaneously resigned from the US companies and accepted positions as full professors at Tianjin University. Tianjin University later formed a joint venture with Pang, Zhang and others under the company name ROFS Microsystem intending to mass produce FBARs.

The indictment alleged that Pang, Zhang and other co-conspirators stole recipes, source code, specifications, presentations, design layouts and other documents marked as confidential and proprietary from the victim companies and shared the information with one another and with individuals working for Tianjin University. The stolen trade secrets enabled Tianjin University to construct and equip a state-of-the-art FBAR fabrication facility, to open ROFS Microsystems, a joint venture located in PRC state-sponsored Tianjin Economic Development Area (TEDA), and to obtain contracts for providing FBARs to commercial and military entities.

The six indicted Chinese nationals were Hao Zhang, aged 36, a former Skyworks employee and a full professor at Tianjin University, charged with conspiracy to commit economic espionage, conspiracy to commit theft of trade secrets, economic espionage and theft of trade secrets. Zhang was arrested upon entry into the United States on May 2015. Wei Pang, aged 35, a former Avago employee and a full professor at Tianjin University, was charged with conspiracy to commit economic espionage, conspiracy to commit theft of trade secrets, economic espionage and theft of trade secrets. Jinping Chen, aged 41, a professor at Tianjin University and a member of the board of directors for ROFS Microsystems. He was charged with conspiracy to commit economic espionage and conspiracy to commit theft of trade secrets. Huisui Zhang (Huisui), aged 34, a citizen of the PRC, studied with Pang and Zhang at a US university in Southern California and received a Master's Degree in Electrical Engineering in 2006. He was charged with conspiracy to commit economic espionage and conspiracy to commit theft of trade secrets. Chong Zhou, aged 26, a Tianjin University graduate student and a design engineer at ROFS Microsystem. He studied under Pang and Zhang, and is charged with conspiracy to commit economic espionage, conspiracy to commit theft of trade secrets, economic espionage and theft of trade secrets. Zhao Gang, aged 39, the General Manager of ROFS Microsystems, was charged with conspiracy to commit economic espionage and conspiracy to commit theft of trade secrets.

Convicted in September 2020, Zhang was sentenced to 18 months' imprisonment and ordered to pay $476,835 in restitution.[19]

* * *

In September 2015 Robert O'Rourke was charged with having illegally downloaded data from his employer, a Woodstock-based manufacturer of cast-iron products. At the time, O'Rourke had already accepted a new job with a rival firm in Jiangsu. Two days later he officially resigned from the Woodstock company but the following week O'Rourke packed up the proprietary information and went to O'Hare International Airport in Chicago to board a flight to China. Federal authorities intervened and seized the stolen electronic data, along with stolen paper documents.

The 13-count indictment charged O'Rourke, aged 57, of Lake Geneva, Wisconsin, with theft of trade secrets. He had worked for the Woodstock company since 1984 as a metallurgist and quality assurance manager. He also helped the company develop international business in China but in December 2013 had opened discussions with a Chinese firm to take a similar job there. After several months of negotiations, O'Rourke accepted the position of Vice President at the Chinese company.

O'Rourke initially advised the Woodstock company on 12 August 2015 that he intended to resign, but did not mention that he was negotiating employment with the Chinese firm, and he continued to work for the Woodstock company for another month, during which he purchased his plane ticket to China and stole the proprietary trade secrets. In October 2019 O'Rourke was sentenced to a year and a day in federal prison.[20]

* * *

In January 2016 Dr Tao Li, aged 45, of San Diego, California, pleaded guilty today to conspiracy to steal trade secrets from GlaxoSmithKline (GSK) to benefit a Chinese pharmaceutical company named Renopharma.

Dr Li and two of his friends, Dr Yu Xue and Dr Yan Mei, created Renopharma in Nanjing, China, supposedly to research and develop

Jerry Chun Shing Lee. A former CIA case officer, 55 year-old Jerry Lee was sentenced in November 2019 to 19 years' imprisonment, having been convicted of spying for the MSS since he settled in Hong Kong in April 2010. Lee's hotel room was searched by the FBI while he was on a visit to Honolulu in August 2012, He was found to be in possession of a thumb-drive containing classified information and was arrested in New York in January 2013.

Benjamin Bishop. In March 2014 a former U.S. Army officer and defence contractor,, Colonel Ben Bishop, based at the U.S. Pacific Command headquarters on Oahu,was sentenced to 87 months' imprisonment, having pleaded guilty to charges relating to passing classified documents to his 27 year-old Chinese girlfriend, a graduate student whom whom he had met in June 2011 at a military conference. The compromised material included details of ballistic missile detection systems and plans for the deployment of nuclear weapons.

Chen Yonglin. A defector from the Chinese consulate-general in Sydney, Chen gave a detailed account of MSS persecution of Falun Hong and was granted political asylum in 2005.

Glenn Shriver In 2010 30 year-old Glenn Shriver was convicted of conspiracy to commit espionage after he admitted having applied to join the U.S. State Department and the CIA on instructions from MSS handlers to whom he had been introduced while studying in Shanghai. Having been sentenced to four years' imprisonment, he was released in 2013.

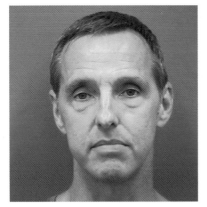

Kevin Mallory. In May 2017 a 61 year-old former CIA officer with experience in Iraq, China and Taiwan, Kevin Mallory was arrested by the FBI in May 2012 and charged with passing classified documents which he had acquired before his retirement in 2012, to his MSScontacts. He was sentenced to 20 years' imprisonment.

Candace Claiborne Having joined the U.S. State Department in 1999, Candace Claiborne was posted to Baghdad, Khartoum, Shanghai and Beijing as an office manager but in July 2019 was sentenced to 40 months' imprisonment for having compromised classified information and maintaining undeclared contacts with the MSS who paid her thousands of dollars.

Ron Rockwell Hansen. A 60 year-old former DIA warrant officer, Ron Hansen was sentenced in September 2019 to ten years' imprisonment for having conspired to pass classified material to the MSS. He had been hired as a civilian contractor in 2006 Ten years lter, when he approached a colleague for information, he was placed under investigation.

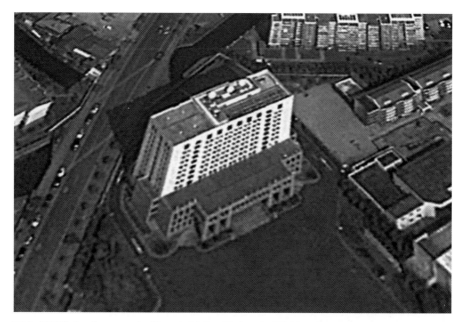

Unit 61398's headquarters in Shanghai. Identified as the PLA's principal cyber warfare organization, 81398 operates from a 12-storey office block located in secure compound on Datong Road in Shnghai's Pudong District which consumes large amount of energy and is conncted to the internet by fibre-optic cables. Criminal entities such as KandyGoo and UglyGorilla have been traced to the building where an estimated 2,000 staff mount hacking attacks on foreign targets

FBI Indictment of named 61938 personnel. In May 2014 five members of the PLA's Unit 61398, Wang Dong, Sun Kailiang, Huang Zhenyu, Gu Chunhui and Wen Xinyu were indicted in Pennsylvani on federal charges of engaging in cyber espionage to attack U.S. companies and nuclear facilities.

Alex Ma In August 2020 a 67-year-old Hong Kong-born CIA retiree, Alexander Yuk Ching Ma, was arrested. He had joined the CIA which had employed his older brother David from 1961 until 1983. Alex resigned in 1989 and in 1995 moved to Shanghai. Ma's espionage for the MSS allegedly began with a three-day interrogation conducted in a Hong Kong hotel in March 2001. The following year he moved back to Hawaii and two years later was employed by the FBI's Field Office as an interpreter, translating Chinese-language documents.

Overhead imagery of the Ministry of State Security headquarters in Beijing.

WANTED
BY THE FBI

YANQING YE

Acting as an Agent of a Foreign Government; Visa Fraud; Making False Statements; Conspiracy

DESCRIPTION

Date(s) of Birth Used: July 22, 1990	**Place of Birth:** Longhai, Fujian, China
Hair: Dark Brown	**Eyes:** Brown
Height: Approximately 5'4"	**Weight:** Approximately 110 pounds
Sex: Female	**Race:** Asian
Nationality: Chinese	**Languages:** English, Chinese

REMARKS

Ye is believed to be in China.

CAUTION

Yanqing Ye is a Lieutenant in the People's Liberation Army (PLA), the armed forces of the People's Republic of China, and a member of the Chinese Communist Party (CCP). Ye studied at the National University of Defense Technology (NUDT), a top military academy directed by the CCP in China. It is alleged that, on her J-1 visa application, Ye falsely identified herself as a "student" and lied about her ongoing military service at the NUDT. During Ye's time in the United States on her J-1 visa, she maintained close contact with her supervisor at the NUDT and other colleagues. While studying at Boston University's Department of Physics, Chemistry and Biomedical Engineering from October of 2017 to April of 2019, Ye allegedly continued to work as a PLA Lieutenant completing numerous assignments from PLA officers such as conducting research, assessing United States military websites, and sending United States documents and information to China.

On January 28, 2020, a federal arrest warrant was issued for Ye in the United States District Court for the District of Massachusetts, Boston, Massachusetts, after she was charged with acting as an agent of a foreign government, visa fraud, making false statements, and conspiracy.

If you have any information concerning this person, please contact your local FBI office or the nearest American Embassy or Consulate.

Field Office: Boston

FBI Wanted Notice for Yanqing Ye. 29 year-old Lieutenant Yanqing Ye , a serving PLA officer. was in 2019 accused of visa fraud, making false statements, and acting as an agent of a foreign government and conspiracy while posing as a Boston University student. After an interview with the FBI she fled the country. The DoJ's last prosecution of the China Initiative, Yanqing had falsely identified herself as a 'student' who, on her J-1 visa application had lied about her military service at the National University of Defense Technology. She was also charged with offences relating to her studies at Boston University's Department of Physics, Chemistry and Biomedical Engineering from October 2017 to April 2019.

Barry Gardner. In 2017 the Labour Member of Parliament for Brent North, and chairman of the Chinese in Britain Parliamntary Group was the subject of an investigation conducted by MI5 because of funds he had received amointing to £182,284 from Christine Lee, the lawyer representing the Chinese embassy in London. A further donation of £200,000 followed, and Gardner employed Lee's son in his Parliamentary office.

Christine Lee.. The legal adviser to the Chinese embassy in London, Lee was publicly identified by MI5 in January 2022 as an agent of the United Front Work Department of the Chinese Communist Party.

MI5 Director-General Ken McCallum and FBI Director Christopher Wray. In July 2022 the Anglo–American counter-intelligence community issued an unprecedented public warning at Thames House about escalating levels of Chinese espionage

英 国

华人世界 杨腾波：推广创业公益平台 促进中英经贸合作

Yang Tengbo. In December 2024 50 year-old Steve Yahg was identified as a suspected MSS agent of influence operating in London under United Front Worker Department cover. His smartphone had been seized at Heathrow in November 2021 and he was subsequently refused entry in February 2023 after compromising reports had been recovered from the encrypted hard-drive. Among them was a message addressed to unknown colleagues boasting of Yang's links to Prince Andrew. A former postgraduate student at the University of York, Yang had attempted to cultivate the Queen's son through an investment scheme for entrepreneurs, but the Prince immediately terminated his links when he received a discreet warning from MI5.

anti-cancer drugs. Actually, Renopharma was used as a repository of stolen information from GSK, and received financial support and subsidies from the Chinese government. At the time, Xue was employed as a research scientist at GSK working on developing biopharmaceutical products. These products typically cost in excess of $1 billion to research and develop.

Xue sent a substantial number of GSK's scientific documents, some of which contained GSK trade secrets, to Li and Mei at Renopharma in China. The data contained information regarding several biopharmaceutical products under development, GSK research data, and GSK processes regarding the research, development, and manufacturing of biopharmaceuticals. Xue typically sent the documents via email or transferred the documents via portable electronic storage devices. Xue sent these documents to Li and Mei with the intention to convert GSK's information for their own benefit. In January 2016, the FBI arrested Li and seized his computer which was found to contain a number of GSK documents containing trade secrets and confidential information which he had received from Xue who had previously pleaded guilty in August 2018. In October 2019 Tao was sentenced to 40 months' imprisonment.[21]

* * *

In May 2017 Wu Yingzhuo, Dong Hao and Xia Lei, all Chinese nationals resident in China, were indicted for computer hacking, theft of trade secrets, conspiracy and identity theft directed at US and foreign employees and computers of three corporate victims in the financial, engineering and technology industries between 2011 and May 2017.

According to the FBI, the three hackers worked for the purported China-based Internet security firm Guangzhou Bo Yu Information Technology Company, better known as 'Boyusec'. The charges alleged that the trio conspired to hack into private companies and steal sensitive internal documents and communications. Some of the victims, identified as Moody's Analytics, Siemens AG and Trimble, Inc., were targeted between December 2015 and March 2016, and lost a large quantity of trade secrets.

The hackers applied familiar techniques, such as spear-phishing emails and infiltrating malicious attachments or links to malware In many instances, the co-conspirators had sought to conceal their activities, location and Boyusec affiliation by using aliases in registering online accounts, intermediary computer servers known as 'hop points' and valid credentials stolen from victim systems.

Allegedly the hackers stole data which including confidential business and commercial information, work product, and sensitive victim employee information, such as usernames and passwords that could be used to extend unauthorised access within the victim systems. The three defendants were Wu Yingzhuo, alas 'mxmtmw,' 'Christ Wu' and 'wyz'. He was described as the founding member and equity shareholder of Boyusec. Dong Hao, alias 'Bu Yi', 'Dong Shi Ye' and 'Tianyu', was also a founding member and equity shareholder of Boyusec, who held the title of 'Executive Director and Manager'. The third, Xia Lei, alias 'Sui Feng Yan Mie', was an employee of Boyusec employee.[22]

* * *

On 23 May 2017 an American citizen, Shan Shi, and a Chinese national, Gang Liu, were arrested in Washington, DC and charged with the theft of trade secrets relating to the development of syntactic foam from a global engineering firm worked on behalf of a Chinese company CBM-Future New Material Science and Technology.

Altogether six defendants were charged with conspiracy to commit theft of trade secrets, and four were US citizens: Shan Shi, aged 52, of Houston, Texas; Uka Kalu Uche, aged 35, of Spring, Texas; Samuel Abotar Ogoe, aged 74, of Missouri City, Texas; and Johnny Wade Randall, aged 48, of Conroe, Texas. Also charged were Kui Bo, aged 40, a Canadian who had been living in Houston, and Gang Liu, aged 31, a Chinese national who had been living in Houston as a permanent resident. Additionally, charges were filed against a Chinese national living in China, Hui Huang, aged 32, an employee of the Chinese manufacturing firm allegedly involved in tasking employees of the Houston company. Reportedly the trade secrets were stolen in order to benefit a manufacturer located in China, which was the only shareholder for a company that had been incorporated in Houston. Between 2012 and 2017, the Chinese manufacturer and employees of its Houston-based company systematically stole the trade secrets of a global engineering firm that was a leader in marine technology. The case involved the development of a technical product called syntactic foam – a strong, light material with military applications, such as oil exploration; aerospace; underwater vehicles and submarines; and stealth technology. The Chinese manufacturer intended to sell syntactic foam to both military and civilian, state-owned enterprises in China – as part of a plan to develop the country's marine engineering industry.

The thefts took place between January and June 2015, and the secrets were passed to people associated with the Chinese manufacturer and the Houston-based company. When the case came to trial plea agreements were made with Uka Kalu Uche, Samuel Abotar Ogoe, Johnny Wade Randall, and Kui Bo. On 29 July 2019 Shan Shi was found guilty of conspiracy to commit theft of trade secrets.[23]

* * *

In August 2017 Dong Liu, alias Kevin, a dual Canadian and Chinese citizen aged 44, was charged in Boston with one count of attempted theft of trade secrets and one count of attempted access to a computer without authorisation.

According to the prosecution, the Medrobotics Corporation, headquartered in Raynham, Massachusetts, manufactured and marketed a unique robot-assisted device that provided surgeons with technology to reach, and visualisation of, hard-to-reach places in the human body for minimally invasive surgery. The company has invested millions of dollars in next-generation robotics that had not yet been patented.

On 28 August 2017, Medrobotics' CEO spotted Liu sitting in a conference room inside the company's secured space with what appeared to be three open laptop computers. He was not a company employee or contractor, so the CEO asked Liu whom he was there to visit. Liu named one company employee whom the CEO knew was out of the country for a few weeks; Liu then identified another employee whom the CEO knew had not scheduled such a meeting; Liu then named the CEO himself, which the CEO knew was not to be true.

Liu claimed to be working with a Chinese patent law firm. He showed the CEO his LinkedIn biography, in which Liu claimed to lead his firm's intellectual property practice in medical devices, among other things. When police responded to the CEO's call and talked with Liu, Liu gave conflicting explanations about how he had entered the building. A check of Medrobotics' visitor log book revealed that neither Liu nor any other visitor had signed into the building that day, despite a company policy that required visitors to log in.

When Liu was arrested by the local police for trespassing, he possessed two laptop computers, an iPad, two portable hard drives, ten cell phone SIM cards, two digital camcorders, at least two flash drives, and other data equipment. Some of these types of equipment can be used to obtain data from computer networks and to video record otherwise-secret physical documents and products. In October 2017 all charges against Lui were dropped.[24]

* * *

In August 2017 Jerry Jindong Xu was arrested in New York, and in October a federal grand jury in Wilmington, Delaware, charged the former Chemours employee with conspiring to steal trade secrets and attempting to monetise them with Chinese investors.

According to the indictment, the conspiracy involved sodium cyanide, a chemical used in mining and of which Chemours is the world's largest producer. Based in Wilmington, Chemours researches and develops sodium cyanide at the Experimental Station in Wilmington. The toxin is most often used to mine gold, silver, and other precious metals, and in 2017 the company had started the construction of a $150 million plant in Mexico. Chemours had been formed in July 2015 after the DuPont Corporation separated its performance chemicals business from its other interests

Xu had moved from China to North America in 2011 while employed by DuPont, and became a Chemours employee when the company was spun off of DuPont in 2015. Xu, terminated by Chemours in 2016, was a marketing professional specialising in sales of sodium cyanide. He was aided by an unnamed co-conspirator, who was also a longtime DuPont employee before leaving the company in 2014 to open a cyanide and mining consulting business.

According to the indictment, Xu's main objective was either to help investors build a competing sodium cyanide plant or become an import competitor in North America. Over the course of a year, while employed at Chemours, he misled colleagues and fabricated assignments in order to accumulate vast amounts of pricing and other information, including obtaining passwords for spreadsheets. He also contacted potential Chinese investors to solicit funding for building a sodium cyanide plant. They communicated in English and Chinese, sometimes over an encrypted Chinese messaging service. Allegedly, Xu explained to one Chinese investor that he wanted to do this project 'for himself and not to slave away at this only to benefit someone else'.

During a 2016 trip to China, Xu accessed Chemours documents and told his accomplice he had 'out-of-the-big [sic] ideas cooking' that he was anxious to discuss. He also asked how much their plant project would be worth. 'Would you say in the millions?' Xu then created a company, made his wife the director, and executed a non-disclosure agreement with his co-conspirator. He also asked for and received a tour of Chemours' sodium cyanide plant, during which he secretly took pictures of plant system diagrams and sent them to himself.

In the week after he was notified of his termination, Xu copied and/or sent himself many Chemours confidential documents, and then falsely certified that he had return   ed all Chemours files. In June 2018 Xu pleaded guilty to one charge of conspiracy to steal trade secrets.[25]

* * *

In January 2018 an electrical engineer was convicted of eighteen federal charges, including engaging in a scheme to illegally obtain integrated circuits with military applications that later were exported to China without the required export licence. After a six-week trial, Yi-Chi Shih, aged 64, a part-time Los Angeles resident, was found guilty in June 2018 of conspiracy to violate the International Emergency Economic Powers Act. He was also found guilty of mail fraud, wire fraud, subscribing to a false tax return, making false statements to a government agency and conspiracy to gain unauthorised access to a protected computer to obtain information. Shih was convicted of all eighteen counts in a federal grand jury indictment.

Allegedly Shih and his co-defendant Kiet Ahn Mai, aged 65, of Pasadena, California, had conspired to illegally provide Shih with unauthorised access to a protected computer of a United States company that manufactured wide-band, high-power semiconductor chips known as monolithic microwave integrated circuits (MMICs).

Shih defrauded the US company out of its proprietary, export-controlled items, including its design services for MMICs. As part of the scheme, Shih accessed the victim company's computer systems via its web portal after Mai obtained that access by posing as a domestic customer seeking to obtain custom-designed MMICs that would be used solely in the United States. Shih and Mai concealed Shih's true intent to transfer the US company's products to China. The MMICs that Shih sent to China required a licence from the Commerce Department but one was never sought or obtained.

The victim company's semiconductor chips have a number of commercial and military applications, and its customers include the US Air Force, Navy and the Defense Advanced Research Projects Agency. MMICs are used in missiles, missile guidance systems, fighter jets, electronic warfare, electronic warfare countermeasures and radar applications.

The semiconductor chips were shipped to Chengdu GaStone Technology Company (CGTC), a Chinese company that was building a MMIC manufacturing facility in Chengdu. Shih was the president of CGTC, which in 2014 was placed on the Commerce Department's Entity List, 'due to its involvement in activities contrary to the national security and foreign policy interest of the United States – specifically, that it had been involved in the illicit procurement of commodities and items for unauthorised military end use in China'.

Shih used a Hollywood Hills-based company he controlled – Pullman Lane Productions LLC – to funnel funds provided by Chinese entities to finance the manufacturing of MMICs by the victim company. Pullman Lane received financing from a Beijing-based company that was also placed on the Entity List the same day as CGTC.

Shih's associate, Kiet Mai, pleaded guilty in December 2018 to one felony count of smuggling and was sentenced to 18 months' probation and a $5,000 fine. In July 2021, following a trial lasting six weeks, Shih was convicted and sentenced to 63 months' imprisonment, fined $300,000 and ordered to pay restitution of $362,000.[26]

* * *

In January 2018 Xiaoqing Zheng, aged 59, of Niskayuna, New York, was convicted of conspiracy to commit economic espionage, following a four-week jury trial that ended on 31 March 2022. He was sentenced to 24 months' imprisonment for conspiring to steal General Electric (GE) trade secrets, knowing or intending to benefit China.

Zheng had been employed at GE Power in Schenectady, New York, as an engineer specialising in turbine sealing technology. He worked at GE from 2008 until the summer of 2018, and conspired with others in China to steal GE's trade secrets surrounding its ground-based and aviation-based turbine technologies, knowing or intending to benefit China and one or more foreign instrumentalities, including China-based companies and universities that research, develop, and manufacture parts for turbines.

According to FBI Assistant Director Alan E. Kohler Jr., 'Xiaoqing Zheng was a Thousand Talents Program member and willingly stole proprietary technology and sent it back to the PRC'.[27]

* * *

In July 2018 Xiaolang Zhang pleaded guilty to stealing trade secrets from Apple, where he worked on a self-driving car project from 2015 to 2018. When he quit his job at Apple, he told his supervisor that he was going to work for Guangzhou Xiaopeng Motors Technology, a

Chinese startup also known as XPeng. A subsequent investigation showed that he had transferred around 24GB of 'highly problematic' data to his wife's laptop via AirDrop and had also taken circuit boards and a server from the company's autonomous vehicle laboratory.

After Zhang was arrested he reached a plea agreement with the prosecution in which he pleaded guilty to the single theft of trade secrets and in January 2023 was sentenced to 24 months' imprisonment.[28]

* * *

In November 2018 a Taiwan-based semiconductor foundry, United Microelectronics Corporation (UMC), pleaded guilty to criminal trade secret theft and was sentenced to pay a $60 million fine, in exchange for its agreement to cooperate with the government in the investigation and prosecution of its co-defendant, a Chinese state-owned-enterprise.

UMC had been indicted in September 2018, along with the Fujian Jinhua Integrated Circuit Company, a Chinese state-owned enterprise, and three individuals for conspiracy to steal, convey, and possess stolen trade secrets of an American semiconductor company, Micron Technology, for the benefit of Fujian Jinhua).

UMC pleaded guilty to one count of criminal trade secret theft and admitted the guilt of three other defendants – Chen Zhengkun, alias Stephen Chen; He Jianting, alias J.T. Ho; and Wang Yungming, alias Kenny Wang – from Micron's Taiwan subsidiary. Allegedly UMC made Chen a senior vice president and assigned him to lead negotiation of an agreement with Fujian Jinhua to develop Dynamic Random Access Memory (DRAM) technology for Fujian Jinhua. The company was fined $60 million.

As a foundry company, UMC previously made logic chips designed by other companies but did not make DRAM memory chips. Chen hired Ho and Wang to join the DRAM development team, and Ho and Wang brought Micron's confidential information to UMC from Micron's Taiwan subsidiary. After UMC's Information Technology Department found Micron's intellectual property on Ho's UMC computer, Chen approved the issuance of two 'off network' laptop computers that allowed UMC employees to access Micron confidential information without further detection by UMC's IT department. In particular, Wang used one file containing Micron's trade secrets to adjust UMC's design rules for the memory in question. Later, when Taiwan authorities searched UMC's offices, Ho and Wang asked another UMC employee to hide papers, notes, USB drives, a personal phone, and a laptop computer while the Taiwan authorities executed their search warrants. Taiwan authorities recovered only one of the two off-network laptops. The hard drive of the other was reformatted and concealed from the Taiwan authorities. Beginning in the month of the Taiwan raids, Chen became president of Fujian Jinhua and took charge of its memory production facility.[29]

* * *

In May 2022, Dr Xiaorong You, alias Shannon You, aged 59, of Lansing, Michigan, was convicted after a 13-day trial at Greeneville, Tennessee, of conspiracy to commit trade secret theft, conspiracy to commit economic espionage, possession of stolen trade secrets, economic espionage and wire fraud. She was sentenced to 168 months' imprisonment, ordered to serve three years of supervised release, and pay a $200,000 fine.

The prosecution alleged that You stole valuable trade secrets related to formulations for bisphenol-A-free coatings for the inside of beverage cans. You was granted access to the trade secrets while working at the Coca-Cola Company in Atlanta, Georgia, and Eastman Chemical Company in Kingsport, Tennessee. The stolen trade secrets belonged to major chemical and coating companies, including Akzo-Nobel, BASF, Dow Chemical, PPG, Toyochem, Sherwin Williams, and Eastman Chemical Company, and cost nearly $120,000,000 to develop.

You stole the trade secrets to set up a new BPA-free coating company in China. You and her Chinese corporate partner, Weihai Jinhong Group, received millions of dollars in Chinese government grants to support the new company. Evidence adduced at her trial showed You's intent to benefit not only Weihai Jinhong Group, but also the governments of China, the Chinese province of Shandong, and the Chinese city of Weihai, as well as her intent to benefit the Chinese Communist Party.

At the time, BPA was used universally to coat the inside of cans and other food and beverage containers to help minimise flavour loss and prevent the container from corroding or reacting with the food or beverage contained therein. However, due to BPA's potential health risks, companies began searching for BPA-free alternatives. As witnesses from the chemical and coating companies testified at trial, developing these BPA-free alternatives was a very complex, expensive and time-consuming process.

From December 2012 through 31 August 2017, You was employed as Principal Engineer for Global Research at Coca-Cola, which had agreements with numerous companies to conduct research and development, testing, analysis, and review of various BPA-free technologies. Because of You's extensive education and experience with BPA and BPA-free coating technologies, she was one of a limited number of Coca-Cola employees with access to BPA-free trade secrets belonging to Akzo-Nobel, BASF, Dow Chemical, PPG, Toyochem, and Sherwin Williams. From approximately September 2017 through June 2018, You was employed as a packaging application development manager for Eastman Chemical Company in Kingsport, Tennessee, where she was one of a limited number of employees with access to trade secrets belonging to Eastman.[30]

* * *

In November 2019 a 36-year-old former associate scientist, Hongjin Tan, was sentenced to 24 months' imprisonment for stealing proprietary information worth more than $1 billion from his employer, the Phillips 66 petroleum company. A Chinese national, Tan pleaded guilty to theft of a trade secret, unauthorised transmission of a trade secret, and unauthorised possession of a trade secret. From June 2017 until December 2018, Tan was employed as an associate scientist at the petroleum company and was assigned to work in a group with the goal of developing next-generation battery technologies for stationary energy storage, specifically flow batteries. In his plea agreement, Tan admitted to intentionally copying and downloading the technologies' research and development materials without authorisation from his employer.

According to the plea agreement, Tan used a thumb-drive to copy hundreds of files containing the proprietary information on 11 December 2018. He subsequently turned in his resignation and was escorted from the premises on the following day, when he returned the thumb drive, claiming that he had forgotten to do so before leaving his employer's property. Upon examination, it was discovered that there was unallocated space on the thumb drive, indicating five documents had previously been deleted. An FBI investigation searched Tan's premises and found an external hard drive. It also discovered that the same five missing files from the thumb drive had been downloaded to the hard drive. Tan maintained the files on a hard drive so he could access the data at a later date.

Upon his conviction Tan was also ordered to pay $150,000 in restitution to his former employer.[31]

* * *

In January 2019 a Chinese national, Jizhong Chen, was convicted of stealing trade secret information about autonomous vehicles from Apple to benefit a competing Chinese firm. A former Apple car engineer, Chen pleaded guilty of theft from the iPhone maker's new self-driving car program.

According to federal prosecutors, Xiaolang Zhang downloaded the plan for a circuit board for Apple's auto-driving after revealing his intentions in 2018 to work for Guangzhou Xiaopeng Motors Technology, a Chinese self-driving car startup business, and thereafter booked an expensive last-minute ticket to China but was detained at San Jose airport after passing security. Zhang had been an active participant in Apple's new electric car project and had worked on it since 2015. A subsequent investigation conducted by Apple revealed that he had transferred nearly 24GB of highly sensitive data to his wife's laptop via AirDrop and had also nabbed circuit boards and a server from the company's autonomous vehicle laboratory.

Initially Zhang had pleaded not guilty to the charges but he reached a plea deal with prosecutors whereby he pleaded guilty to the theft. Along with Zhang, Jizhong Chen, the other former Apple engineer charged with trade secret theft, has pleaded not guilty.[32]

* * *

On 26 May 2022 Haoyang Yu was convicted in Boston of possessing a stolen trade secret, being proprietary information removed from Analog Devices (ADI), a US semiconductor company. Aged 43, Yu was convicted following a month-long jury trial of possessing the prototype design of a microchip, known as the HMC1022A, which was owned and developed by the semiconductor company headquartered in Wilmington.

From 2014 to 2017, Yu worked at ADI, where he designed microchips used by the communications, defence and aerospace industries. Accordingly, Yu had access to ADI's present and future microchip designs, including their schematic files, design layout files and manufacturing files. While he was an ADI employee, Yu started his own microchip design firm, Tricon MMIC, LLC, and used the stolen HMC1022A design to manufacture a knock-off version of ADI's chip. Yu began selling his version of HMC1022A prior to ADI's release of its chip. ADI cooperated fully in the government's investigation.

The jury acquitted Yu of other counts of possessing stolen trade secrets, wire fraud, immigration fraud, and the illegal export of controlled technology.[33]

* * *

In September 2019 59-year-old Zhongsan Liu was convicted on a charge of fraudulently obtaining J-1 research scholar visas for Chinese government officials. According to the prosecution, Liu had operated an office of the China Association for the International Exchange of Personnel (CAIEP), a Chinese government agency, based in Fort Lee, New Jersey. Among other activities, it was alleged that CAIEP engaged in talent-recruitment, including recruiting US scientists, academics, engineers and other experts to work in China. Between 2017 and September 2019, Liu worked with others to fraudulently procure J-1 research scholar visas for Chinese government employees so they could work for CAIEP in the United States without informing the US Department of State and the Department of Homeland Security. The J-1 research scholar program permits foreign nationals to come to the United States for the primary purpose of conducting research at a corporate research facility, museum, library, university or other research institution. Liu worked with others to obtain a J-1 research scholar visa for a prospective CAIEP employee, Sun Li, based on the false representation that Sun Li would conduct research at a US university, and to conceal the activities of another CAIEP employee, Liang Xiao, who was present in the United States on a J-1 visa sponsored by a US university.

In April 2018 Liang Xiao applied for and received a J-1 visa to conduct research at that US university. Although Liang claimed she was entering the United States for the primary purpose of conducting research at the university, her actual purpose was to work for CAIEP. Liu helped Liang to pretend to be a false research scholar by, among other things, directing Liang to report to the university upon her arrival in the United States; ensuring that Liang obtained a local driver's licence; and disguising Liang's CAIEP salary as a subsidy for a research scholar's living expenses. In addition, Liu enabled Sun Li to obtain a J-1 visa under false pretences by contacting various US universities seeking to arrange invitations for her.[34]

* * *

In September 2019 Xuehua 'Edward' Peng was convicted on a charge of acting as an illegal foreign agent for his delivering of classified information to the Chinese Ministry of State Security, and sentenced to 48 months' imprisonment, and ordered to pay a $30,000 fine for acting as an undeclared agent.

According to the prosecution, Peng, a 56-year-old US citizen living in Hayward, California, participated in scheme to conduct pickups known as 'dead drops' and transport Secure Digital (SD) cards from a source in the United States to the MSS operatives in China. As part of his guilty plea, Penk admitted that in March 2015, a Chinese official had introduced himself while Peng was on a business trip to China. The official asked Peng to use his citizenship in the United States to assist China and Peng eventually came to understand that he was an MSS officer. Peng admitted that in March of 2015, he had received instructions regarding how to use dead drops to exchange money for items to deliver to China. He also admitted that the officer directed him to locate and reserve hotel rooms where he was to leave money and then depart for several hours. Peng would return later and retrieve small electronic storage devices that the source would leave for him. Thereafter, Peng was to fly to China and deliver the retrieved devices to his MSS handler. Peng never met the individual who left the devices for him and was instructed not to access the information stored on the cards.

According to his confession, Peng participated in five dead drops involving drop-offs of cash and/or pick-ups of SD cards, after a practice run in June 2015. After he participated in two dead drops in the San Francisco Bay area between October 2015 and April 2016, Peng began making dead drops in Columbus, Georgia. After three dead drops in Georgia, Peng informed his handler that he wanted to resume dead drops in the San Francisco Bay area. Peng did not complete a seventh dead drop before his arrest by the FBI in September 2019. When interviewed, Peng also admitted that he had been paid at least $30,000 for his role as an MSS courier.[35]

* * *

In July 2020 Saw-Teong Ang, a 63-year-old University of Arkansas professor, was indicted for wire fraud for his acceptance of US contracting funds related to NASA and the Air Force while being employed by Chinese entities, In a plea agreement Professor Ang pleaded guilty to one count out of fifty-nine charges – making a false statement to a federal agent.

Ang had worked as a researcher at the University of Arkansas in Fayetteville, Arkansas since 1988 and had served as the Director of the High Density Electronics Center until May 2020. He was fired by the University of Arkansas less than two months after his arrest, and was sentenced one year and one day in prison in June 2022.[36]

* * *

In July 2020 two Chinese nationals, Li Xiaoyu and Dong Jiazhi, were charged by the FBI for hacking the US Department of Energy on behalf of the MSS. The two allegedly had committed economic espionage, extortion, computer fraud, and the theft of intellectual property over the course of 11 years.

A federal grand jury in Spokane, Washington, had returned an indictment earlier in June charging two hackers, both nationals and residents of China, with hacking into the computer systems of hundreds of victim companies, governments, non-governmental organisations, and individual dissidents, clergy and democratic and human rights activists in the United States and abroad, including Hong Kong and China. The defendants in some instances acted for their own personal financial gain, and in others for the benefit of the MSS or other Chinese government agencies. The hackers stole terabytes of data which comprised a sophisticated and prolific threat to US networks.

The 11-count indictment alleged LI Xiaoyu, aged 34, and Dong Jiazhi, aged 33, who were trained in computer applications technologies at the same Chinese university, conducted a hacking campaign since 2009 targeting companies in countries with high technology industries, including the United States, Australia, Belgium, Germany, Japan, Lithuania, the Netherlands, Spain, South Korea, Sweden, and the United Kingdom. Targeted industries included, among others, high tech manufacturing; medical device, civil, and industrial engineering; business, educational, and gaming software; solar energy; pharmaceuticals; and dfence. In at least one instance, the hackers had sought to extort cryptocurrency from a victim entity, by threatening to release the victim's stolen source code on the Internet. More recently, the defendants probed for vulnerabilities in computer networks of companies developing COVID-19 vaccines, testing technology and treatments.

According to the prosecution, the cybercrimes were first discovered on computers of the Department of Energy's Hanford Site in eastern Washington. As the grand jury charged, the computer systems of many businesses, individuals and agencies throughout the United States and worldwide have been hacked and compromised with a huge array of sensitive and valuable trade secrets, technologies, data, and personal information being stolen. The hackers operated from China both for their own gain and with the assistance and for the MSS.

To conceal the theft of information from victim networks and otherwise evade detection, the defendants typically packaged victim data in encrypted Roshal Archive Compressed files (RAR files), changed

RAR file and victim documents' names and extensions (e.g., from '.rar' to '.jpg') and system timestamps, and concealed programs and documents at innocuous-seeming locations on victim networks and in victim networks' 'recycle bins'. The defendants frequently returned to re-victimise companies, government entities, and organisations from which they had previously stolen data, in some cases years after the initial successful data theft.

The indictment charged the defendants with conspiring to steal trade secrets from at least eight known victims, which consisted of technology designs, manufacturing processes, test mechanisms and results, source code, and pharmaceutical chemical structures.[37]

* * *

In October 2020 Lei ('Jason') Gao was charged with conspiring to steal trade secrets from a US oil and gas manufacturer to benefit a Chinese firm. Allegedly he stole trade secrets between 2019 and 2020 and, with others created a scheme to obtain trade secrets from a Houston-based manufacturer of advanced coiled tubing, resulting in economic harm to the victim company. The prosecution claimed that Gao used the stolen trade secrets to assist in the development of an advanced coiled tubing product which they introduced to the market for sale in 2020. Gao left the United States for China in 2019 and has not returned.

A federal arrest warrant was issued for Gao on 29 October 2020, in Houston, Texas, when he was charged with conspiracy to commit theft and possession of trade secrets, receiving and buying trade secrets and aiding and abetting, and attempted receiving and buying trade secrets.[38]

* * *

In November 2020 Wei Sun, a 49-year-old electrical engineer with Raytheon, was sentenced to 38 months' federal imprisonment for transporting sensitive missile technology to China on his laptop. A Chinese national and naturalised citizen of the United States, Wei had pleaded guilty to one felony count of violating the Arms Export Control Act. He had been employed in Tucson for ten years as an electrical engineer with Raytheon Missiles and Defense, a company that develops and produces missile systems for use by the United States military. During his employment with the company, Wei had access to information directly related to defence-related technology. Some of this technical information constituted what is defined as 'defence articles', which are controlled and prohibited from export without a licence the International Traffic in Arms Regulations and the arms export regulation.

From December 2018 to January 2019, Wei travelled from the United States to China on a personal trip and carried unclassified technical information in his company-issued computer, including data associated with an advanced missile guidance system that was controlled and regulated under the arms control export regime. Thus, despite having been trained to handle these materials correctly, Sun knowingly transported the information to China without the required export licence.[39]

* * *

In December 2020 Yu Zhou, 51, of Dublin, Ohio, who had been arrested in California in July 2019, pleaded guilty to charges of the theft of scientific trade secrets related to exosomes and exosome isolation from Nationwide Children's Hospital's Research Institute for his own personal financial gain, and conspiracy to commit wire fraud. He was sentenced to 33 months' imprisonment for conspiring to steal exosome-related trade secrets concerning the research, identification and treatment of a range of paediatric medical conditions.

According to the prosecution, Zhou and his co-conspirator and 48-year-old wife Li Chen worked in separate medical research laboratories at the Research Institute for 10 years each (Zhou from 2007 until 2017 and Chen from 2008 until 2018). They pleaded guilty to conspiring to steal at least five trade secrets related to exosome research from Nationwide Children's Hospital. Chen was sentenced in February to 30 months' for her role.

During the trial the court heard that exosomes play a key role in the research, identification and treatment of a range of medical conditions, including necrotizing enterocolitis, a condition found in premature babies), liver fibrosis and liver cancer. Allegedly Zhou and Chen conspired to steal and then monetize one of the trade secrets by creating and selling exosome 'isolation kits'. Zhou's research at Nationwide Children's included a novel isolation method in which exosomes could be isolated from samples as small as one drop of blood. This method was vital to the research being conducted in Zhou's laboratory because necrotising enterocolitis is a condition found primarily in premature babies, only small amounts of fluid can safely be taken from them.

Zhou and Chen started a company in China to sell the kits and were encouraged to do so by financial incentives provided by the Chinese government, including the State Administration of Foreign Expert

Affairs and the National Natural Science Foundation of China. Zhou and Chen were also part of application processes related to multiple Chinese government programmes, including talent plans, a method used by China to transfer foreign research and technology to the Chinese government.

The couple was ordered to forfeit approximately $1.45 million, 500,000 shares of common stock of Avalon GloboCare Corp. and 400 shares of common stock of GenExosome Technologies Inc. They were also ordered to pay $2.6 million in restitution.[40]

* * *

In January 2020 an indictment was unsealed charging Cheng Bo, also known as Joe Cheng, a 45-year-old Chinese national, with participating in a criminal conspiracy from 2012 to 2015 to violate US export laws by shipping US power amplifiers to China.

Cheng's former employer, Avnet Asia Pte. Ltd., a Singapore company and global distributor of electronic components and related software, agreed to pay a financial penalty to the United States of $1,508,000 to settle criminal liability for the conduct of its former employees, including Cheng. As part of a non-prosecution agreement, Avnet Asia admitted responsibility for Cheng's unlawful conspiracy to ship export-controlled US goods with potential military applications to China, and also for the criminal conduct of another former employee who, from 2007 to 2009, illegally caused US goods to be shipped to China and Iran without a licence in violation of the International Emergency Economic Powers Act. Avnet Asia also agreed to pay an additional $1,721,000 as part of a $3,229,000 administrative penalty to resolve violations of the Export Administration Regulations.

'The People's Republic of China is relentless in its pursuit of US technology, much of which can be used for military purposes,' said Assistant Director Alan E. Kohler Jr. of the FBI's Counterintelligence Division. 'The FBI is just as relentless in identifying and stopping those who violate export controls while doing business with China. Let us be clear, this is not business as usual. It is illegal and individuals and companies will pay a price for such violations.'

According to the prosecution, Cheng was a sales account manager with Avnet Asia, and operated as a sales representative to a Hong Kong-based customer with whom Cheng had an ownership interest. Cheng submitted paperwork on behalf of the customer to purchase export-controlled US goods, including power amplifiers and made false statements to the US manufacturer of power amplifiers in which he had asserted that that his customer would use the amplifiers in Hong Kong when, in fact, Cheng knew that the goods would be illegally shipped from there to China.

Avnet Asia admitted that from 2012 to 2015, Cheng sent at least eighteen separate shipments of export-controlled goods from the United States to Hong Kong, knowing that the goods were intended to be subsequently shipped to China, and that their value was at least $814,000. Avnet Asia also conceded that another sales account manager, this one based in Singapore, conspired to violate US export control laws and economic sanctions from 2007 through 2009. He had helped two Singapore business organisations to ship US goods to Iran and China, by helping to create documents which falsely stated that the goods were destined only for Singapore. The Singapore-based sales account manager caused at least twenty-nine separate Avnet Asia shipments of goods to be exported from the United States, knowing that the goods were intended to be subsequently shipped to Iran or China. The value of these goods was at least $347,000, and neither Avnet Asia nor anyone else applied for an export licence from US government authorities.[41]

* * *

In January 2021 Professor Gang Chen of the Massachusetts Institute of Technology, a naturalised US citizen born in China, was charged with wire fraud for failing to disclose connections to various entities in China and was alleged to have received approximately $29 million in foreign funding since 2013, including $19 million from China's Southern University of Science and Technology. The indictment accused Chen of attempting to defraud the US Department of Energy by means of materially false and fraudulent pretences. However, when the case came before the court, the charges were dismissed.

Dr Chen studied heat transfer and was working on the development of a semiconductor that could convert heat from car exhaust into electricity, or fabric for clothing that could cool the body. The prosecution had alleged that Chen, in applications for $2.7 million in grants from the US Energy Department, had failed to disclose certain affiliations with China. Prosecutors announced that they had received new information indicating that Dr Chen had not been obliged to disclose those affiliations, undercutting the basis of the case.

The dismissal had a significant impact on the DoJ's China Initiative, which had been created in November 2018 to counter China's economic and scientific espionage. Many of the prosecutions pursued under the programme, like the case against Dr Chen, did not allege espionage or theft of information, but the simpler issue of a failure to disclose Chinese affiliations in grant applications to US agencies.

The son of two mathematics teachers who were sent to teach on farms during China's Cultural Revolution, Dr Chen grew up without any hope of becoming a scientist. His parents, the descendants of landowners, had a 'bad classification' from the Chinese government, and were viewed suspiciously. His father warned him he would probably spend his life as a farmer.[42]

* * *

In April 2021, Mingqing Xiao, a mathematics professor at Southern Illinois University (SIU), was indicted on two counts of wire fraud and one count of making a false statement in regards to a National Science Foundation grant application made on behalf of the university. If convicted, Mingqing Xiao could have faced up to 20 years in federal prison and a $250,000 fine.

Xiao had been a resident of the United States since 1991 and a citizen since 2006. In 2000 he worked on the faculty of the SIU's Department of Mathematics, having been granted promotion to full professor in 2007. His research area was mainly in applied mathematics, such as differential equations and computational science but it was not of a sensitive nature and was published widely. At the time Xiao had authored or co-authored over 100 peer-reviewed journal articles, book chapters and refereed conference publications. He had received five National Science Foundation grants on SIU's behalf and in 2016, the SIU College of Science named Xiao its Outstanding Scholar. The Justice Department began its 'China Initiative' in November 2018. While purported to counter Chinese national security threats and reinforce the former president's overall national security strategy, it quickly became apparent that this initiative was primarily accumulating prosecutions against Chinese-American academics.

In 2015 Xiao had initiated a relationship with Shenzhen University, based in Xiao's native Guangdong province. In addition to traveling there to present lectures twice during his summer vacations, he established a joint Ph.D. program between Shenzhen and SIU. Xiao's collaborative efforts followed a pattern encouraged for decades to recruit Chinese students to SIU, which has suffered a significant enrolment decline over the past decade, including a specific Memorandum of Understanding between SIU and Shenzhen to engage in joint research and educational activities. Xiao's sponsorship of this project resulted in the autumn of 2018, with the arrival of a group of undergraduates from Shenzhen who paid full tuition to attend SIU.

The university was not able to fund Xiao's trips to China after the initial 2015 visit, so Shenzhen University agreed to reimburse his travel expenses by requiring him to open a bank account in Shenzhen, into which two payments were made.

In December 2020 Xiao was interviewed by the FBI and described his collaboration with Shenzhen on behalf of SIU and disclosed the bank account in China. He was indicted in April 2021 and placed on administrative leave by the university. At his trial Xiao was acquitted on three charges but convicted of four felony tax charges.[43]

* * *

Shuren Qin, aged 44, a Chinese national living in Wellesley, Massachusetts, entered the United States through the EB-5 Immigrant Investor Visa Program in 2014 and established LinkOcean Technologies which he used to export goods and technology with underwater and marine applications to China. In April 2021 he pleaded guilty to one count of conspiracy to unlawfully export items from the United States to North Western Polytechnical University without first obtaining the required export licences; one count of visa fraud; two counts of making false statements to law enforcement agents regarding his customers and the types of parts he exported from the United States to China; four counts of money laundering; and two counts of smuggling hydrophones from the US to China.

The university had been involved in the development of unmanned aerial vehicles, autonomous underwater vehicles and missile proliferation projects, and in 2001 had been placed on the US Department of Commerce's (DoC) Entity List for national security reasons. Qin communicated with and received purchase orders from the university to obtain items used for anti-submarine warfare. Between approximately July 2015 and December 2016 Qin sent at least sixty hydrophones to the university without obtaining the required export licences from the DoC. Qin and his company, LinkOcean, did so by concealing from the US hydrophone manufacturer that the university was the true end-user and by filing false end-user information. In addition, on four occasions Qin engaged in money laundering by transferring more than $100,000 from Chinese bank accounts to banks in the United States.

In July 2016 Qin engaged in visa fraud with his visa application by falsely certifying that he had not committed any crime for which he was not arrested since becoming a conditional permanent resident.

In addition, Qin made false statements to federal agents on two occasions regarding LinkOcean's customers and its export activities. Specifically, during a November 2017 interview with Customs officers, Qin falsely stated that he only exported instruments that attach to a buoy. However, Qin had exported and caused the export of remotely operated side-scan sonar systems, unmanned underwater vehicles, unmanned surface vehicles, robotic boats and hydrophones. The items had military applications and several of these items were delivered to military end-users in China. In July 2018 Qin lied to investigators when he stated that he did not have any customers on the DoC's Entity List when he had at least two such customers North West Polytechnical University and the National University of Defense Technology. At the time, the National University was on the DoC's Entity List and was involved in the modernisation of China's armed forces

By the end of the summer of 2017, investigators learned that Qin was interested in procuring both AUVs and sonobuoys, thereby raising concerns that Ultra Electronics was at that same time developing 'an AUV that worked in conjunction with [a] sonobuoy . . . strictly for military use by the US Navy'. Qin also lied when questioned during the secondary inspection at the border regarding the types of parts he exported, concealing his 'interest in procuring side-scan sonar systems, AUVs, and sonobuoys'.[44]

* * *

In September 2018 a federal grand jury in San Francisco indicted a Chinese state-owned enterprise and three individuals with crimes related to a conspiracy to steal, convey and possess stolen trade secrets of an American semiconductor company for the benefit of a company controlled by the Chinese government. All of the defendants were also charged with conspiracy to commit economic espionage. In addition, prosecutors filed a civil lawsuit to enjoin the further transfer of the stolen trade secrets and to enjoin certain defendants from exporting to the United States any products manufactured by United Microelectronics Corporation (UMC) or Jinhua that were created using the trade secrets at issue. The prosecution alleged that the plot involved a Taiwanese company, and three Taiwan citizens planned to steal trade secrets from Micron, an Idaho-based semi-conductor company.

According to the indictment, the defendants were engaged in a conspiracy to steal the trade secrets of Micron Technology, a leader in the global semiconductor industry specialising in the advanced research, development, and manufacturing of memory products, including dynamic random-access memory (DRAM). DRAM is a leading-edge memory storage device used in computer electronics. Micron is the only United States-based company that manufactures DRAM. According to the indictment, Micron maintains a significant competitive advantage in this field due in large part from its intellectual property, including its trade secrets that include detailed, confidential information pertaining to the design, development, and manufacturing of advanced DRAM products.

Hitherto, China did not possess DRAM technology, and the Central Government and the PRC's State Council publicly identified the development of DRAM and other microelectronics technology as a national economic priority. The defendants were UMC, a Taiwan semiconductor foundry; Fujian Jinhua Integrated Circuit, Co., Ltd. ('Jinhua'), a state-owned enterprise of the PRC; and three Taiwan nationals: Chen Zhengkun, alias Stephen Chen, aged 55; He Jianting, alias J.T. Ho, aged 42; and Wang Yungming, alias Kenny Wang, aged 44. UMC was described as a publicly listed semiconductor foundry company traded on the New York Stock Exchange; headquartered in Taiwan; and has offices worldwide, including in Sunnyvale, California. UMC mass produces integrated-circuit logic products based on designs and technology developed and provided by its customers. Jinhua is a state-owned enterprise of the PRC, funded entirely by the Chinese government, and established in February 2016 for the sole purpose of designing, developing, and manufacturing DRAM.

According to the indictment, Chen was a General Manager and Chairman of an electronics corporation that Micron acquired in 2013. Chen then became the president of a Micron subsidiary in Taiwan, Micron Memory Taiwan (MMT), responsible for manufacturing at least one of Micron's DRAM chips. Chen resigned from MMT in July 2015 and began working at UMC almost immediately. While at UMC, Chen arranged a cooperation agreement between UMC and Fujian Jinhua whereby, with funding from Fujian Jinhua, UMC would transfer DRAM technology to Fujian Jinhua to mass produce. The technology would be jointly shared by both UMC and Fujian Jinhua. Chen later became the President of Jinhua and was put in charge of its DRAM production facility. While at UMC, Chen recruited numerous MMT employees, including Ho and Wang, to join him at UMC. Prior to leaving MMT, Ho and Wang both stole and brought to UMC several Micron trade secrets related to the design and manufacture of DRAM. Wang downloaded over 900 Micron confidential and proprietary files before he left MMT and stored them on USB external hard drives or in personal cloud storage, from where he could access the technology while working at UMC.

If convicted, the individual defendants face a maximum sentence of 15 years imprisonment and a $5 million fine for economic espionage charges, and 10 years imprisonment for theft of trade secrets charges. If convicted, each company faces forfeiture and a maximum fine of more than $20 billion.

The Attorney General Sessions said. 'The worldwide supply for DRAM is worth nearly $50 billion; Micron controls about 20 to 25 per cent of the dynamic random access memory industry – a technology not possessed by the Chinese until very recently. As this and other recent cases have shown, Chinese economic espionage against the United States has been increasing – and it has been increasing rapidly. I am here to say that enough is enough. With integrity and professionalism, the DoJ will aggressively prosecute such illegal activity.'

'The theft of intellectual property is not only unfair, but stifles technological innovation by disincentivizing investment in long-term research and development,' said US Attorney Alex Tse. 'The theft of intellectual property on a continuing basis by nation-state actors is an even more damaging affront to the rule of law. We in the Northern District of California, one of the world's great centres of intellectual property development, will continue to lead the fight to protect US innovation from criminal misappropriation, whether motivated by personal greed or national economic ambition.'

'No country presents a broader, more severe threat to our ideas, our innovation, and our economic security than China,' said FBI Director Christopher Wray. 'The Chinese government is determined to acquire American technology, and they're willing use a variety of means to do that – from foreign investments, corporate acquisitions, and cyber intrusions to obtaining the services of current or former company employees to get inside information. If China acquires an American company's most important technology – the very technology that makes it the leader in a field – that company will suffer severe losses, and our national security could even be impacted. We are committed to continuing to work closely with our federal, state, local, and private sector partners to counter this threat from China.'[45]

* * *

In October 2018 two Chinese intelligence officers and their group of computer hackers were charged with conspiracy to steal sensitive commercial aviation and technological data. Their purpose was to steal, among other data, intellectual property and confidential business information, including information related to a turbofan engine used in commercial airliners.

The charged intelligence officers, Zha Rong and Chai Meng, and other co-conspirators, worked for the Jiangsu Province Ministry of State Security (JSSD), headquartered in Nanjing, which was described as the provincial foreign intelligence arm of China's MSS.

From at least January 2010 to May 2015, JSSD intelligence officers and their team of hackers, including Zhang Zhang-Gui, Liu Chunliang, Gao Hong Kun, Zhuang Xiaowei and Ma Zhiqi, focused on the theft of technology relating to the turbofan engine used to power US and European commercial airliners. This engine was under development by a partnership between a French aerospace manufacturer with an office in Suzhou, Jiangsu province, China, and a company based in the United States. Members of the conspiracy, assisted and enabled by JSSD-recruited insiders Gu Gen and Tian Xi, hacked the French aerospace manufacturer. The hackers also accessed the systems of other companies that manufactured parts for the turbofan, including aerospace companies based in Arizona, Massachusetts and Oregon. At the time, a Chinese state-owned aerospace company was working to develop a comparable engine for use in commercial aircraft manufactured in China and elsewhere.

Zhang Zhang-Gui was also charged, along with Chinese national Li Xiao, in a separate hacking conspiracy, which alleged that both men had he leveraged the JSSD-directed conspiracy's intrusions, including the hack of a San Diego-based technology company, for their own criminal purposes.

On 10 October the DoJ announced that a JSSD intelligence officer had been charged with attempting to steal trade secrets related to jet aircraft engines, and in September, in the Northern District of Illinois, a grand jury indicted a US Army recruit accused of working as an agent of a JSSD intelligence officer.

The FBI's investigation showed that the JSSD intelligence officers and hackers masterminded illicit access to networks to steal non-public commercial and other data. The hackers used a range of techniques, including spear-phishing, sowing multiple different strains of malware into company computer systems, using the victim companies' own websites as 'watering holes' to compromise website visitors' computers, and domain hijacking through the compromise of domain registrars.

The first alleged hack began no later than 8 January 2010, when members of the conspiracy infiltrated Capstone Turbine, a Los-

Angeles-based gas turbine manufacturer, in order to steal data and use the Capstone Turbine website as a 'watering hole'. The same hackers also sought repeatedly to access a San Diego-based technology company from at least August 2012 to January 2014, to similarly steal commercial information and use its website as a 'watering hole'.

The Chinese intelligence personnel also co-opted victim company employees, and from at least November 2013 to February 2014, two Chinese nationals working at the direction of the JSSD, Tian Xi and Gu Gen, were employed in the French aerospace company's Suzhou office. In January 2014, after receiving malware from an identified JSSD officer acting as his handler, Tian infected one of the French company's computers with malware at the JSSD officer's direction. A month later, in February 2014, Gu, the French company's head of Information Technology and Security in Suzhou, warned the conspirators when he learned that the company had been alerted to the existence of malware on the company systems. That same day, acting on that tip-off, Chai Meng and Liu Chunliang tried to protect the JSSD by deleting the domain linking the malware to an account controlled by members of the conspiracy.

The group's hacking attempts continued through at least May 2015, when an Oregon-based company, which, like many of the other targeted companies, built parts for the turbofan jet engine used in commercial airliners, identified and removed the conspiracy's malware from its computer systems.

Count Two of the indictment charged that a separate conspiracy to hack computers in which Zhang Zhang-Gui had supplied his friend, Li Xiao, with variants of the malware that had been developed and deployed by hackers working at the direction of the JSSD on the hack into Capstone Turbine. Using malware supplied by Zhang, as well as other malware, Li launched repeatedly accessed a San Diego-based computer technology company for more than 18 months, causing immense damage to protected computers.[46]

* * *

In October 2018 an MSS officer, Yanjun Xu, alias Qu Hui, alias Zhang Hui, was extradited to the United States where he was arrested and charged with conspiring and attempting to commit economic espionage and steal trade secrets from multiple US aviation and aerospace companies.

'This unprecedented extradition of a Chinese intelligence officer exposes the Chinese government's direct oversight of economic espionage against the United States,' said FBI Assistant Director Bill Priestap.

Yanjun, described as a Deputy Division Director with the MSS's Jiangsu State Security Department, Sixth Bureau, had been arrested in Belgium in April and then indicted by a federal grand jury in the Southern District of Ohio, charging Xu with conspiring and attempting to commit economic espionage and theft of trade secrets. According to the indictment:

> Beginning in at least December 2013 and continuing until his arrest, Xu targeted certain companies inside and outside the United States that are recognized as leaders in the aviation field. This included GE Aviation. He identified experts who worked for these companies and recruited them to travel to China, often initially under the guise of asking them to deliver a university presentation. Xu and others paid the experts' travel costs and provided stipends.[47]

* * *

Ji Chaoqun, aged 27, a Chinese citizen residing in Chicago, was arrested there in October 2018 for acting within the United States as an illegal agent of the People's Republic of China. Allegedly, Ji had worked at the direction of a high-level intelligence officer in the Jiangsu Province Ministry of State Security. Allegedly Ji had been tasked with providing the intelligence officer with biographical information on eight individuals for possible recruitment by the JSSD, among them Chinese nationals who were working as engineers and scientists in the United States, some of whom were US defence contractors.

Ji had been born in China and arrived in the United States in 2013 on an F1 Visa to study electrical engineering at the Illinois Institute of Technology in Chicago. In 2016, Ji enlisted in the US Army Reserves as an E4 Specialist under the Military Accessions Vital to the National Interest (MAVNI) program, which authorises the US Armed Forces to recruit certain legal aliens whose skills are considered vital to the national interest. In his application to participate in the MAVNI program, Ji specifically denied having had contact with a foreign government within the past seven years. In a subsequent interview with a US Army officer, Ji again failed to disclose his relationship and contacts with the intelligence officer. In January 2023 he was sentenced to eight years' imprisonment.[48]

* * *

In April 2018 Shan Shi, 53, a US citizen from Houston, Texas, and Gang Liu, 32, a Chinese national, were among six individuals indicted in June 2017 on charges of conspiracy to commit theft of trade secrets, conspiracy to commit economic espionage count against Shi and Liu, as well as a federal money laundering conspiracy count against Shi.

CBM-Future New Material Science and Technology (CBMF), a Chinese company based in Taizhou, and its Houston-based subsidiary, CBM International (CBMI), had also been indicted on all three charges. The other defendants included Uka Kalu Uche, aged 36, a US citizen from Spring, Texas; Samuel Abotar Ogoe, aged 75, a US citizen from Missouri City, Texas; Kui Bo, 41, a Canadian citizen who had been residing in the Dallas area; and Hui Huang, 33, a Chinese national. All the defendants pleaded not guilty in 2017 to the charges in the original indictment, with the exception of Huang, who had not been apprehended and was believed to remain at large in China. A seventh defendant previously pleaded guilty in December 2017 to a charge of conspiracy to commit theft of trade secrets.

According to the indictment, China has promoted military, social and economic development initiatives with a goal of making the country a marine power and has prioritised the development of engineered components of deepwater buoyancy materials. The charges in the indictment involve the development of syntactic foam, a strong, lightweight material that can be tailored for commercial and military uses, including oil exploration, aerospace and stealth technologies, and underwater vehicles, such as submarines.

Allegedly, from at least 2013 to May 2017 Shi had operated on behalf of CBMF, which intended to create a facility in China to sell syntactic foam. CBMF received research funds from state funding in China and was part of a collaborative innovation centre with Chinese government entities. Accordingly, Shi and Liu conspired with the other defendants to steal trade secrets from a global engineering firm that is a producer in the global syntactic foam market.

In March 2014 Shi incorporated CBMI, which was owned and funded by CBMF, in Houston. CBMF employees then wired approximately $3.1 million to CBMI between June 2014 and May 2017. Shi and others recruited and hired current and former employees of the company in Houston, including Liu, for the purpose of aiding CBMF's capability to make syntactic foam. Liu previously worked for the company as a material development engineer and had access to proprietary and trade secret data. He and others were accused of passing along those trade secrets. According to the indictment, the technology was ultimately destined for China, to benefit the government and other state-owned enterprises. In February 2020 Shi was sentenced to 20 months' imprisonment.[49]

* * *

A 51-year-old Chinese national and US legal permanent resident living in Manhattan, Kansas, Zhang Weiqiang worked as a rice breeder for Ventria Bioscience in Junction City, Kansas. Ventria develops genetically programmed rice to express recombinant human proteins, which are then extracted for use in the therapeutic and medical fields. Zhang had a master's degree in agriculture from Shengyang Agricultural University in China and a doctorate from Louisiana State University.

According to trial evidence, Zhang acquired without authorisation hundreds of rice seeds produced by Ventria and stored them at his residence in Manhattan. The rice seeds have a wide variety of health research applications and were developed to produce either human serum albumin, contained in blood, or lactoferrin, an iron-binding protein found, for example, in human milk. Ventria spent millions of dollars and years of research developing its seeds and cost-effective methods to extract the proteins, which are used to develop lifesaving products for global markets. Ventria used locked doors with magnetic card readers to restrict access to the temperature-controlled environment where the seeds were stored and processed.

In the summer of 2013, personnel from a crop research institute in China visited Zhang at his home in Manhattan. Zhang drove the visitors to tour facilities in Iowa, Missouri and Ohio. On 7 August 2013, US Customs officers found seeds belonging to Ventria in the luggage of Zhang's visitors as they prepared to leave the United States for China.

Zhang was convicted in February 2017 of one count of conspiracy to steal trade secrets, one count of conspiracy to commit interstate transportation of stolen property and one count of interstate transportation of stolen property. He was sentenced to 121 months in a federal prison for conspiring to steal samples of a variety of rice seeds from a biopharmaceutical research facility.[50]

* * *

Xu Jiaqiang, aged 31, formerly of Beijing, China, was sentenced in January 2018 to five years' imprisonment for economic espionage and theft of a trade secret in connection with Xu's theft of proprietary source code from his former employer, with the intent to benefit the National Health and Family Planning Commission of the People's Republic of China. Xu previously had pleaded guilty to all six counts with which he was charged.

According to the allegations filed against Xu, from November 2010 to May 2014, he had worked as a developer for a particular US company. He enjoyed access to certain proprietary software as well as that software's underlying source code. The proprietary software was a clustered file system developed and marketed by the company in the United States and other countries. A clustered file system facilitated faster computer performance by coordinating work among multiple servers. The company took significant precautions to protect the proprietary source code as a trade secret. Among other things, the proprietary source code was stored behind a company firewall and could be accessed only by a small number of trusted employees. Before receiving proprietary source code access, employees were required to first request and receive approval from a particular official. The staff also agreed in writing at both the outset and the conclusion of their employment that they would maintain the confidentiality of any proprietary information. The proprietary software and the proprietary source code were very valuable.

In May 2014 Xu voluntarily resigned from the company but subsequently was in touch with an undercover FBI officer who posed as a financial investor aiming to start a large-data storage technology company, and with another undercover officer who pretended to be a project manager. In their communications, Xu discussed his past experience with the company and indicated that he had experience with the proprietary software and the proprietary source code. On 6 March 2015, Xu sent both FBI undercovers a code, which Xu stated was a sample of his prior work with the company. Another company employee later confirmed that the code sent by Xu included proprietary material that related to the proprietary source code.

Xu subsequently informed one of the FBI undercovers that Xu was willing to consider providing him with the proprietary source code as a platform for his company to develop of its own data storage system. Consequently, in early August 2015 the FBI arranged for a computer network to be set up consistent with Xu's specifications. Files were then remotely uploaded to the FBI-arranged computer network and soon afterwards, Xu and FBI undercover confirmed that the upload had been received. In September 2015, the FBI made the Xu upload available to a company employee who had expertise regarding the proprietary software and the proprietary source code. Based on an analysis of technical features of the Xu upload, it appeared that it contained a functioning copy of the proprietary software.

On 7 December 2015, Xu met with one of the FBI undercovers at a hotel in White Plains, New York and stated that he had used the proprietary source code to make software to sell to customers, and mentioned that he knew the proprietary source code to be the product of decades of work on the part of the company, and that he had used the proprietary source code to build a copy which he had uploaded and installed on the FBI's network. Xu also claimed that he had altered the copy so as to remove any incriminating copyrighted material.[51]

* * *

In January 2016 four state-owned Chinese companies were indicted on charges of conspiring to commit economic espionage and related crimes. Reportedly the companies conspired and attempted to engage in economic espionage by seeking to acquire misappropriated trade secrets for the production technology for chloride-route titanium dioxide from E.I. du Pont de Nemours & Company.

According to the indictment, between 1998 and 2011 Pangang Group Company, Ltd (also known as Panzhihua Iron and Steel (Group) Co., Ltd) conspired with Chinese nationals Hou Shengdong and Dong Yingjie as well as three of the company's subsidiaries and others to acquire stolen or misappropriated trade secrets. The defendant subsidiary companies were the Pangang Group Steel Vanadium & Titanium Company, Ltd; the Pangang Group Titanium Industry Company Ltd; and the Pangang Group International Economic & Trading Company.

The trade secrets relate to TiO^2 technology from DuPont which had developed the technology and controlled a significant amount of the world's TiO^2 sales. The defendants were accused of having obtained confidential trade secret information including photographs related to TiO^2 plant technologies and facilities. Further, the prosecution alleged that an Oakland company was paid at least $27 million between 2006 and 2011 for assistance with TiO^2 technology, including obtaining DuPont trade secrets. The defendants also allegedly attempted, between 2008 and 2011, to commit economic espionage related to DuPont's TiO^2 processes. The four companies pleaded not guilty to all charges.[52]

* * *

In August 2016 Wenxia Man, alias Wency Man, aged 45, of San Diego, was sentenced to 50 months' imprisonment for conspiring to export and cause the export of fighter jet engines, an unmanned aerial vehicle and related technical data to China in violation of the Arms Export Control Act.

On 9 June 2016, Man was convicted by a federal jury in Florida on one count of conspiring to export and cause the export of defence articles without the required licence. According to the prosecution, between approximately March 2011 and June 2013, Man conspired with Xinsheng Zhang, who was located in China, to illegally acquire and export to China defence articles including: Pratt & Whitney F135-PW-100 engines used in the F-35 Joint Strike Fighter; Pratt & Whitney F119-PW-100 turbofan engines used in the F-22 Raptor fighter jet; General Electric F110-GE-132 engines designed for the F-16 fighter jet; the General Atomics MQ-9 Reaper/Predator B Unmanned Aerial Vehicle, capable of firing Hellfire missiles; and technical data for each of these defence articles. During the course of the investigation, when talking to an a Customs Enforcement's Homeland Security Investigations undercover agent, Man referred to Zhang as a 'technology spy' who worked on behalf of the Chinese military to copy items obtained from other countries and stated that he was particularly interested in stealth technology.[53]

* * *

In May 2017 a Chinese national Si ('Cathy') Chen pleaded guilty to participating in a scheme that illegally exported sensitive space communications technology to China was sentenced today to serve 46 months' in federal imprisonment. Aged 33, and resident in Pomona, California, Si had been in custody since her arrest in May 2017.

Chen, who used various aliases, included 'Cathy Chen,' pleaded guilty in July to conspiracy to violate the International Emergency Economic Powers Act, to money laundering and using a forged passport with her photo but a different name that appeared to have been issued by China.

According to court documents, from March 2013 through the end of 2015, Chen purchased and smuggled sensitive items to China without obtaining the required licences from the US Department of Commerce. Those items included components commonly used in military communications 'jammers'. Additionally, Chen smuggled communications devices worth more than $100,000 that are commonly used in space communications applications. Chen falsely undervalued the items on the shipping paperwork to avoid arousing suspicion. Chen received payments for the illegally exported products through an account held at a bank in China by a family member.

In addition to participating in the scheme to violate export controls, Chen used several aliases and a forged Chinese passport to conceal her smuggling activities. Chen used a Chinese passport bearing her photo and a false name – 'Chunping Ji' – to rent an office in Pomona where she took delivery of the export-controlled items. After receiving the goods, Chen shipped the devices to Hong Kong, and from there they were transhipped to China. The parcels shipped to Hong Kong bore her false name, along with false product descriptions and monetary values, all done in an effort to avoid attracting law enforcement scrutiny.[54]

* * *

In March 2016, a Chinese national and resident of China pleaded guilty to participating in a years-long conspiracy to hack into the computer networks of major US defence contractors, steal sensitive military and export-controlled data and send the stolen data to China. A criminal complaint filed in 2014 and subsequent indictments filed in Los Angeles charged Su Bin, also known as Stephen Su and Stephen Subin, a China-based businessman in the aviation and aerospace fields, for his role in the criminal conspiracy to steal military technical data, including data relating to the C-17 strategic transport aircraft and certain fighter jets produced for the US military. Su was initially arrested in Canada in July 2014 and consented to his extradition in February 2016. In the plea agreement, Su admitted to conspiring with two persons in China from October 2008 to March 2014 to gain unauthorised access to protected computer networks in the United States, including computers belonging to the Boeing Company in Orange County, California, to obtain sensitive military information and to export that information illegally from the United States to China. As part of the conspiracy, Su would email the co-conspirators with guidance regarding what persons, companies and technologies to target during their computer intrusions. One of Su's co-conspirators would then gain access to information residing on computers of US companies and email Su directory file listings and folders showing the data that the co-conspirator had been able to access. Su then directed his co-conspirator as to which files and folders his co-conspirator should steal. Once the co-conspirator stole the data, including by using techniques to avoid detection when hacking the victim computers, Su translated the contents of certain stolen data from English into Chinese.

In addition, Su and his co-conspirators each wrote, revised and emailed reports about the information and technology they had acquired by their hacking activities, including its value, to the final beneficiaries of their hacking activities. Su's plea agreement made clear that the information he and his co-conspirators intentionally stole included data listed on the US Munitions List contained in the International Traffic in Arms Regulations. Su also admitted that he engaged in the crime for the purpose of financial gain and specifically sought to profit from selling the data he and his co-conspirators illegally acquired.[55]

* * *

In June 2016 Kan Chen, aged 26 of Ningbo, China, in Zhejiang Province, was sentenced to 30 months' imprisonment and three years of supervised release for conspiring to violate the Arms Export Control Act and International Traffic in Arms Regulations; attempting to violate the Arms Export Control Act and International Traffic in Arms Regulations; and violating the International Emergency Economic Powers Act.

On 16 June 2015, Chen was arrested by US Immigration and Customs Enforcement's Homeland Security Investigation agents on the Northern Marianas island of Saipan following an eight-month long investigation and has remained in custody. He pleaded guilty to the charges in March 2016.

According to court documents, from July 2013 through to his arrest in June 2015, Chen illegally exported over 180 export-controlled items, valued at over $275,000, from the United States to China. Over forty of those items – purchased for more than $190,000 – were sophisticated night vision and thermal imaging scopes, which are designated by the International Traffic in Arms Regulations as US Munitions List defence articles and can be mounted on automatic and semi-automatic rifles and used for military purposes at night.

Given the sensitivity surrounding these military-grade items, Chen devised a scheme to smuggle these items through Delaware and outside the United States. He purchased the devices via the internet and telephone and had them mailed to several reshipping services in New Castle, Delaware, which provided an American shipping address for customers located in China, accept packages for their customers and then re-ship them to China. In order to further conceal his role Chen arranged for the re-shippers to send the devices to several intermediaries who in turn forwarded the devices to Chen in China. Chen then sent the devices to his customers.[56]

* * *

In February 2015 a company based in Arlington Heights, Illinois, its president, and a former employee were charged with unlawfully exporting and importing military articles, including components used in night vision systems and on the M1A1 Abrams main battle tank.

Allegedly Vibgyor Optical Systems, Inc. purported to manufacture optics and optical systems, including items that were to be supplied to the US Department of Defense. However, instead of manufacturing the items domestically, as it claimed, Vibgyor illegally sent the technical data for, and samples of, the military articles to manufacturers in China, then imported the items from China to sell to its customers – including DoD prime contractors. Vibgyor's president, Bharat 'Victor' Verma, and Urvashi 'Sonia' Verma, a former Vibgyor employee and owner of a now-defunct company that operated as a subcontractor for Vibgyor, were also charged in the indictment. According to the indictment, between November 2006 and March 2014, the defendants conspired to defraud the United States and violate both the Arms Export Control Act and International Traffic in Arms Regulations. Vibgyor won subcontracts to supply optical components and systems to DoD prime contractors by misrepresenting the location of the manufacture of the items it supplied. Bharat Verma falsely claimed that the items Vibgyor supplied were manufactured domestically, when they actually had been manufactured in China, based on information illegally exported to Chinese manufacturers. In addition to illegally providing technical data for a military item to China, Urvashi Verma attempted to ship an example of one of the military items to the Chinese manufacturer. Vibgyor, Bharat Verma, and Urvashi Verma were charged with one count of conspiracy to violate the arms control regulations, one count of conspiracy to defraud the United States, and one count of violating the arms control regulations. Vibgyor and Bharat Verma were also charged with international money laundering.[57]

* * *

In Jane 2015, Hui Sheng Shen, alias 'Charlie,' was sentenced in New Jersey to 49 months 'imprisonment and a fine of $200. His accomplice, Huan Ling Chang, alias 'Alice', was sentenced to time served and a $200 fine. Both Taiwanese nationals, each pleaded guilty to one count of conspiracy to violate the Arms Export Control Act and one count of conspiracy to import illegal drugs.

In April 2012 Shen and Chang had been charged separately with conspiracy to violate the Arms Export Control Act. Both had been arrested in February 2012 in New York on charges of conspiring to import and importing crystal methamphetamine from Taiwan to the United States. Allegedly, during negotiations with undercover FBI agents over the meth deal, Shen and Chang asked FBI undercover agents if they could obtain an E-2 Hawkeye reconnaissance aircraft for a customer in China. In subsequent conversations, they indicated they were also interested in stealth technology for the F-22 fighter jet, as well as missile engine technology, and various Unmanned Aerial Vehicles (UAVs), including the RQ-11b Raven, a small hand-launched drone. Shen and Chang stated that their clients were connected to the Chinese government and its intelligence service which had sent undercover agents a code book to facilitate communications relating to the proposed arms exports, and opened a bank account in Hong Kong to receive and disburse funds related to the transactions. On a visit to New York in February 2012, the pair examined a Raven RQ-11b UAV and manuals relating to the RQ-4 Global Hawk provided by the FBI that they allegedly intended to export to China. Shen and Chang were arrested shortly thereafter.[58]

* * *

In December 2014, Janice Kuang Capener, a Chinese citizen resident in Salt Lake City, was sentenced in Utah to 90 days' imprisonment, 24 months' supervised release, a $100 special assessment, and a $3,000 fine. Capener pleaded guilty in September 2014 to a charge of stealing trade secrets.

In May 2012 Capener, Jun Luo and two companies, Sunhills International LLC, a California company established by Capener, and Zhejiang Hongchen Irrigation Equipment Company, were charged with theft of trade secrets, wire fraud, and conspiracy to commit wire fraud in connection with the alleged theft of trade secrets from Orbit Irrigation Products, an irrigation company headquartered in Utah. According to court documents, Capener had worked at Orbit from June 2003 through November 2009, including serving as the chief of operations at Orbit's manufacturing plant in Ningbo, China. Capener allegedly stole Orbit's trade secrets relating to sales and pricing and used that information for herself and others to the detriment of Orbit. Capener also allegedly worked with Luo, Sunhills International and Zhejiang Hongchen Irrigation Equipment to devise a scheme to undermine Orbit's position in the marketplace using illegally obtained proprietary pricing information.

Capener and Luo were arrested in May 2012 but in August 2012, all charges against Luo, also a Chinese citizen, were dismissed. Zhejiang

Hongchen Irrigation Equipment Co., Ltd., a Chinese company under contract with Orbit, pleaded guilty to Counts 1–5 of the original indictment and was sentenced to 36 months' probation, and ordered to pay a fine of $100,000 and restitution of $300,000 for its role in a scheme to defraud and conspiracy to commit wire fraud.[59]

* * *

In July 2014, in Massachusetts, Qiang Hu aka Johnson Hu, a Chinese national and resident of Shanghai, was sentenced to 34 months' federal imprisonment and a $100 special assessment. Hu had pleaded guilty on October 2013 for his role in a conspiracy scheme to export dual-use pressure transducers from the United States to China. Previously, in June 2012, Hu had been charged with conspiracy to illegally export from the United States to China and elsewhere dual-use pressure transducers, in violation of the International Emergency Economic Powers Act Hu was arrested in May 2012, after he arrived in Massachusetts for a business meeting.

According to the prosecution, the pressure transducers in question, manufactured by MKS Instruments headquartered in Andover, Massachusetts, are controlled for export by the Commerce Department because they can be used in gas centrifuges to enrich uranium and produce weapons-grade uranium. Specifically, they can be used to measure gas pressure of uranium hexafluoride in centrifuge cascades. The indictment claimed that Hu worked as a sales manager for a subsidiary of MKS Instruments in Shanghai, where he had been employed since 2008. Hu and his co-conspirators allegedly caused thousands of MKS export-controlled pressure transducers, worth more than $6.5 million, to be illegally exported from the United States to unauthorised end-users in China and elsewhere using export licences fraudulently obtained from the Department of Commerce. Reportedly, Hu and his co-conspirators used two primary means of deception to export the pressure transducers. First, they used licences issued to legitimate MKS business customers to export the pressure transducers to China, and then caused the parts to be delivered to other end-users who were not themselves named on the export licences or authorised to receive the parts. Second, the conspirators obtained export licences in the name of a front company and then used these fraudulently-obtained licences to export the parts to China, where they were delivered to the actual end-users.[60]

* * *

In July 2014, in Connecticut, charges against United Technologies Corporation (UTC) and Hamilton Sundstrand Corporation (HSC) were dismissed but count three of the information against Pratt & Whitney Canada Corp (PWC) was upheld.

Previously, in June 2012, PWC, a Canadian subsidiary of Connecticut-based defence contractor UTC, had pleaded guilty to violating the Arms Export Control Act and making false statements in connection with the illegal export to China of US-origin military software that was used in the development of China's first modern military attack helicopter, the Z-10. In addition, UTC, its US-based subsidiary HSC and PWC all agreed to pay more than $75 million as part of a global settlement with the DoJ in connection with various export violations, including those related to the Z-10, and for making false and belated disclosures to the US government about the illegal exports for the Z-10. Consequently, a three-count criminal information was filed against the companies. Count one charged PWC with violating the Arms Export Control Act for the illegal export of defence articles to China for the Z-10 helicopter.

Specifically, in 2002 and 2003 PWC had exported HSC military software used to test and operate PWC engines to China for the Z-10 without any US export licence. PWC knew from the start of the Z-10 project in 2000 that the Chinese were developing an attack helicopter and that supplying it with US-origin components would be illegal.

According to court documents, PWC's illegal conduct was driven by profit. PWC anticipated that its work on the Z-10 attack helicopter would open the door to a far more lucrative civilian helicopter market in China potentially worth as much as $2 billion to PWC. Count two of the charges alleged PWC, UTC, and HSC with making false statements about these illegal exports to the State Department in their belated disclosures, which did not begin until 2006.

Count three charged PWC and HSC for their failure to timely inform the State Department of the unlawful export of defence articles to China, an embargoed nation, as required by US export regulations. While PWC pleaded guilty to counts one and two, prosecution of PWC, UTC, and HSC on the other charges was deferred for two years, provided that the companies abided by the terms of a deferred prosecution agreement with the Justice Department. In addition to the resolution of the criminal charges, as part of a global settlement, UTC also resolved over 500 additional administrative charges with the State Department. Those charges involved more than 800 exports in violation of the Arms Export Control Act from the mid-1990s to 2011. In connection with the global settlement with the Justice and

State Departments, PWC, UTC, and HSC agreed to pay more than $75 million in penalties, subject themselves to independent monitoring for several years, and be required to comply with an extensive training and remedial action program to strengthen their export compliance.[61]

* * *

In April 2014 Yufeng Wei, a Chinese national, was re-sentenced to 23 months' imprisonment, 2 years of supervised released, and a $1,100 special assessment. Previously, in September 2013, Wei's now ex-husband Zhen Zhou Wu, also a Chinese national, was re-sentenced to 84 months' imprisonment, 2 years' supervised release, a $1,700 special assessment, and ordered to pay a $15,000 fine. Wei and Wu were re- sentenced for conspiring over a 10-year-period to illegally export military and sophisticated electronics used in military phased array radar, electronic warfare, and missile systems to China, and illegally exporting sensitive electronic components to China between 2004 and 2007, After serving their convictions, both Wu and Wei, a permanent resident, were to be deported.

In March 2013, a successful appeal led to the quashing of the two counts of the convictions for illegally exporting parts designated on the United States Munitions List. However, the court confirmed that 'from 1996 until 2008, Wei and Wu shipped tens of millions of dollars' worth of sophisticated electronic components from the United States to China with little regard for whether the parts that they sold were export-controlled'. It was further stated that Wu's company 'specifically pursued military customers; and Wu promoted himself as both an exporter of military supplies and an export compliance expert.' And noted that 'Wu and Wei repeatedly attempted to disguise the fact that they were exporting to China and that they lacked the necessary licences to do so.' Because two counts of both Wei and Wu's convictions were vacated, the case was remanded for re-sentencing hearings. Wei and Wu were originally sentenced in 2011. Wei was sentenced in January 2011 to 36 months' imprisonment, while in January 2011, Wu, was sentenced to 97 months' imprisonment. Their company, Chitron Electronics, Inc., was fined $15.5 million. Wei, Wu and Chitron Electronics, Inc. were convicted at trial in May 2010 on charges relating to the illegal export of military electronic components to China through Hong Kong. They were also found to have illegally exported Commerce Department-controlled electronics components to China with military applications such as electronic warfare, military radar, and satellite communications systems. Wu founded and controlled Chitron, with headquarters in Shenzhen, China and a US office located in Waltham, Massachusetts, where Wei had worked as manager. Wu and Chitron sold electronics from the US to Chinese military factories and military research institutes, including numerous institutes of the China Electronics Technology Group Corporation, which was responsible for the procurement, development and manufacture of electronics for the Chinese military. Since as early as 2002, Wu referred to Chinese military entities as Chitron's major customer and employed an engineer at Chitron's Shenzhen office to work with Chinese military customers. By 2007, 25 per cent of Chitron's sales were to Chinese military entities. Shenzhen Chitron Electronics Company Limited, Wu's Chinese company through which US electronics were delivered to the Chinese military and other end-users, was also indicted. In February 2011 Chitron-Shenzhen received a fine of $1.9 million for refusing to appear for trial. On 22 July 2010, co-defendant Bo Li, alias Eric Lee, pleaded guilty and was sentenced to time served for making false statements on shipping documents.[62]

* * *

In March 2014, General Technology Systems Integration was sentenced in California to 5 years' probation and a special assessment of $400. Previously, in October 2010, York Yuan Chang, also known as David Zhang, and his wife, Leping Huang, were arrested on charges of conspiring to export restricted electronics technology to China without a licence and making false statements. According to the October 2010 criminal complaint, the defendants were the owners of General Technology Systems Integration, Inc. (GTSI), a California company involved in the export of technology to China. GTSI allegedly entered into contracts with the 24th Research Institute of the China Electronics Technology Corporation Group in China to design and transfer to China technology for the development of two types of high-performance analogue-to-digital converters. The defendants allegedly hired two engineers to design the technology and provide training to individuals in China. Twice in 2009, US Customs stopped the engineers upon their return to the United States and found computer files and documents indicating illegal technology transfer involving GTSI and China. According to the prosecution, Chang and Huang sought to cover up the project after the authorities contacted the engineers. The devices that the defendants allegedly attempted to export to China were subject to export controls for reasons of national security and counter-terrorism.[63]

* * *

In December 2013, a Chinese citizen and former California Department of Transportation engineer, Philip He, was sentenced in Colorado for exporting radiation-hardened integrated circuits from the United States to China, in violation of the Arms Export Control Act, He was sentenced to 36 months' imprisonment followed by 3 years of supervised release. He pleaded guilty in September 2013. According to the prosecution, he had been arrested as he attempted to deliver the circuits onto a Chinese ship at the Long Beach, California port. During a search of He's vehicle, agents located more than 300 space-qualified and radiation-hardened computer circuits concealed inside plastic infant formula containers. The circuits are used in satellite communications and had a total value of nearly $550,000. He did not have a State Department licence. A December 2011 indictment charged He with conspiracy to violate the Arms Export Control Act (AECA) and to smuggle goods; attempted violation of the arms control regulations; and smuggling. According to the charges, He, the only employee of an Oakland company called Sierra Electronic Instruments, arranged for the purchase of more than 300 radiation-hardened circuits from Aeroflex, a Colorado manufacturer, in May 2011. He arranged for the purchase after a co-conspirator sent him wire transfers totalling nearly $490,000 from a bank in China. He then provided false certification to Aeroflex that the items would remain in the United States. He received the first shipment of 112 circuits from Aeroflex in July 2011 and later travelled from Mexico to Shanghai in September. In October 2011, he received a second shipment of 200 circuits from Aeroflex. He drove to the Port of Long Beach in December 2011 and met with two men in front of a docked Chinese-flagged ship that was registered to a subsidiary of a China state-owned corporation. The ship had recently arrived from Shanghai and was scheduled to return on 15 December 2011. He had allegedly concealed the 200 circuits in infant formula containers within boxes labelled 'milk powder' in the trunk of his vehicle. He was arrested on 11 December 2011 at the port.[64]

* * *

In December 2013, Ming Suan Zhang, a Chinese citizen, was sentenced in New York to 57 months' imprisonment. Previously, in August 2013, Zhang had pleaded guilty to violating the International Emergency Economic Powers Act by attempting to export massive quantities of aerospace-grade carbon fibre from the United States to China. In September 2012 had been charged Zhang with attempting to illegally export thousands of pounds of aerospace-grade carbon fibre from the United States to China. According to the prosecution, Zhang was arrested in the United States after trying to negotiate a deal to acquire the specialised carbon fibre, a high-tech material used frequently in the military, defence and aerospace industries, and which is therefore closely regulated by the US Department of Commerce to combat nuclear proliferation and terrorism. It was further alleged that Zhang came to the attention of federal authorities after two Taiwanese accomplices attempted to locate large quantities of the specialised carbon fibre via remote internet contacts. In July 2012 Zhang allegedly told an accomplice: 'When I place the order, I place one to two tons. However, the first shipment will be for 100 kg [kilograms].' Shortly thereafter, Zhang contacted an undercover law enforcement agent in an effort to finalise the deal to export the carbon fibre from New York to China. In one recorded conversation, Zhang stated that he had an urgent need for the carbon fibre in connection with the scheduled test flight of a Chinese fighter plane. Zhang then arranged a meeting with an undercover agent to take possession of a carbon fibre sample, which was to be shipped to China and analysed to verify its authenticity. Zhang was subsequently placed under arrest.[65]

* * *

In November 2013 Zhifu Lin, a Chinese national and resident of West Virginia, was sentenced to 108 months' imprisonment, 3 years' supervision and a $100 special assessment. Previously, in October 2012, Lin had pleaded guilty to violating the Arms Export Control Act and engaging in illegal weapons trafficking. Lin's plea came after co-defendant Joseph Debose, a resident of North Carolina and former staff sergeant in a US Special Forces National Guard unit, pleaded guilty in September 2012 to violating the Arms Export Control Act. Lin, Debose and others exported multiple shipments of firearms from the US to China by secreting them in packages and transporting them to shipping companies, including one in Queens, New York, to be sent to China. The weapons included numerous semiautomatic handguns, rifles, and shotguns. The smuggling scheme came to light after authorities in China seized a package containing firearms with defaced serial numbers shipped from Queens. Thereafter, US agents travelled to China and examined the firearms. Using forensic techniques, agents learned that one of the seized weapons had originally been purchased in North Carolina. Among the weapons seized in China were those Debose had provided to his associates for export. On 20 May 2012, Debose was arrested in Smithfield, North Carolina, and charged with illegally exporting firearms to China without the required licences. Lin and another Chinese national, co-defendant Lilan Li, were also arrested and charged in connection with the case in an April 2012 indictment. Debose was sentenced in July 2013 to 24 months' imprisonment, 3 years' supervised release, and a $100 special assessment. Li pleaded guilty in June 2012.[66]

* * * *

In May 2013 Lisong Ma, alias 'Ma Li', was sentenced in New York to 46 months' imprisonment after pleading guilty to an information charging him with attempting to illegally export one or more spools of Toray T-800 carbon fibre from the United States to China without the required licences from the Department of Commerce.

According to charges filed in March 2013, Ma contacted undercover law enforcement officers in February 2013 seeking carbon fibre for export to China. Ma then travelled to the United States where he met with undercover agents about obtaining samples of carbon fibre. Ma paid $400 for a spool of T-800 carbon fibre and allegedly arranged for it to be shipped via Federal Express from the United States to China, falsely labelled as 'clothing' and without a licence. The package was intercepted before leaving the United States. According to the prosecution, Type T-800 carbon fibre is extremely high-grade and is used primarily in aerospace and military applications. It is controlled for export by the Department of Commerce for nuclear non-proliferation and national security reasons.[67]

* * *

In April 2013 a former General Motors (GM) engineer, Shanshan Du, was sentenced to 12 months and one day along with a $12,500 fine. Her husband, Yu Qin, was sentenced to 36 months on each count to be served concurrently along with a $25,000 fine. Both defendants had been found guilty by a federal jury in November 2012 for conspiring to steal hybrid technology trade secrets from GM with the intent to use them in a joint venture with an automotive competitor in China. Du and Qin were also convicted of unlawful possession of trade secrets after a month-long trial in November 2012. Qin was also convicted of wire fraud and obstruction of justice. The evidence at trial showed that from December 2003 through May 2006, the defendants conspired to steal GM's trade secret information.

Du, while employed with GM's hybrid vehicle technology group, provided GM trade secret information relating to hybrid vehicles to her husband, Qin, for the benefit of their private company, Millennium

Technology International Inc. (MTI), which the defendants jointly owned and operated. Approximately five days after Du was offered a severance agreement by GM in January 2005, she copied more than 16,000 GM files, including trade secret documents, to an external computer hard drive used for MTI business. A few months later, Qin proceeded with a business venture to provide hybrid vehicle technology to Chery Automobile, an automotive manufacturer based in China and a competitor of GM. In May 2006 a search conducted by the FBI recovered multiple computer devices containing GM trade secret information on several computer and electronic devices located in the defendants' residence. Shortly after the FBI search team left the defendants' residence, the defendants drove to a dumpster behind a grocery store, where defendant Qin discarded plastic bags containing shredded documents, including GM trade secret information relating to MTI and hybrid vehicles, a cache valued at more than $40 million.[68]

* * *

In April 2013, Kevin Zhang, alias Zhao Wei Zhang, was sentenced in California to time served and three years' supervised release. Previously, in February 2013, Zhang had pleaded guilty for his role in a conspiracy to export defence equipment from the United States to China without a licence. In July 2012, Zhang was arrested as he attempted to cross the border from Canada in Washington state.

Zhang had been charged in January 2011 with one count of conspiracy to export defence articles (specifically G-200 Dynamically Tuned Gyroscopes) from the United States to China without a licence. According to the indictment, these particular gyroscopes may be used in tactical missile guidance and unmanned aircraft systems. Zhang allegedly instructed individuals in the United States to obtain and export defence articles, including the gyroscopes, to China and sought to employ a courier to smuggle the gyroscopes out of the US. The indictment alleged that Zhang, acting on behalf of a client in China, sought to purchase three gyroscopes for $21,000 from an individual in the United States as a prelude to future purchases of gyroscopes.[69]

* * *

In March 2013, Sixing Liu, alias 'Steve Liu,' a native of China with a PhD in electrical engineering who worked as a senior staff engineer for Space & Navigation, a New Jersey-based division of L-3 Communications, was sentenced in New Jersey to 70 months' imprisonment for exporting sensitive US military technology to China, stealing trade secrets and lying to federal agents. In September 2012 Liu was convicted on nine of eleven counts, specifically six counts of violating the Arms Export Control Act, one count of possessing stolen trade secrets in violation of the Economic Espionage Act, one count of transporting stolen property, and one count of lying to federal agents. The jury acquitted Liu on two counts of lying to federal agents. According to documents filed in the case and evidence presented at trial, in 2010, Liu stole thousands of electronic files from his employer, L-3 Communications, Space and Navigation Division. The stolen files detailed the performance and design of guidance systems for missiles, rockets, target locators, and unmanned aerial vehicles. Liu stole the files to position and prepare himself for future employment in China. As part of that plan, Liu delivered presentations about the technology at several Chinese universities, the Chinese Academy of Sciences, and conferences organised by Chinese government entities. However, Liu was not charged with any crimes related to those presentations.

On 12 November 2010, Liu boarded a flight from Newark to China and upon his return to the United States on 29 November agents found him in possession of a non-work-issued computer found to contain the stolen material. The following day, Liu lied to federal agents about the extent of his work on US defence technology. The State Department later verified that several of the stolen files on Liu's computer contained technical data that relates to defence items listed on the United States Munitions List. The prosecution also alleged that Liu's company trained him about the United States' export control laws and told him that most of the company's products were covered by those laws. Liu was first arrested in March 2010 in Chicago on a complaint filed in New Jersey charging him with one count of exporting defence-related technical data without a licence.[70]

* * *

In January 2013, Ji Li Huang, a Chinese business owner, and his employee, Xiao Guang Qi, pleaded guilty and were sentenced in Missouri for conspiring to steal trade secrets from Pittsburgh Corning Corporation, which produces Foamglas insulation. Huang was the CEO of Ningbo Oriental Crafts Ltd., which employed 200 factory workers to manufacture promotional products for export to the United States and Europe. Huang was sentenced to 18 months' imprisonment and ordered to pay a fine of $250,000. Qi was sentenced to time served and ordered to pay a fine of $20,000.

Pittsburgh Corning, headquartered in Pittsburgh, Penn., manufactures various grades or densities of cellular glass insulation sold under the trade name Foamglas. That material is used to insulate buildings, industrial piping systems and liquefied natural gas storage tank bases. Pittsburgh Corning considers the product formula and manufacturing process for Foamglas proprietary and trade secrets. By pleading guilty, Huang and Qi admitted that they attempted to illegally purchase trade secrets of Pittsburgh Corning for the purpose of opening a plant in China to compete with Pittsburgh Corning. The court ruled that the intended loss to Pittsburgh Corning exceeded $7 million, based on the company's investment of time and resources to research, develop and protect the proprietary information the defendants attempted to steal. Huang and Qi were arrested when they met with an individual they believed to be an employee of Pittsburgh Corning who had stolen documents that contained trade secret information and was willing to sell it to them for $100,000. That employee, however, was cooperating with law enforcement and the meetings in Kansas City were a sting operation that led to their arrests in September 2012.[71]

* * *

In January 2013, Timothy Gormley was sentenced to 42 months' imprisonment, three years' supervised release and a $1,000 fine in Pennsylvania for five counts of violating the International Emergency Economic Powers Act. On 17 October 2012, Gormley, the former export control manager of AR Worldwide/Amplifier Research in Souderton, Pennsylvania, pleaded guilty in connection with the illegal export of over fifty-seven microwave amplifiers, which are controlled for National Security reasons due to their applications in military systems, including radar jamming and weapons guidance systems.

The August 2012 charges alleged that between 2007 and 2011 Gormley failed to obtain the required licences on behalf of the company for shipments sent to destinations requiring such licences for the shipment of these goods. The information cited specific shipments of amplifiers from the United States to customers in India and China that Gormley caused without the required export licence. This investigation was conducted by the Department of Commerce.[72]

* * *

In December 2012, federal prosecutors in Oregon unsealed a 12-count indictment charging Wan Li Yuan, alias 'Nicholas Bush', a Chinese national and another Chinese resident known as 'Jason Jiang', with export and money laundering violations in connection with their alleged efforts to obtain dual-use programmable logic devices (PLDs) from the United States for export to China. According to the indictment, while operating from China, Yuan and Jiang created a sophisticated scheme to conceal their true identity and location in order to mislead US companies into believing they were dealing with American customers so they could procure and send sensitive technologies to China without the required export licences. Yuan and Jiang allegedly sought to procure PLDs made by Lattice Semiconductor Corporation in Oregon, which are designed to operate at extreme temperature ranges and which can have military applications such as in missiles and radar systems. To further his efforts, the indictment alleges that Yuan created a fake website and email addresses using the name of a legitimate New York-based company. Yuan requested US companies to ship the desired parts to the address of a freight forwarder in New York, which he also falsely represented as being associated with the New York company whose business name Yuan had stolen.

Through the investigation and use of an undercover operation, the FBI and Department of Commerce were able to seize approximately $414,000 in funds sent by Yuan as down payments for the Lattice PLDs. Lattice Semiconductor cooperated with the government in the investigation, which was conducted by the FBI and the Department of Commerce.[73]

* * *

In October 2012, Fu-Tain Lu was sentenced in California to 15 months' imprisonment, 3 years' supervised release, a $100 special assessment and a $5,000 fine. Previously, on 17 November 2011, Lu pleaded guilty to selling sensitive microwave amplifiers to China without the required licence. Lu was the owner and founder of Fushine Technology, Inc., corporation formerly located in Cupertino, California. Fushine was an exporter of electronic components used in communications, radar and other applications. At the time of the offence, Fushine had a sales representative agreement with Miteq Components, Inc., a New York-based manufacturer of microwave and satellite communications components and subsystems. Lu admitted that, in March 2004, Fushine submitted a purchase order to Miteq for one microwave amplifier and requested that Miteq notify Fushine immediately if an export licence was required. Miteq responded that the part was controlled for export to China. Nonetheless, in April 2004, Fushine exported the amplifier to co-defendant Everjet Science and Technology Corporation, located in China, without a licence from the Department of Commerce. Lu further admitted that the amplifier he shipped was restricted for export to China for reasons of national security. Lu, along with the two corporate defendants, Fushine and Everjet, was first indicted on 1 April 2009. A further indictment was returned on 17 February 2010. In addition to the count of conviction, the indictment also charged him with conspiring to violate US export regulations, and lying to federal agents who were investigating that conduct. The superseding indictment quoted from an internal company email in which an Everjet employee told a Fushine employee, 'Since these products are a little bit sensitive, in case the maker ask [sic] you where the location of the end user is, please do not mention it is in China.' As part of the plea agreement, Lu also agreed to forfeit thirty-six additional microwave amplifiers seized on March 2010, but that were not included in the superseding indictment. In October 2012, the prosecution moved to dismiss all charges against Fushine Technology.[74]

* * *

In October 2012 Chi Tong Kuok, a resident of Macau, was sentenced in California to time served, after having pleaded guilty in July 2012 to one count of conspiracy to illegally export defence articles and to smuggle goods from the United States. According to the plea agreement, Kuok and others conspired to purchase and export from the United States defence articles, including communication, precision location and cryptographic equipment, without a licence. Kuok also caused $1,700 to be sent to the United States for the purchase and unlicensed export of a KG-175 Taclane Encryptor. According to court documents, the KG-175 Taclane Encryptor was developed by General Dynamics under a contract with the National Security Agency for use by the US military to encrypt Internet Protocol communications. Kuok was first arrested in June 2009 in Atlanta, Georgia, after he arrived from Paris to catch a connecting flight to Panama in order to meet with undercover federal agents to take possession of controlled US technology. An indictment returned in July 2009 and on 11 May 2010, Kuok was convicted of conspiracy to export defence articles without a licence and smuggling goods to Macau and Hong Kong, smuggling goods; attempting to export defence articles without a licence; and money laundering. On 13 September 2010, Kuok was sentenced to 96 months' imprisonment.

Kuok appealed and in July 2012 his convictions on counts three and four were quashed and a new trial was ordered on counts one and two. However, Kuok pleaded guilty prior to the second trial.[75]

* * *

In September 2012 Chunlai Yang, a former senior software engineer for Chicago-based CME Group, Inc., pleaded guilty in Illinois to two counts of theft of trade secrets for stealing source code and other proprietary information while at the same time pursuing plans to improve an electronic trading exchange in China. Yang admitted that he downloaded more than 10,000 files containing CME computer source code that made up a substantial part of the operating systems for the Globex electronic trading platform. The government maintained that the potential loss was between $50 million and $100 million. Yang began working for CME Group in 2000 and was a senior software engineer at the time of his arrest. Between late 2010 and June 2011, Yang downloaded more than 10,000 computer files containing CME computer source code from CME's secure internal computer system to his CME-issued work computer. He then transferred many of these files from his work computer to his personal USB flash drives, and then transferred many of these files from his flash drives to his personal computers and hard drives at his home. Yang also admitted that he downloaded thousands of other CME files. Yang admitted that he and two unnamed business partners developed plans to form a business referred to as the Tongmei (Gateway to America) Futures Exchange Software Technology Company (Gateway), whose purpose was to increase the trading volume at the Zhangjiagang, China, chemical electronic trading exchange (the Zhangjiagang Exchange). The Zhangjiagang Exchange was to become a transfer station to China for advanced technologies companies around the world. Yang expected that Gateway would provide the exchange with technology through written source code to allow for high trading volume, high trading speeds, and multiple trading functions. Yang was indicted in September 2011.[76]

* * *

In August 2012 Hanjuan Jin, a former software engineer for Motorola, was sentenced in Illinois to four years' imprisonment for stealing trade secrets from Motorola, specifically Motorola's proprietary iDEN telecommunications technology, for herself and for Sun Kaisens, a company that developed products for the Chinese military. According to court documents filed in the case, Motorola spent more than $400 million researching and developing iDEN technology in just a matter of years. In February 2012, Jin was found guilty of three counts of stealing trade secrets. Jin, a naturalised US citizen born in China, possessed more than 1,000 electronic and paper Motorola proprietary documents when she was stopped by US authorities at Chicago's O'Hare International Airport as she attempted to travel to China on 8 February 2007. The judge presiding over the case found her not guilty of three counts of economic espionage for the benefit of the government of China and its military. According to the prosecution, Jin began working for Motorola in 1998, and took medical leave in February 2006. Between June and November 2006, while still on sick leave, Jin pursued employment in China with Sun Kaisens. Between November 2006 and February 2007, Jin returned to China and did work for Sun Kaisens on projects for the Chinese military. On 15 February 2007, Jin returned to the United States from China and reserved a flight to China scheduled to depart on 28 February 2007. Jin advised Motorola that she was ready to return to work at Motorola, without informing Motorola that she planned to return to China to work for Sun Kaisens. On 26 February 2007, she returned to Motorola, and accessed hundreds of technical documents belonging to Motorola on its secure internal computer network. As she attempted to depart from Chicago to China, federal agents seized material which provided a description of communication feature that Motorola incorporates into its telecommunications products. Authorities also recovered classified Chinese documents describing telecommunication projects for the Chinese military. Jin was charged with theft of trade secrets in an indictment dated 1 April 2008. A further indictment was returned in December 2008 charged her with economic espionage.[77]

* * *

In May 2012, Yuan Li, a former research chemist with the global pharmaceutical company Sanofi-Aventis, was sentenced in New Jersey to 18 months' imprisonment, 2 years of supervised release, a $100 special assessment and restitution of $131,000. Previously, in January 2012, Li had pleaded guilty to stealing Sanofi's trade secrets and making them available for sale through Abby Pharmatech, Inc., the US subsidiary of a Chinese chemicals company. According to court documents, Li worked at Sanofi headquarters in Bridgewater, New Jersey, from August 2006 through June 2011, where she assisted in the development of several compounds (considered trade secrets) that Sanofi viewed as potential building blocks for future drugs.

While employed at Sanofi, Li was a 50 per cent partner in Abby, which sells and distributes pharmaceuticals. Li admitted that between October 2008 and June 2011, she accessed internal Sanofi databases and downloaded information on Sanofi compounds and transferred this information to her personal home computer. She also admitted that she made the stolen compounds available for sale on Abby's website.[78]

* * *

In May 2012 Hing Shing Lau, also known as Victor Lau, a foreign national living in Hong Kong, was sentenced in Ohio to 10 months' imprisonment followed by 2 years' supervised release.

Previously, on 3 May 2012, Lau had pleaded guilty to two counts of violating export control laws. On 9 June 2009, a federal grand jury had indicted Lau on charges of trying to buy twelve infrared thermal-imaging cameras from a Dayton-area company in order to illegally export the cameras to Hong Kong and China. On three occasions, he wire-transferred a total of $39,514 from Hong Kong to the US as partial payment for the cameras. The indictment charges Lau with two counts of violating export control laws and four counts of money laundering. Canadian authorities arrested Lau on 3 June 2009 at Toronto's International Airport.

On 23 April 2012, Jason Jian Liang, the owner and operator of Sanwave International Corporation in Huntington Beach, California, was sentenced to 46 months' imprisonment and 3 years' supervised release after pleading guilty in July 2011 to violations stemming from his illegal exports of thermal-imaging cameras to Hong Kong and China. Liang was first indicted in June. 2010. A further indictment dated August 2010 charged Liang with illegally exporting more thermal-imaging cameras to China without first having obtained the required licences. The cameras in question were manufactured by L-3 Communications Infrared Products and were designated by the Commerce Department as an export-controlled item that could not be exported to China for national security reasons. Ultimately Liang admitted making seven illegal exports of 300-D thermal-imaging cameras over a 31-month period. All told, he exported sixty-three cameras.[79]

* * *

In January 2012, Wen Chyu Liu, aka David W. Liou, a former research scientist at Dow Chemical Company in Louisiana, was sentenced in Louisiana to 60 months' imprisonment, 2 years' supervised release, a $25,000 fine and was ordered to pay $600,000 in restitution. Liu was convicted in February 2011 of one count of conspiracy to commit trade secret theft for stealing trade secrets from Dow and selling them to companies in China, and he was also convicted of one count of perjury. According to the evidence presented in court, Liu came to the United States from China for graduate work. He began working for Dow in 1965 and retired in 1992. Dow is a leading producer of the elastomeric polymer, chlorinated polyethylene (CPE). Dow's Tyrin CPE is used in a number of applications worldwide, such as automotive and industrial hoses, electrical cable jackets and vinyl siding. While employed at Dow, Liu worked as a research scientist on various aspects of the development and manufacture of Dow elastomers, including Tyrin CPE. The evidence at trial established that Liu conspired with at least four current and former employees of Dow's facilities in Plaquemine, Louisiana, and in Stade, Germany, who had worked in Tyrin CPE production, to misappropriate those trade secrets in an effort to develop and market CPE process design packages to Chinese companies.

Liou travelled throughout China to market the stolen information, and he paid current and former Dow employees for Dow's CPE-related material and information. In one instance, Liou bribed a then-employee at the Plaquemine facility with $50,000 in cash to provide Dow's process manual and other CPE-related information.[80]

* * *

In January 2012 Yan Zhu, a Chinese citizen in the US on a work visa, was sentenced in New Jersey to three years' probation and a special assessment of $700. Previously, on 6 April 2011, Zhu was convicted in New Jersey on seven counts of wire fraud in connection with his scheme to steal confidential and proprietary business information relating to computer systems and software with environmental applications from his New Jersey employer. He was acquitted on the charge of conspiracy to steal trade secrets and two counts of unauthorised transmission of trade secrets in interstate or foreign commerce. On 10 April 2009, Zhu was arrested on charges of theft of trade secrets, conspiracy, wire fraud and theft of honest services fraud in connection with a plot to steal software from his former US employer and sell a modified version to the Chinese government after he was fired. Zhu was employed as a senior environmental engineer from May 2006 until his termination in

July 2008. Zhu worked for a comprehensive multimedia environmental information management portal that developed a proprietary software program for the Chinese market which allows users to manage air emissions, ambient water quality, and ground water quality.[81]

* * *

In December 2011 Kexue Huang, a Chinese national and former resident of Indiana, was sentenced to 87 months' imprisonment and 3 years' supervised release stemming from his plea of guilty in October 2011 to charges of economic espionage to benefit a foreign university tied to China and theft of trade secrets. Huang also pleaded guilty on 19 September 2011 to one count of an indictment filed in the District of Minnesota for stealing a trade secret from a second company, Cargill Inc. Previously, in June 2010, Huang had been charged in Indiana with misappropriating and transporting trade secrets to China while working as a research scientist at Dow AgroSciences LLC. On 18 October 2011, a separate indictment in Minnesota charging Huang with stealing a trade secret from Cargill Inc. was unsealed. According to court documents, from January 2003 until February 2008, Huang had been employed as a research scientist at Dow. In 2005, he became a research leader for Dow in strain development related to unique, proprietary organic insecticides marketed worldwide. Huang admitted that during his employment at Dow, he misappropriated several Dow trade secrets.

According to plea documents, from 2007 to 2010, Huang transferred and delivered the stolen Dow trade secrets to individuals in Germany and China. With the assistance of these individuals, Huang used the stolen materials to conduct unauthorised research to benefit foreign universities tied to the PRC. Huang also admitted that he pursued steps to develop and produce the misappropriated Dow trade secrets in China. After Huang left Dow, he was hired in March 2008 by Cargill, an international producer and marketer of food, agricultural, financial and industrial products and services. Huang worked as a biotechnologist for Cargill until July 2009.

Huang admitted that during his employment with Cargill, he stole one of the company's trade secrets – a key component in the manufacture of a new food product – which he later disseminated to another person, specifically a student at Hunan Normal University in China. According to the plea agreement, the aggregated loss from Huang's conduct exceeds $7 million but was less than $20 million. On 27 December 2011, Huang received a sentence in the Minnesota case to 87 months' imprisonment and three years' supervised release, to be served concurrently with the term imposed in the defendant's case in Indiana.[82]

* * *

In October 2011 Lian Yang, a resident of Woodinville, Washington, was sentenced to 18 months' imprisonment and a $10,000 fine. On 24 March 2011, Yang pleaded guilty to conspiring to violate the Arms Export Control Act by trying to sell radiation-hardened military and aerospace technology to China. Yang was arrested on 3 December 2010 on charges him with conspiracy to violate the Arms Export Control Act. According to the prosecution, Yang attempted to purchase and export from the United States to China 300 radiation-hardened, programmable semiconductor devices that are used in satellites and are also classified as defence articles under the US Munitions List. It was further alleged that Yang had contemplated creating a shell company in the United States that would appear to be purchasing the parts, concealing the fact that the parts were to be shipped to China. Yang allegedly planned that false purchasing orders would be created indicating that parts that could be legally exported were being purchased, not restricted parts. Yang and his co-conspirators allegedly wire-transferred $60,000 to undercover agents as partial payment for a sample of five devices. As part of the conspiracy, Yang negotiated a payment schedule with the undercover agents for the purchase and delivery of the remaining 300 devices in exchange for a total of $620,000.[83]

* * *

In September 2011, Hong Wei Xian, alias 'Harry Zan', and Li Li, alias 'Lea Li', were sentenced in Virginia to 24 months' imprisonment for conspiracy to violate the Arms Export Control Act and conspiracy to smuggle goods unlawfully from the United States, in connection with their efforts to export to China radiation-hardened microchips that are used in satellite systems and are categorised as defence articles.

The defendants were arrested on 1 September 2010 in Budapest by Hungarian authorities on a US provisional arrest warrant. On 4 April 2011, following extradition from Hungary, they made their initial court appearance in federal court in Virginia. Both defendants pleaded guilty to the charges on 1 June 2011.

According to court documents, Zan and Li operated two companies in China, Beijing Starcreates Space Science, and Technology Development Company Limited. This firm was allegedly in the business of selling technology to China Aerospace and Technology Corporation, a Chinese government-controlled entity involved in the production and design of missile systems and launch vehicles. The prosecution alleged that from April 2009 to September 2010, the defendants contacted a Virginia company seeking to purchase and export thousands of Programmable Read-Only Microchips (PROMs). The defendants ultimately attempted to purchase forty PROMs from the Virginia firm and indicated to undercover agents that the PROMs were intended for China Aerospace and Technology Corporation.[84]

* * *

In September 2011 the Staff Gasket Manufacturing Corporation, a defence contracting company in New Jersey, was sentenced in New Jersey to five years' probation and ordered to pay $751,091 in restitution and an $800 special assessment. Eric Helf, Staff Gasket's president was sentenced to three years' probation, a $500 fine and a final order of forfeiture was entered for $49,926. On 19 April 2011 Staff Gasket pleaded guilty to Arms Export Control Act and wire fraud violations, while Helf pleaded guilty to one count of wire fraud. From August 2004 to March 2006, Staff Gasket entered into contracts with the Department of Defense to provide replacement parts for use in military operations. Many of the parts to be supplied were critical application items and were thus required to be manufactured in the United States. Nonetheless, Staff Gasket contracted with foreign manufacturers, including in China, and many of the parts ultimately supplied to the Defense Department, including lock pins for helicopters, were made overseas, substandard, and failed in the field. As a result, Staff Gasket caused the Defense Department to sustain losses of some $751,091 in connection with the fraudulent contracts.[85]

* * *

In July 2011, Swiss Technology (Swiss Tech), Inc., a company based in Clifton, New Jersey. that makes equipment for the US military, pleaded guilty to a one-count criminal information charging the firm with conspiracy to violate the Arms Export Control Act from August 2004 to about July 2009. On 15 November 2011 Swiss Tech was sentenced to two years' probation and ordered to pay restitution in the amount of $1.1 million to the Defense Department in connection with fraudulent contracts.

Swiss Tech was under contract with the Department of Defense to manufacture components for the M249 machine gun. In order to lower its manufacturing costs, Swiss Tech sent defence articles, including specification drawings and parts samples, to a company in China so that it could make these machine-gun components for Swiss Tech. Swiss Tech did not have the required State Department licence for exports of these munitions to China. After receiving the components from the Chinese company, Swiss Tech then shipped the defence articles and other parts to the Department of Defense, purporting that the defence articles were made by Swiss Tech in conformance with its contract. Among other things, Swiss Tech illegally exported to China specifications for the production of M249 machine-gun parts, as well as components for the M249 machine gun, and M16 or M4 rifle.[86]

* * *

In April 2011 Xiang Dong Yu, alias Mike Yu, was sentenced in Michigan to 70 months' imprisonment. Previously, on 17 November 2010, Dong, a product engineer with Ford Motor Company pleaded guilty to two counts of theft of trade secrets. According to the plea agreement, Yu was a product engineer for Ford from 1997 to 2007 and had access to Ford trade secrets, including Ford design documents. In December 2006, Yu accepted a job at the China branch of a US company. On the eve of his departure from Ford and before he told Ford of his new job, Yu copied some 4,000 Ford documents onto an external hard drive, including sensitive design documents. Ford spent millions of dollars and decades on research, development and testing to develop and improve the design specifications set forth in these documents. On 20 December 2006, Yu travelled to the location of his new employer in Shenzhen, China, taking the Ford trade secrets with him. On 2 January 2007 Yu emailed his Ford supervisor from China and informed him that he was leaving Ford. And in November 2008, Yu began working for Beijing Automotive Company, a direct competitor of Ford. On 19 October 2009, Yu returned to the US and upon arrival, he was arrested. At that time, Yu had in his possession his Beijing Automotive Company laptop computer and during an FBI examination, forty-one Ford system design specifications documents were found to have been copied. The FBI also discovered that each of those design documents had been accessed by Yu during the time of his employment with Beijing Automotive Company.[87]

* * *

In March 2007 the ITT Corporation pleaded guilty in Virginia to two criminal counts of violating the Arms Export Control Act stemming from its illegal exports of restricted military night vision data to China, Singapore, and the United Kingdom and omission of statements of material fact in required arms exports reports. As part of the plea agreement, ITT Corporation agreed to invest $50 million toward the development of the most advanced night vision systems in the world for the US armed forces. On 12 April 2011, the Justice Department announced that a government motion to dismiss the remaining deferred criminal charge against the ITT Corporation, the leading manufacturer of military night vision equipment for the US armed forces, had been granted by the court. The Justice Department agreed to dismiss the remaining criminal charge against ITT after the corporation implemented an extensive remedial plan overseen by an independent monitor to prevent future Arms Export Control Act violations.[88]

* * *

In January 2011 a federal judge in the District of Hawaii sentenced Noshir Gowadia, 66, of Maui to 32 years' imprisonment for communicating classified national defence information to China, illegally exporting military technical data, as well as money laundering, filing false tax returns and other offences. On 9 August 2010, a federal jury in the District of Hawaii found Gowadia guilty of fourteen criminal violations after a 40-day trial and six days of deliberation. These included five criminal offences relating to his design for China of a low-signature cruise missile exhaust system capable of rendering a PRC cruise missile resistant to detection by infrared missiles. The jury also convicted Gowadia of three counts of illegally communicating classified information regarding lock-on range for infrared missiles against the US B-2 bomber to persons not authorised to receive such information. Gowadia was also convicted of unlawfully exporting classified information about the B-2, illegally retaining information related to US national defence at his home, money laundering and filing false tax returns for the years 2001 and 2002.

Gowadia was an engineer with Northrop Grumman Corporation from 1968 to 1986, during which time he contributed to the development of the unique propulsion system and low observable capabilities of the B-2 bomber. Gowadia continued to work on classified matters as a contractor with the US government until 1997, when his security clearance was terminated. Evidence at trial revealed that from July 2003 to June 2005, Gowadia took six trips to China to provide defence services in the form of design, test support and test data analysis of technologies for the purpose of assisting China with its cruise missile system by developing a stealthy exhaust nozzle and was paid at least $110,000 by the PRC. The jury convicted Gowadia of two specific transmissions of classified information: a PowerPoint presentation on the exhaust nozzle of a Chinese cruise missile project and an evaluation of the effectiveness of a redesigned nozzle, and a computer file providing his signature prediction of a PRC cruise missile outfitted with his modified exhaust nozzle and associated predictions in relation to a US air-to-air missiles. The prosecution also produced evidence which documented Gowadia's use of three foreign entities he controlled, including a Liechtenstein charity purportedly for the benefit of children, to disguise the income he received from foreign countries.[89]

* * *

In December 2010 David Yen Lee, a former chemist for Valspar Corporation, a Chicago paint manufacturing company, was sentenced to 15 months' imprisonment for stealing trade secrets involving numerous formulas and other proprietary information valued up to $20 million as he prepared to go to work for a competitor in China. Lee, formerly a technical director in Valspar Corp's architectural coatings group since 2006, pleaded guilty in September 2010 to using his access to Valspar's secure internal computer network to download approximately 160 original batch tickets, or secret formulas for paints and coatings. Lee also obtained raw materials information, chemical formulas and calculations, sales and cost data, and other internal memoranda, product research, marketing data, and other material from Valspar. Lee admitted that between September 2008 and February 2009, he had negotiated employment with Nippon Paint, in Shanghai, China and accepted employment with Nippon as vice president of technology and administrator of research and development. Lee was scheduled to fly from Chicago to Shanghai on 27 March 2009 but did not inform Valspar that he had accepted a job at Nippon until he resigned on 16 March. Between November. 2008 and March 2009 Lee downloaded technical documents and materials belonging to Valspar, including the paint formula batch tickets. He further copied certain downloaded files to external thumb drives to store the data, knowing that he intended to use the confidential information belong to Valspar for his own benefit. However, there was no evidence to show that he actually disclosed any of the stolen trade secrets.[90]

* * *

In October 2010, Hong Meng, a former research chemist for DuPont, was sentenced to 14 months' imprisonment and $58,621 in restitution for theft of trade secrets after he had pleaded guilty on 8 June 2010. Meng was involved in researching Organic Light Emitting Diodes during his tenure at DuPont. In early 2009, DuPont's diode research efforts resulted in the development of a breakthrough chemical process (considered a trade secret) that increased the performance and longevity of diode displays. In the spring of 2009, while still employed at DuPont and without DuPont's permission or knowledge, Meng accepted employment as a faculty member at Peking University College of Engineering. Department of Nanotechnology in Beijing, and thereafter began soliciting funding to commercialise his research at the university. In June 2009, he emailed to his university account the protected chemical process from DuPont. He also downloaded the chemical process from his DuPont work computer to a thumb drive which he uploaded to his personal computer. In August 2009, he mailed a package containing 109 samples of DuPont intermediate chemical compounds to a colleague at Northwestern University and instructed his colleague at Northwestern to forward the material to Meng's office at the university. Eight of the 109 samples were trade secret chemical compounds. Meng also made false statements to the FBI when questioned about these sample.[91]

* * *

In June 2010 the Rocky Mountain Instrument Company (RMI), a Colorado corporation located in Lafayette, Colorado, pleaded guilty to one count of exporting defence articles without a licence in violation of the Arms Export Control Act. The company was then immediately sentenced to five years' probation and ordered to forfeit $1 million. Between April 2005 and October 2007, RMI exported from the United States to Turkey, South Korea, China, and Russia, prisms and technical data related to various optics used in military applications, which were designated as defence articles on the US Munitions List, without having first obtained the required export licences. The military technology that RMI illegally exported consisted of guidance or targeting systems used in such military items as unmanned aerial vehicles, AC-130 gunships, Abrams tanks, TOW anti-tank missile systems, and Bradley fighting vehicles. RMI was originally charged on 17 March 2010.[92]

* * *

In May 2010 Sam Ching Sheng Lee, part-owner and chief operations manager of Multimillion Business Associate Corporation (MBA), pleaded guilty to conspiracy to violate the International Emergency Economic Powers Act for the illegal export of national security-controlled thermal-imaging cameras to China. His nephew, Charles Yu Hsu Lee, pleaded guilty the same day to a felony for the same activity. Sam Lee was sentenced on 18 February to 12 months' imprisonment and a $10,000 fine, while Charles Lee was sentenced on 15 December 2010 to six days and a $3,000 fine. The Lees had been arrested on 10 December 2008 in Hacienda Heights, California, on an indictment issued on 15 December 2008 charging them with conspiracy to export and exporting national security-controlled equipment without a licence. The indictment alleged that the defendants, doing business as MBA, an import-export business located in Hacienda Heights, assisted contacts in China illegally procure export controlled thermal-imaging cameras. During the period between April 2002 and July 2007, the defendants allegedly exported a total of ten thermal-imaging cameras to China in circumvention of export laws. After being advised of strict export restrictions, Charles Lee allegedly purchased the cameras from US suppliers for approximately $9,500 apiece by withholding the fact that the devices were destined for China. His uncle, Sam Lee, then received the devices and, through his company, arranged for their shipment to Shanghai, China without obtaining proper licences. One of the recipients is alleged to be an employee of a company in Shanghai engaged in the development of infrared technology. The thermal-imaging cameras are controlled for export to China by the Department of Commerce for national security and regional stability reasons because of their use in a wide variety of military and civilian applications.[93]

* * *

In February 2010 a former Rockwell and Boeing engineer, Dongfan 'Greg' Chung, was sentenced to 188 months' imprisonment and three years' supervised release after his conviction on 16 July 2009 charges of economic espionage and acting as an illegal agent of China, for whom he stole restricted technology and Boeing trade secrets, including information related to the Space Shuttle program and the Delta IV rocket. According to the prosecution, Chung had served as an illegal agent of China for more than 30 years and kept more than 300,000 pages of documents reflecting Boeing trade secrets stashed in his home as part of his mission of steal aerospace and military trade secrets from

Boeing to assist the Chinese government. Chung sent Boeing trade secrets to China via the mail, via sea freight, via the Chinese consulate in San Francisco, and via a Chinese agent named Chi Mak. On several occasions, Chung also used the trade secrets that he misappropriated from Boeing to prepare detailed briefings that he later presented to Chinese officials in China.

Chung was originally arrested on 11 February 2008, in Southern California after being indicted on eight counts of economic espionage, one count of conspiracy to commit economic espionage, one count of acting as an unregistered foreign agent, one count of obstruction of justice, and three counts of making false statements to the FBI.[94]

* * *

In April 2015 Bo Cai, a Chinese national, was sentenced in New Mexico to 24 months' imprisonment. On the same day, his cousin Wentong Cai, a Chinese national living in the US on a student visa, was also sentenced to 18 months' imprisonment. Both men were ordered to be deported after completing their prison sentences. Bo Cai and Wentong Cai were charged in a three-count superseding indictment with a scheme to illegally export sensors primarily manufactured for sale to the US Department of Defense for use in high-level applications such as line-of-sight stabilisation and precision motion control systems, without first obtaining the required export licence. Previously, on 16 December 2014, Wentong Cai, pleaded guilty to conspiring with Bo Cai to violate the Arms Export Control Act and the International Traffic Arms Regulations. Bo Cai pleaded guilty on 23 July 2014. Allegedly Cai and Wentong Cai had participated in a scheme to illegally export defence articles with military applications to China. According to court documents, in March 2012 Bo Cai was employed by a technology company in China when he embarked on an illegal scheme to smuggle sensors out of the US to China for one of his customers despite knowledge that the sensors could not be exported without a licence and that the US did not issue licences to export the sensors to China. Bo Cai enlisted his cousin Wentong Cai to acquire the sensors under the ruse that he planned to use the sensors at Iowa State University where he was a graduate microbiology student.

The investigation of this case began in October 2013 when an undercover Homeland Security agent responded to Wentong Cai's overtures. After negotiations by telephone and email, Bo Cai and Wentong Cai travelled to New Mexico in December 2013 where they obtained a sensor from undercover agents and developed a plan for smuggling the sensor out of the US to China. On 11 December 2013, Bo Cai was arrested at an airport in Los Angeles after the sensor was discovered concealed in a computer speaker in his luggage as he prepared to board a flight to China. Wentong Cai was arrested in Iowa in January 2014.[95]

* * *

In August 2015, Yue Wu, alias David Wu, a Chinese national, was sentenced in Washington to 18 months' imprisonment, a $100 special assessment, and deportation after completion of his sentence following a plea of guilty on 36 May 2015 to conspiracy to violate the Arms Export Control Act. Previously, on 22 October 2014, Wu had been indicted for violating the same Act. According to court documents, between December 2011 and October 2014, Wu directed others to contact a United States manufacturer and request the purchase of QA3000 accelerometers for export to China without first obtaining a licence from the State Department. Wu and another person met with an undercover agent in San Francisco in an effort to order thirty accelerometers from him. Wu had explained that he was attempting to acquire the accelerometers on behalf of a customer in China and requested that the equipment be concealed in a housing to evade US export restrictions, providing the agent with schematics for the construction of the housing. The prosecution further alleged that Wu suggested that the agent ship the accelerometers to Wu's associate in Switzerland, who, in turn, would trans-ship the accelerometers into China.[96]

* * *

In April 2016 Fuyi Sun, alias 'Frank', a Chinese citizen, was arrested in New York in connection with a scheme to illegally export to China, without a licence, high-grade carbon fibre that is used primarily in aerospace and military applications. Sun was arrested after traveling to New York to meet with undercover federal agents in an effort to obtain the specialised fibre, which – due to its military and aerospace applications – required an export licence for export to China. The three charges filed on 13 April 2016, accused Sun of: Count One – attempt to violate the International Emergency Economic Powers Act; Count Two – conspiracy to violate the same Act; and Count Three – attempt to smuggle goods from the United States. According to the prosecution Sun attempted for years to acquire high-grade carbon fibre for illegal export to China. After traveling to New York from China to finalise the deal, Sun told the undercover agents that the carbon fibre he sought was headed to the Chinese military. He then paid tens of thousands of dollars in cash to purchase two cases of it. To avoid detection, Sun directed the undercovers to ship the carbon fibre in unmarked boxes and to falsify the shipping documents regarding the contents of the boxes. Since approximately 2011, Sun had attempted to acquire extremely high-grade carbon fibre, including Toray type M60JB-3000-50B carbon fibre. M60 Carbon Fiber has applications in aerospace technologies, unmanned aerial vehicles and other government defence applications. Accordingly, M60 Carbon Fiber is strictly controlled – including that it requires a licence for export to China – for nuclear non-proliferation and anti-terrorism reasons. In furtherance of his attempts to illegally export M60 Carbon Fiber from the US to China without a licence, Sun contacted what he believed was a distributor of carbon fibre – but which was, in fact, an undercover entity created by Homeland Security Investigations and 'staffed' by undercover federal agents. Sun inquired about purchasing the M60 Carbon Fiber without the required licence. In the course of his years-long communications with the undercovers and the company, Sun repeatedly suggested various security measures that he believed would protect them from 'US intelligence'. Among other such measures, at one point, Sun instructed the undercovers to use the term 'banana' instead of 'carbon fibre' in their communications. Consequently, soon thereafter he inquired about purchasing 450kg of 'banana' for more than $62,000. In order to avoid detection, Sun also suggested removing the identifying barcodes for the M60 Carbon Fiber, prior to transshipment, and further suggested that they identify the M60 Carbon Fiber as 'acrylic fibre' in customs documents. On or about 11 April 2016, Sun travelled from China to New York to buy the M60 Carbon Fiber from the undercover company. During meetings with the federal agents, in April 2016, Sun repeatedly suggested that the Chinese military was the ultimate end-user for the M60 Carbon Fiber he sought to acquire. Sun claimed to have personally worked in the Chinese missile program. Sun also asserted that he maintained a close relationship with the Chinese military, had a sophisticated understanding of the Chinese military's need for carbon fibre, and suggested that he would be supplying the M60 Carbon Fiber to the Chinese military or to institutions closely associated with it. On 12 April 2016, Sun agreed to purchase two cases of M60 Carbon Fiber from the undercovers and paid them $23,000 in cash for the consignment. He also paid an additional $2,000 as compensation for the risk he believed they were taking to illegally export the carbon fibre to China without a licence.[97]

* * *

On 2 March 2016 Louis Brothers was sentenced in Kentucky to 93 months' imprisonment for illegally exporting sophisticated technology equipment to China and concealing the unlawful proceeds. The sentence also included a monetary judgment of $1.1 million.

A former president and CEO of Valley Forge Composite Technologies, Brothers pleaded guilty to the offences in July 2015, admitting that from 2009 until 2013, he unlawfully exported microcircuits to China.

According to his plea agreement, Brothers intentionally avoided notifying the Department of State about his activity and labelled his shipments as 'computer parts' in order to conceal the true identity of the items. Brothers further admitted that he falsified paperwork to make it appear that the proceeds he received from his business with the PRC were actually profits from a business he owned in Kentucky.[98]

* * *

In February 2016 Song Il Ki, alias Kim Song II, was convicted in Utah of violating the Arms Export Control Act. The prosecution alleged that he had exported from the United States, defence items including PVS-7 and PVVS-14 Night Vision Optics and a THOR 320 Thermal Imaging Weapons Sight, without having first obtained a licence. Kim was sentenced 40 months' imprisonment, with credit for time served, 36 months of supervised release, and a $100 special assessment.[99]

* * *

In February 2021 a former University of Florida professor and researcher and resident of China was indicted for fraudulently obtaining $1.75 million in federal grant money from the National Institutes of Health (NIH) by concealing support he received from the Chinese government and a company that he founded in China to profit from that research.

Lin Yang, aged 43, who lived in Tampa, Florida, at the time of the offences, was charged with six counts of wire fraud and four counts of making false statements to an agency of the United States.

According to the indictment, Yang obtained a $1.75 million grant from NIH to develop and disseminate an imaging informatics tool for muscles known as 'MuscleMiner'. Between September 2014 and July 2019, Yang served as the principal investigator for the NIH grant at his university and was responsible for conducting and administering the grant in compliance with applicable federal law and institutional policies. Among other things, Yang was required to disclose his foreign research support and financial conflicts of interest, including his ownership of, or interest in, a foreign company.

However, during that same period in 2016 Yang established a business, 'Deep Informatics', in China and promoted it by claiming that its products were the result of years of research supported by millions of dollars of US government funding. Simultaneously, Yang applied for and was accepted into the Thousand Talents program in connection with Northwestern Polytechnical University, in Xi'an, China.

Yang was alleged to have concealed his conflicts of interest and other support in connection with his Chinese business and his participation in a Chinese government talent plan and affiliation with a Chinese research university. On multiple occasions, Yang submitted disclosures to NIH containing false statements and material omissions concerning his affiliations and research endeavours with a foreign government and company. Additionally, in January 2019, the University of Florida's College of Engineering required all faculty to provide, in writing, updated disclosures concerning activities with foreign entities in China and two other countries. The indictment alleges that Yang provided the University with a written response that falsely stated he had no affiliation with any business, entity, or university in China. Yang travelled to China in August of 2019 and did not return.[100]

* * *

These cases follow a theme with, at the very least, the Beijing authorities turning a Nelsonic eye to some very obvious law-breaking in terms of money-laundering and customs irregularities. In many examples the degree of collaboration has been such that collusion is more than a mere suspicion. In a counter-espionage environment in which the requirements on the prosecution to achieve a conviction are often too onerous, the US Justice Department turned to the 'Al Capone' expedient of pursuing suspected commercial and economic spies with abuse of the currency regulations, visa fraud, export licence lapses, failures to make mandatory declarations, income tax evasion, etc. Although the penalties are never enough to act as a deterrent, they did have the merit of disrupting the adversaries' illegal operations. The DoJ's China Initiative would gradually wind down, in part because of political pressure applied by academics who found that colleagues had been penalized for having failed to disclose foreign funding for their research projects. About seventy-seven federal prosecutions were considered part of the programme, of which nineteen involved scientists who had failed to make the necessary declarations about support received from the Thousand Talents project. Of that nineteen, fourteen were accused of 'violation of integrity standards'.

In retrospect, it is clear that the DoJ's China Initiative was intended to raise awareness of the economic threat from Beijing and was not likely to survive long because of perceptions about racial profiling of the kind that had dogged the investigations conducted by the FBI and Department of Energy into leaks from Los Alamos that had culminated in the controversial prosecution of Dr Peter Lee in March 1998. On the other hand, the programme did deliver close coordination between the various hitherto competing branches of federal law enforcement, such as the FBI, Customs & Border Protection, Homeland Security Investigations and the Defense Counterintelligence and Security Agency which created federal task forces to identify and prosecute offenders.

Chapter X

TAIWAN

China will employ all methods and the issue [of Chinese espionage] is more serious than ever.

Peng Sheng-chu
Director, National Security Bureau
10 March 2017

As one of the MSS's 'five poisons', along with the democracy movement, Uighur activists, Tibetan independence and adherents of Falun Gong, Taiwan has been designated as a priority intelligence collection target by the Chinese Communist Party. The challenge of recruiting and managing Taiwanese citizens, with their long history of opposition to the Communists, was complicated by the labyrinthine nature of family relationships and mixed loyalties, as exemplified by PLANESMAN, the MSS veteran at the heart of the elite surrounding Mao Zedong who defected in Hong Kong in 1985 and subsequently was given asylum and resettled in the United States. For all his impeccable credentials, PLANESMAN turned out to have an aunt who was a wealthy banker in Hong Kong, and an uncle who was a senior military officer in Taipei.

In spite of the apparently obvious political and kinship obstacles to the recruitment of human sources, the MSS has been widely credited with penetrating almost every level of Taipei's political and military establishment. Analysis of counter-espionage cases investigated by the National Security Bureau (NSB) suggests that up to 80 per cent of detected spies were military personnel, with the remainder having civilian occupations. This disparity may either reflect greater vigilance within the armed forces, where all ranks receive regular security awareness briefings, or may suggest a response to reporting priorities as set by the PLA, an organisation that has had almost no combat experience and whose planners are justifiably cautious at the task of launching an amphibious invasion by an estimated two million troops of the heavily fortified island state.[1] Owing to the 'one child' policy, there will also be an element of doubt about the PLA's willingness to fight, or their parents' support for a shooting war.

In the absence of a well-informed defector such as PLANESMAN, who has enjoyed an unusually broad view of his organisation's structure, personalities and operations, counter-intelligence assessments indicating a significant investment of resources in a particular field can be misleading, and may only be an indicator of the increased efficiency of the local security apparatus. Interpreting, for example, arrest or conviction statistics for evidence of a change in an adversary's targeting requirements can be a fool's errand as the figures may have been skewed by a single event, such as a single spy-ring succumbing to penetration, or the domino effect of a successful arrest. On the other hand, in an information vacuum, analysts are likely to grasp at any potential indicators.[2]

In Far East geopolitical terms Taiwan has always been a potential flashpoint and Beijing's insistence that the islands are a Chinese province, and not a sovereign independent nation, has elevated a long-standing territorial dispute into a permanent source of East/West friction. It has also developed a reputation as one of the world's centres of espionage, not least because the ruling political parties have consistently taken a very enlightened view of Chinese intelligence operations and maintained the penalties for most cases of espionage as months of imprisonment, rather than years. Accordingly, in the absence of a realistic deterrent, the consequences of exposure are far from dire, and represent a mild inconvenience rather than the draconian sentences that elsewhere generate cooperation and defections.

According to the NSB, some sixty investigations were conducted between 2002 and 2017, of which forty-two have been conducted since August 2009 when travel links with the mainland were opened. Indeed, the NSB itself became a target for hostile penetration and in May 2017,[3] Major Wang Hung-ju, a retired Special Service Command military police officer who had been assigned to the NSB's fifty-strong bodyguard unit in 2002 as a protection officer for Vice President Annette Lu, reportedly admitted to having been recruited by the Tianjin Sate Security Bureau while on a visit to China in 2009, Wang was indicted on charges of spying for China, having attempted to recruit an officer named Tseng. His offer to Tseng was a large sum of cash and resettlement on the mainland. He also pitched another friend, then working at the Military Police Command. Reportedly Wang, who retired in 2003, was exposed during a Ministry of Justice Investigation

Bureau check on a local businessman, Ho Chih-Chiang, who in 2010 had been imprisoned for 14 months on a charge of having attempted in 2007 to suborn another NSB officer whom he had asked to supply information about NSB personnel posted abroad.[4]

In June 2012 an academic at Taiwan's Central Police University, Dr Wang Chang-yu, was arrested and accused of having been recruited by the MSS during a visit to Beijing, allegedly by a handler who identified himself as Xiao Zhang of the Taiwan Affairs Office.

In September 2013 retired Vice Admiral Ko Cheg-Sheng, the navy's former deputy commander, was imprisoned for 14 months for collecting classified information he passed to a naturalised Australian businessman, Shen Ping-kang, who was said to have worked for the MSS since the 1990s. Reportedly Ko, who had been handled through the United Front Work Department, had agreed to try and recruit contacts who had served as his subordinates during his distinguished naval career.

In August 2014 the deputy director of Taiwan's Mainland Affairs Council, Chang Hsien-yao, resigned his post after an investigation that lasted two years. He was accused of having leaked sensitive material to Beijing through an intermediary, a Taiwanese businessman, but the case was eventually dropped.[5]

In January 2014 a Taiwanese Air Force officer, with the rank of lieutenant-colonel, was sentenced to life imprisonment for espionage. The sentence was unusually long by Taiwanese standards, but no details were released either during or after the trial.

Another air force officer, Yuan Hsiao-feng, together with Lieutenant Chen Web-jen, also spied for the PLA2. Reportedly Yuan copied huge quantities of classified data on thumb-drives before he retired in 2007. Four years later they were arrested after they had attempted to recruit two junior officers who reported the incident. Both Yuan and Chen were sentenced to life imprisonment.[6]

In February 2014 two former naval officers, Lieutenant Chien Ching-kao and Lieutenant Lu Chun-chun, were imprisoned for 10 months, having been convicted of espionage. According to the prosecution, in 2009 Lu had persuaded Chien to join the Communist Party, and the pair had then arranged for the MSS to pay for overseas trips for themselves and for their potential recruits. Among those they cultivated was a former commander based at the navy's meteorology and oceanography branch. Lu had retired from Taiwan's missile command centre in 2005, and Chien, who was accused of having compromised details of the navy's warships and their deployments, had been discharged from the navy in 2009.[7]

In May 2017 Major-General Hsieh Chia-kang, then serving as deputy commander of the Matsu Defence Command and formerly the commander of Air Defence Command, had been active as a spy since 2009. Hsieh had been recruited by a retired colonel, Hsin Peng-sheng, who was also detained in May 2017. He admitted to having recruited Hsieh when they had served together, and said that he had been approached while leading a tour group in China. Later he had travelled to Malaysia and Thailand to report to his handlers. After their arrest the homes of both men, in Kaohsiung and Pingtung County, were searched for incriminating evidence. Of particular concern was the sensitivity of the information that Hsieh had current access to, such as the specifications and capabilities of various missile systems, including the specifications of all the nation's missiles, including the newly-installed US-manufactured MIM-104F Patriot batteries, and the domestically-developed Tien Kung III and Hsiung Feng 2E cruise missiles.[8]

In April 2016 a former PLA officer, Captain Zheng Xiaojiang, was sentenced to 4 years' imprisonment, and a Taiwanese retiree, Major-General Hsu Nai-chuan, was imprisoned for 34 months. Originally from Xiamen, Fujian Province, Zhen had become resident in Hong Kong in 2005 and often visited Taiwan on a tourist visa. During one of these trips he recruited Hsu, but there was no evidence that the spy-ring he planned ever became operational. Indeed, Zhen agreed to confess and cooperate with the prosecution, naming his principal handler as Mao Shangyu, based in Xiamen City.[9]

The arrest of Captain Zheng in September 2014 was considered highly significant because he was the first case, in several decades, of someone from the mainland engaging in espionage. Hitherto, the spies had been home-grown. According to the NSB, Zheng's network included an army retiree, Major-General Hsu Nai-chuan, Air Force Lieutenant Colonel Chou Chih-li, Air Force pilot Sung Chia-lu, retired army officer Yang Jung-hua, retired air force pilot Ma Po-le, and Lee Huan-yu, the owner of a Kaohsiung karaoke bar which was a popular venue with military personnel. Zheng, who allegedly paid his agents around US $9,400, along with free trips to Southeast Asian tourist destinations, was deported to Hong Kong in July 2018.

Also implicated was the deputy commander of the Air Force Academy's flight training section, an officer named Ke, who spied for 4 years before his retirement in 2013. Ke was also accused of having recruited a subordinate, Lieutenant-Colonel Lou.

Hsu's last military appointment had been as garrison commander of 193 Brigade on Matsu, and had retired from the army in 2007. He was then given a government administrative post in Kinmen Island County, and twice unsuccessfully ran for elected office in 2012 and 2014. Hsu's links to the disputed islands of Matsu and Kinmen, just off the Chinese coast, was probably no coincidence as details of the military strengths there would have been a priority for the PLA2.[10]

According to the prosecution, the spy-ring had collected information about the Dassault Mirage 2000 fighter, the long-range early-warning radar installed by Raytheon on Leshan Mountain in Hsinchu County, and the air force procurement plans for advanced technology. Reportedly, other topics of interest to PLA2 included the E-2K Hawkeye early-warning aircraft, the PAC-2 anti-ballistic missile and the Hawk anti-aircraft system. Given the American political commitment to Taiwan's independence, and the quality of advanced hardware supplied to support the local defences and enhance the scale of deterrence, penetration of the Taiwanese military must have been regarded in Beijing as an attractive backdoor which offered access to the most advanced US technology.

* * *

Among the most prominent espionage cases has been Zhou Hongxu, an MBA student who had graduated from the National Chengchi University in July 2016 and was arrested in March 2017. Zhou was an exchange student from Zhejiang University and in his confession he admitted that he had been recruited in Shanghai in July 2014 by an MSS handler working in the Taiwan Affairs Office who instructed him to enrol at the university and cultivate 'government personnel and other people of influence'. After graduation Zhou had returned to Taiwan in February 2017 on a business visa to work for a local firm.

Zhou had then approached a civil servant employed in the Ministry of Foreign Affairs in August 2016, offering payment of $40,000 a quarter, a pitch that was reported to the NSB. Zhou was convicted of espionage and sentenced to 14 months' imprisonment.[11]

In June 2023 a former presidential bodyguard named Sun was imprisoned for 32 months, while his nephew Wang was sentenced to 16 months. According to Sun, he had moved to China to work for a law firm when in 2018 he was recruited by an MSS officer named Fang who paid him $1,500 a month and suggested he contact his nephew who had recently been promoted to the presidential office's guard unit.

A military intelligence officer, Lo Chi-cheng, was found in 2010 to have been acting as a double agent for China since 2007. Lo, who worked at the Ministry of National Defence's Military Intelligence Bureau, was sentenced to life in prison plus 27 years for spying for China, taking bribes and extortion. He was also accused of having colluded with Lo Pin, a mainland-based Taiwanese businessman, to disclose classified information. Additionally, Lo was convicted of having insinuated deliberately fabricated false information into Taiwan's intelligence assessment system. According to the prosecution, Lo Pin had been recruited by Lo Chi-cheng in 2003, and from February 2004 to October 2005, Lo Pin had made ten visits to China to meet his handlers who had paid him $1,500 a month. However, the MSS severed the connection in 2000, apparently suspecting compromise, and paid him off with almost $30,000.[12]

However, during a visit to China in July 2006 Lo Pin was detained and invited to 'redeem himself through good service'. The price for his release was to be the recruitment of Lo Chi-cheng who agreed to receive carefully doctored intelligence reports and pass them into Taiwan's Ministry of Defence. Over the next three years Lo Pin acted as an intermediary or 'cut-out' and made numerous visits to Hong Kong to pass on Lo Chi-cheng's reports, and receive the false material to take to Taipei. According to the prosecution, Lo had been awarded bonuses for his supply of 'chicken-feed' while Lo Pin had earned received some $46,000 from his Chinese handlers. Both men were arrested in October 2010 as they exchanged documents at Taipei's Kunyang metro station. Under interrogation, Lo Pin confessed to espionage and was released on bail.

MSS willingness to adopt ruthless tactics was demonstrated in July 2006 when two Taiwanese Military Intelligence Bureau officers, Colonels Hsu Chang-kuo and Colonel Chu Kung-hsun, flew to Vietnam to negotiate terms for the defection someone described as a high-level Chinese official. The prize was too tempting to ignore, but both men were abducted after a short struggle with eight Chinese, and shipped to China for interrogation. The incident, which took place at a Vietnamese checkpoint in an area near the border with China's south-western Guangxi Province only became known because Hsu was able to send a text message seeking help. The bait turned out to be an elaborate trap which ensnared the two hapless victims and kept them hostage for the next 9 years, their death sentence have been commuted to 20 years' imprisonment. They would be released in November 2015 in exchange for Li Zhihao, then aged 70, who had been imprisoned in 1999. It remains unclear whether Chu and Hsu ever had any prospect of negotiating with a genuine defector, or if he was always part of a scheme to seize the two Taiwanese officers. The spy-swap had been arranged in anticipation of President Ma Ying-Jeau's scheduled meeting with President Xi Jinping in Singapore later the same month. No details of Li Zhihao or his conviction were ever disclosed, beyond the acknowledgment that he had been paroled from a life sentence.[13]

Another strategy embraced by the MSS and PLA2 in relation to Taiwan was the 'false-flag' in which MSS personnel represent themselves as Taiwanese intelligence professionals, and used the fake nationality as leverage to gain cooperation that otherwise would have been absent. Classic among such cases is the suborning of Gregg Bergersen, a weapons system policy analyst employed by the Defense Security Cooperation Agency, the US Department of Defense unit in the Pentagon responsible for supervising the sale of defence equipment to foreign buyers. Bergersen was arrested in February 2008 and charged with passing classified information to Kuo Tai Shen, a Taiwanese with a furniture manufacturing business in New Orleans, after Bergersen had been led to believe that Kuo was working for Taiwan when in fact he had been recruited by a PLA2 contact in Guangzhou. Accordingly, he supplied Kuo with information and documents that were supposedly intended to assist him in developing defence exports to Taiwan. Among the items passed were details of the Broad Victory project, which was designed to upgrade existing Taiwanese command-and-control systems; blueprints of the Defense Department's Global Information Grid communications network; and pages of the secret 2007 Javis Report, which listed Defense Security Cooperation Agency sales planned over the next five years.

Also involved in the false-flag operation was Kang Yuxin, a Chinese woman who was sentenced to 18 months' imprisonment for her part in a persuading Bergersen to hand over secret military documents to Kao. Kang had pleaded guilty in May 2008 to aiding an undeclared foreign government agent by serving as an intermediary between Bergersen and Kuo. Aged 58, Kuo was sentenced to 188 months' imprisonment and required to forfeit $40,000 for conspiracy to deliver national defence information to China. Kuo pleaded guilty to this offence on 13 May 2008, having been arrested in February 2008.[14]

During the course of the conspiracy, Kuo had cultivated a friendship with Bergersen, giving him gifts, cash, dinners, and trips to such places as Las Vegas. Kuo also led Bergersen to believe that he would make him a part owner or an employee of a company selling US defence technology to Taiwan after Bergersen's retirement from government service. Unbeknownst to Bergersen, Kuo passed his documents and information to his MSS handler who directed Kuo to obtain specific documents and information, for which he was paid approximately $50,000.

On 11 July 2008 Bergersen was sentenced to 57 months' imprisonment and 3 years' supervised release after pleading guilty on 31 March 2008 to conspiracy to deliver national defence information to a person not entitled to receive it, On 1 August 2008, Kao's accomplice, Kang ('Katie') Yu Xin Kang, was sentenced to 18 months' imprisonment for aiding and abetting an unregistered agent of a foreign government. She pleaded guilty to this offence on 28 May 2008.

A fourth co-conspirator was James Fordren, who was also jailed. In May 2009 he was a senior Department of Defense officer based at the Pentagon, and was arrested and charged with espionage for China, apparently having been duped by Kuo. However, a month later his indictment was changed to accuse him of having worked for Beijing for more than a decade. Aged 62, US Air Force Lieutenant-Colonel Fondren held Top Secret clearances as deputy director of the Washington liaison office for the US Pacific Command. He was charged with passing secrets to Kuo, whom he had first met at a country club in Houma, Louisiana. According to the indictment, Fondren wrote an email in 1998 stating that Kuo was using opinion papers on Taiwanese military issues that Fondren provided to ingratiate himself with the Chinese government. Then in 1999 the two men travelled together to the coastal town of Zhuhai to meet a government official, Lin Hong, to whom Fondren promised to obtain reports on missile defences in Taiwan. He would later exchange more than forty emails with the Chinese in 1999 and 2000.

Between June 1998 and January 2000, Kuo paid nearly $8,000 to Fondren's consultancy, Strategy Inc. After his official retirement, Fondren returned as a contractor to the Defense Department, and Kuo apparently claimed to be working for Taiwan. Convicted in September 2009 on one count of passing classified information to an agent of a foreign government, Fondren was sentenced to three years' imprisonment on 22 January 2010.[15]

From a counter-intelligence perspective, the entire charade appeared to have been choreographed to either exploit Fondren and Bergersen's naivete, or to provide them with a plausible cover-story intended to give the impression that they were neither mercenary or adherents of the regime in Beijing. Either way, the operation showed considerable sophistication, not least in the PLA2's ability to recruit such high-level sources in key positions in the Defense Department.

* * *

In January 2011 Major-General Lo Hsien-che, the electronic communications and information bureau chief, was arrested and charged with having sold Taiwan's military secrets to mainland China since 2004. In April 2012 he was convicted of espionage and sentenced by a court martial to life imprisonment.[16]

Born in 1959 to a military family, Lo's father was an NCO who retired from the army to farm in Guanshan, Taitung, and his elder brother also served in the army, reaching the rank of colonel. Lo himself attended Taiwan's Military Academy, and upon graduation was assigned to the 51st Communications Section. He also studied in the US Defense Language Institute in Monterey, California, and went on courses at the Colleges of Army and Warfare of the National Defense University. In 2000, he was promoted to colonel and appointed commander of the 73rd Communications unit of the 6th Army Corps. Between 2002 and 2005 he was posted to Bangkok as military attaché, and in 2006 was selected as deputy director of international intelligence affairs. He was then made head of the army's electronic communications and information branch before his last promotion, in January 2008 to the rank of major-general.

Reportedly Lo, who was married, had been honey-trapped in Thailand in 2004 by a woman holding an Australian passport who traded sex for secrets, although she also paid him up to $1 million on several occasions. Their illicit affair was compromised when Lo travelled with her on holiday to the United States where the relationship was noted by a federal agency and reported to Taipei. Lo remains the most senior officer ever to have been caught spying for Beijing, but the official damage assessment remains classified so the extent of the harm he inflicted has yet to published.

In January 2012 Lin Linghui, who was married to a Taiwanese colonel working in military intelligence, was detained in China and instructed to summon her husband. Reportedly, the plot failed, but it suggested that the MSS had been motivated to seize a hostage in order to gain access to what some MSS officer regarded as a target recruit. In a similar episode in October 2013 a retired Taiwanese intelligence officer, Major Shen Shu-lung, was employed to lure a target to Shanghai where he underwent three days of interrogation before he was released.[17]

Ubiquitous hostile surveillance in mainland Chinese cities has served as a significant deterrent to Taiwan's intelligence collection efforts, which have been severely curtailed by political decisions in Taipei where such operations had been conducted by the Military Intelligence Bureau (MIB). The high-water level of these recruitments, often achieved through family links, was in August 1999 when several assets were rolled up in China. For example, in June two senior officials, Xiong Tianjun and Xi Shiguo, were sentenced to life imprisonment, having been convicted of spying for the MIB.

Later in 1999 retired 58-year-old Major-General Liu Liankun, who had headed the PLA's logistics department, was executed with another spy, 56-year-old Colonel Shao Zhengzhong. The pair were estimated to have received $1.6 million, and were said to have been actively engaged in espionage over the past five years.[18]

* * *

In January 2018 it was reported that the Taipei District Prosecutors Office was investigating if classified information regarding the Airborne Special Service Company was passed on to Zhou Hongxu who had been convicted already for violating the National Security Act.

In March 2018, a retired colonel was charged with breaching the National Security Act by the Kaohsiung District Prosecutors Office, which alleged that the colonel shared classified personal information and planned to develop a spy ring in Taiwan.

In April 2018, Hung Chin-hsi, a Macao-born businessman, was accused of developing a spy-ring in the Ministry of Justice, on behalf of China. In 2022, Taipei District Prosecutors Office charged retired major General Chien Yao-tung and retired Lieutenant-Colonel Wei-Hsien-yi for developing a spy network for China. They were accused of working for a Hong Kong resident named Tse, who would visit Taiwan to recruit retired officers and cultivate those on active duty. Chien and Wei tried unsuccessfully to recruit Chang Che-ping, who was a deputy minister of national defence before serving as a strategic adviser to President Tsai Ing-wen. Initially Chang was considered a suspect, but was later acquitted of complicity and renamed as a witness.[19]

* * *

Taiwan's integrated circuit fabrication industry has often been cited as the nation's best protection against Chinese aggression and even invasion. In commercial terms the economic consequences of military action would be profound for the mainland, and would be global in magnitude. Nevertheless, short of invasion, or the imposition of a maritime blockade, Beijing is inclined to sabre-rattling in the Straits of Taiwan and continues to pursue a policy of territorial claims across the South China Sea and is active in militarising the region.

While Taiwan remains dominant in the development and production of integrated circuits, Beijing persists in sponsoring deniable technology-transfer operations, as manifested when a source inside Nanya Technology stole designs for dynamic random-access memory (DRAM) on behalf of Tsinghua Holdings. Hsu Chih-Peng, an engineer for Taiwan Semiconductor Manufacturing Co. stole microchip designs after being solicited by the Chinese government-owned Shanghai Huali Microelectronics.

According to the prosecution, engineer Wang Yongming (on behalf of Fujian Jinhua Integrated Circuit) engaged in espionage to steal Micron Technology microchip designs via the Taiwanese company UMC. Micron claimed that UMC hired Micron's engineers, tasking them to steal files on advanced memory chips. The files Wang stole were said to be production secrets, including testing procedures related to metallization, and the DR25nmS design protocol.

In some respects the tension between Taipei and Beijing is reminiscent of the anomalous status of the German Democratic Republic where the divided population meant family ties were necessarily severed and it was not unusual to find closely-related kinsmen with very different political loyalties, a scenario created by geographic necessity rather than conscious choice.

Chapter XI

THE CHINA THREAT

I think the challenge of the rise of China absolutely raises huge questions for the future of the Western alliance . . . none of us can give a confident long-term answer to exactly how the balance of power plays out globally across the next few decades but it is clear for all of us that this is, I think, the central intelligence challenge for us across the next decade.

Ken McCallum, Director-General, MI5
December 2020

China's undisguised interest in contributing to, if not taking control of, Western critical infrastructure was plain to see, and in October 2020 MI5 advised that 'a lot of the China intent is very public'.[1] However, the reaction has been timid, late, and uncoordinated.

In Britain the Parliamentary Security and Intelligence Committee, drawn from both Houses of Parliament, is the only legitimate access to details of the procedures, resources and performance of the five principal entities, being GCHQ, SIS, MI5, the Defence Intelligence Staff and the Joint Intelligence Organisation. Created in 1994, the ISC receives written and oral evidence in private, has the power to initiate its own enquiries, and issues annual reports on selected topics, which are published after their submission to the Prime Minister. The ISC is emphatically not a committee of either House, and the membership is appointed by the prime minister. Unfortunately the single member of staff employed to conduct independent enquiries for the Committee, John Morrison, a civilian analyst and former deputy chief of Defence Intelligence and head of the Defence Intelligence Analysis Staff, was removed from his post in 2004 and was not replaced. Considering that the US Congressional equivalents are supported by dozens of former professionals, the ISC would appear to be seeking to fulfil its remit at a considerable disadvantage. In contrast, the French equivalent employs eighteen staff, the Greek fifty-two, the Canadian eleven, and the German nine. The US Senate Select Committee has a staff of around fifteen, while the House has about twenty.

In terms of the Chinese threat, the ISC published a series of statistics to show how each of the four agencies had devoted resources to the issue. The first to undergo examination was SIS, which explained that following the hand-over of Hang Kong in 1997 (and maybe the change of government in London, with Robin Cook's appointment as Foreign Secretary) intelligence collection priorities in the Far East had changed:

After 1997, SIS effort on China reduced, but since 2004/05 it has been seeking to rebuild resources: The percentage of operational effort dedicated to China has [XXX] over the past 20 years, ranging between [XX] % (1999) and [XXX] % (2003).

For 2018/19 the figure stood at [XXX] % (for comparative purposes, the figure for Russia was [XXX] %).

This equated to a financial spend of £ [XXX] (out of £ [XXX]).

In 2020, the figure increased to [XXX] %, and a financial spend of £ [XXX] (out of £ [XXX]).

In terms of staff dedicated to China, figures show [XXX] from [XXX] full-time equivalent (FTE) (2005/06) to [XXX] FTE for 2019/20.

Of these, [XXX][2]

For understandable operational reasons none of the agencies, nor any other security or intelligence organisation, is too keen on disclosing publicly the resources devoted to a particular sector, and this information might assist an adversary, and the same kind of redactions were applied to the three other subjects of scrutiny:

GCHQ statistics show a similar picture: Between 2000 and 2019, the number of GCHQ and National Cyber Security Centre (NCSC) staff working on China increased from [XXX] FTE to [XXX] FTE.

In 2020, this increased to [XXX] FTE.

The percentage of operational effort dedicated to China has increased from [XX] % in 2000 to [XXX] % in 2019.

Operational effort on China rose to [XXX[% in 2020.

MI5 statistics provide an overall picture of work on Hostile State Activity (HSA), of which China is only one strand: For the financial year 2019/20, HSA2 was allocated a total spend of £ [XXX] (International Counter-Terrorism and Northern Ireland-related terrorism received £ [XXX] and £ [XXX] respectively).

Of that £ [XXX], work on China received £ [XXX].

This was an increase of £ [XXX] from the previous year (but it nevertheless only represents a return to the levels of [XXX]).

The proportion of mission effort on China is around [XXX] %. This roughly equates to [XXX] people.

The Joint Intelligence Organisation similarly has found it difficult to disaggregate exactly: In March 2021, the JIO China Team contained [XXX] FTE staff with [XXX] due to be advertised (an increase from [XXX] FTE pre-2017 and [XXX] FTE in early 2019). In addition, there [XXX] dedicated to China open-source work.

The allocation of effort has increased [XXX] over the past two decades from[XXX] % in 1999 to [XXX] in 2019 and then [XX] % in 2020.

Towards the end of 2020, the JIC Chair told us:[XXX] *In terms of my time, I would say that I probably spend about [XXX] % of my time on China, something of that sort.'*

Other organisations

Defence Intelligence statistics for 2020 show that: [XXX] analysts spent 50% or more of their time on China (a decrease from [XXX] last year) and [XXX} analysts spent less than 50% of their time on China (an increase from [XXX] last year).

DI spends £ [XXX] on China-related activity.294 Alongside broader politico-military analysis, this includes: [XXX] partnership programme with the defence industry in order to ensure that insights [XXX] are then shared in an appropriate manner with the defence industry to advise them about how they can protect themselves;

DI has previously told the Committee that it does not hold comprehensive records relating to allocations of effort on China for past years. We found that difficult to understand. DI explained that *'allocation of effort is challenging* [for it] *to calculate given the range of intelligence capabilities and specialisms within DI, many of which cover multiple geographic areas '*. Notwithstanding that, we are surprised that information on allocation of effort on an area as supposedly significant as China is not readily to hand so that it can be kept under constant review.

Homeland Security Group statistics for 2020 show that: Approximately [XXX] staff worked on China [XXX].

This is a decrease from 2019, when [XXX] FTE staff worked on China. In 2019, the Committee was told that [XXX] due to be recruited, which would raise the number of dedicated staff to [XXX] FTE. Then in 2020, we were informed that the figure *'will rise to [XXX] FTE* [XXX] At the time of taking evidence, we had yet to receive confirmation that this uplift had taken place.

The National Security Secretariat has [XXX] staff working on China with an administrative spend of £ [XXX] per annum. This includes a secretariat for the China National Security Council (NSC) strategy and National Strategy Implementation Group (NSIG), co-ordination of cross-cutting policy in support of that strategy, and provision of advice to the Prime Minister.

Potential for increase in resourcing

When we took evidence in autumn 2019, the Intelligence Community told us that any increase in resources on China would have to be viewed as necessary by the NSC (and the Treasury) and it may be that the threat posed by Russia, Iran or counter-terrorism could be considered as more in need of increased resourcing. In the past, such balancing of priorities has seen resources being diverted away from China onto acute counter-terrorism priorities. As Director General MI5 explained to the Committee:

[XXX] *there are some difficult choices when the CT* [counter-terrorism] *thing has not reduced in its scale and its sharpness … we need to figure out how much of these kinds of capabilities feels enough or proportionate against this threat.*[3]

The ISC report on China sought to drill down on these figures and examine the amount of resources devoted to the threat, rather than the opaque statistical change that had taken place over the past five years, and included the inter-agency Joint States Threat Assessment Team (JSTAT):

Under the Security Services Act 1989, MI5 is responsible for countering Hostile State Activity (HSA), i.e. *'protection against threats from espionage, terrorism and sabotage* [and] *from the activities of agents of foreign powers'*. In May 2019, MI5 had around [XXX] full-time equivalent (FTE) staff working on State Threats – predominantly on counter-intelligence and counter-espionage but also on counter-proliferation and state-sponsored terrorism work. The HSA team primarily focuses on Russia, China and Iran but they also have a 'Rest of the World' remit.

MI5 also has responsibility for the Joint State Threats Assessment Team (JSTAT). JSTAT provides assessments and a holistic view on the national security threat posed by: espionage; assassination; interference in our democracy and society; threats to the UK's economic security; and threats to the UK's people and assets overseas.

It therefore looks in depth at the threats from [XXX] activity, as well as niche and emerging threats, and provides assessment for a wide range of government departments.

JSTAT works under MI5's legal authorisations. It is governed by a Board [XXX], and draws its staff from across government, including policy departments, MI5, DI, SIS and GCHQ. In 2019, the Committee was told that JSTAT had around [XXX] analysts, [XXX] of whom were working on China in February 2020 (the previous Committee was told that the intention was to increase that [XXX] by the end of the financial year 2019/20).322 By late 2020, the number had risen [XXX] and the intention was for a further increase [XXX] in 2021, subject to the outcome of the Spending Review. MI5 explained that JSTAT was vital to countering the threat from China:

So we have already clocked that we need to bolster how we are bringing together a fragmentary complex intelligence picture, mixing that with what is in the public domain, because, as I have said, a lot of the China intent is very public, and then using that to inform the security aspect of the judgement that then is part of informing Ministers and the Departments about the overall balance.

MI5's objectives in relation to HSA are to '*seek those trying to pass sensitive UK information and equipment to other countries and ensure they don't succeed* ' (counter-espionage) and to '*disrupt the actions of foreign intelligence officers where these are damaging to our country's interests* ' (counter-intelligence). MI5 told us that its role is spread across a range of areas, including investigating activity against UK interests both within the UK and abroad (as well as remotely online) [XXX]. MI5 also has responsibility for detecting (and countering) '*penetration of government, or the Agencies themselves for that matter* '[XXX]. MI5 told the Committee that: '*the MI5 role is clearly central on the counter-intelligence element* [XXX]

In 2020, [XXX] of MI5's operational effort was focused on China. [XXX] in order to counter the breadth of the China threat, MI5 has prioritised its efforts [XXX] MI5 told us that it was working on a number of areas relating [XXX], including: HMG – attempts to penetrate the UK Intelligence Community and wider HMG [XX];

[XXX]

Science and Technology – attempts to obtain sensitive UK defence technology [XXX]

[XXX]

[XXX]

[XXX] and

Cyber – developing HMG's understanding [XXX].

Although MI5 argued that the measures it was taking were proving to be effective, it also accepted that [XXX]. Director General MI5 told us:

We've built up quite an experience base now [XXX]. So I don't think we are likely to be[XXX] . Clearly that's in some ways not that different to the version I face of that around counter-terrorism, for example [XXX].[4]

While heavily redacted, to the point of being impossible to interpret, there are clues in the China Report which suggest that the agencies' response to the China threat had been too little too late, as can be discerned from the Committee's comment that:

MI5 is responsible for countering Hostile State Activity, and the Centre for the Protection of National Infrastructure and the National Cyber Security Centre play a key role in engaging with those within and outside government to protect national security. There is a wide array of defensive tools, which are being used to good effect, but the Government has come late to the party and has a lot of catching up to do. Our closest allies identified the need to use such tools against China long ago and we must learn from their experience and knowledge.[5]

It would seem that MI5 in particular had been slow to react to the China threat, and this poor performance had put the organisation's record over the unusually prolonged period of five years under uncomfortable scrutiny. Accordingly, MI5s' evidence to the Committee sounded quite defensive, explaining the challenges of countering Chinese espionage:

Much of the impact that China has on national security is overt – through its economic might, its takeovers and mergers, its interaction with Academia and Industry – as opposed to covert activity carried out by its intelligence officers [XXX]. This means that 'interference' operations can be less easy to point to than traditional 'spying' operations [XXX].

The UK Intelligence Community have been open with the Committee about the challenges of detecting Chinese interference operations:

China's blended approach – its intertwining of overt and covert activity – poses significant challenges. [XXX]. Unpicking this is difficult.

The JIC Chair acknowledged that [XXX] *some of it is legitimate activity, some of it . . .* [is not] *legitimate but not necessarily illegal '*. MI5 clarified the role that the UK Intelligence Community plays in identifying Chinese interference operations:

[XXXX] *A lot of that will be visible, open, what I think diplomacy is about, that fostering of understanding, but we worry about where it is more covert or more nefarious.*[6]

The impression given by the Committee's own commentary reinforces the impression that the British intelligence community had been caught off-guard, and was engaging in a belated game of catch-up. For example, the Committee remarked that, 'The JIO, working with NSS and JSTAT, told this Inquiry that they were working to "map" foreign interference [XXX]' which implies that the process of analytical mapping is ongoing, and is still in the early research stage, with the agencies not yet fully engaged in the investigation of actual cases. This view is reinforced by the comment 'The UK Intelligence Community have been open with the Committee about the challenges of detecting Chinese interference operations. [XXX]'. Indeed, in 2019 that same community had disclaimed responsibility for confronting the threat, a lapse that would be characterised as a 'lack of understanding':

> One of the factors in the lack of understanding is that, until recently, the Agencies did not recognise that they had any responsibility for countering Chinese interference activity in the UK, since they considered that the policy community had mandated them to focus on other threats. In 2019, they told the Committee that:

> *Responsibility for mitigating the more overt aspects of the* [Chinese] *threat to the UK . . . rests with government policy departments [XXX]*

> Historically, this resulted in an intelligence gap as it meant that not only were the Agencies not taking responsibility for tackling it, they were not even proactively seeking to identify it. Instead, it 'fell through the cracks' as the Government was relying on government departments to identify and then tackle the threat posed by China on their policy areas. (This was not unusual – we reported a similar historic problem in our *Russia* Report.) Yet the whole-of-state approach used by China meant that various UK government departments were trying to tackle different versions of the same problem – that of Chinese nationals, whether employed by the Chinese Communist Party or private individuals, actively working for China's benefit. For example, at the time of taking evidence, the Department for Education (alongside the (then) Department for Business, Energy and Industrial Strategy) was responsible for identifying and tackling Chinese interference in UK Academia.

> However, there is no evidence that Whitehall policy departments have the necessary resources, expertise or knowledge of the threat to investigate and counter the Chinese whole-of-state approach. The nature of China's engagement, influence and interference activity in the UK is difficult to detect, but even more concerning is the fact that the Government may not previously have been looking for it. [XXX].

> Since the Committee began taking evidence and questioning the Agencies on their lack of involvement in tackling overt aspects of the Chinese threat, there appears to have been a change in approach. [XXX] [XXX].

> MI5 told us that this decision was part of a '*gradual widening of our aperture* ' to look beyond the traditional focus [XXX] This allowed it to increase its work on influence alongside espionage. MI5 says that it is exploring [XXX]'

The expansion of MI5's role into the new but ill-defined field of countering influence and interference would lead the organisation to research Chinese students in the UK, and their college faculties, noting that there were about 151,000 currently enrolled, supported by twenty-nine Confucius Institutes. Partly funded by Hanban, a branch of the Chinese Communist Party's propaganda department, the Confucius Institutes exercise both influence and discipline over its (mainly) ethnic Chinese membership while promoting Mandarin language courses and Chinese culture.

When explaining the Security Service's interest in October 2020, Ken McCallum had drawn attention to the legal position, which stood in stark contrast to the campaign waged in the United States by the Justice Department. Put simply, the Chinese intelligence professionals were not breaking any laws.

> There is some good work happening, which is informing a range of policy action, and one recent example would be [XXX]. That work has in part been stimulated by some very good analysis and assessment work which has brought together that picture.'[8]

The ISC observed that 'the fact remains that there have been no prosecutions and only one arrest of a [XXX]'. This is partly down to the difficulty in prosecuting espionage offences (discussed further in the chapter on Legislation) as Director General MI5 explained: '[XXX] more often it is information that confers a UK advantage but isn't necessarily a ... state official secret, which is one of the reasons why the proposed new legislation is something that we see advantage in.'[9]

Perhaps the only unintended advantage of the China Report taking so long to prepare, over three different premierships, was the element of continuity, with much the same witnesses being confronted with their earlier testimony. This elongated continuity also served to highlight Whitehall's lack of attention to the China threat in the post-1997 era.

In October 2020, the Acting National Security Adviser (David Quarrey) told the Committee that there was now 'an enormous amount of work underway, and of course it is not perfect at the moment, but it shows, I think, that we are joining up more effectively across government and between the covert side and the overt side, to get our arms around the scale of the threat'. Director GCHQ also told us that the situation was improving. However, the Director also noted that there was a tension between centralising the response and empowering the lead government department to address the issue (which had, in the past, resulted in a lack of co-ordination).[10]

Turning to SIS, the picture was much the same:

Operational effort within SIS and GCHQ is broken down into different 'missions' (as explained in the chapter on HMG Resourcing). As at 2020, SIS allocated [XXX] % of its overall operational effort to China and GCHQ allocated [XXX] % of its operational effort to China. The China mission is then further broken down into the different 'requirements' on China which the Government has set for SIS and GCHQ.

> In evidence in 2020, SIS broke down its operational effort in relation to China as [XXX]

[XXX]

[XXX]

This split has been broadly static since 2019.
In 2019, GCHQ noted that its operational effort was similarly divided but with an additional focus on [XXX] A year later, Director GCHQ told us that there were between [XXX] and [XXX] active Chinese cyber groups, and that GCHQ was able to cover [XXX].[11]

The Committee noted that because of a change in the methodology adopted by SIS and GCHQ made it difficult to distinguish between, and therefore judge, the relative performance of each, noting that 'it is now not possible to establish to what extent SIS and GCHQ are individually responsible for any progress made against these outcomes – and therefore how their effectiveness or performance can be meaningfully assessed. We question the logic behind this.'[12]

Despite this criticism, the Committee had been impressed with a GCHQ's project code-named WINDERMERE by the ISC, first disclosed in 2019, which had been designed to counter Chinese cyber-attacks.

> . . . the UK is leading internationally on countering the cyber threat from China. [Given that there has been a lot of public reporting regarding the UK's limited focus on China by comparison with its Five Eyes partners, it is interesting that the UK Intelligence Community consider that they are leading internationally on responding to the Chinese cyber threat.]
>
> Operation WINDERMERE is a cross-UK Intelligence Community strategy to address Chinese cyber activity, led by GCHQ [XXX]. It aims to *reduce the impact of the Chinese State's cyber programme on UK'* [XXX]

The strategy focuses on taking intelligence [XXX] and using it for defence means (in order to make UK cyber space a hard operating environment) [XXX].[13]

Overall, the Committee appeared unimpressed by what SIS and GCQH had accomplished since 2019, and tried to source the complacency by questioning the Intelligence Coverage and Effects (ICE) management tool employed to assess the value of particular operations and campaigns.

Although SIS and GCHQ were judged by the Cabinet Office to be meeting or exceeding most of their ICE targets on China in 2018, this seems largely due to expectation management, as most targets were set to 'some' or 'limited' contribution – so, although they met their targets, the targets themselves were set rather low.

When the Committee asked Director GCHQ in 2019 if he felt '*that in the circumstances* [GCHQ was] *not doing too badly* ', the Director agreed with that assessment - but also said that it was still very much at the starting point.[XXX]

SIS noted that the 'coverage' targets in the 2018 ICE Plan had enabled it to start work, jointly with GCHQ and MI5, on [XXX] – this, rather worryingly, implies that little had actually been achieved at that point. When, in 2019, we pressed on why there appeared to be so little work [XXX], GCHQ told us that: *coverage leads directly to intelligence reporting, which can have an impact and does have an impact and affects the way we position the UK's policy, it affects the way we are conducting our international relations and it affects the way we are laying down our capability investments in the future. So* [XXX] *then I think that is probably a more precise way of thinking about that. The answer to . . . why so much* [is directed] *at* [XXX] *at the moment is because* [XXX].

When we asked again, in late 2020, what had now been achieved, GCHQ said that the increase in effort could be seen in all areas of activity, including the collection of intelligence, effects work [XXX], and in the defensive aspects of the cyber effort. The progress [XXX] meant that: *we have made massive headway, such that the issue is starting to be how do we deal with the scale of the information at our disposal? How do we get into and focus the effort on the things that we most care about* [XX].

It is at this point that the ISC Report undergoes a change in tone, and expresses some healthy scepticism:

However, when we asked, again, in 2020, how SIS and GCHQ had performed against the requirements set by the Cabinet Office, we were told that the pandemic meant that there had not been a Cabinet Office review of whether either Agency had met its targets.

It is clear that there has been progress in terms of 'offensive' work since we started our Inquiry – for instance, an increase in 'effects' work. However, given what appears to be the extremely low starting point, this is not cause for celebration [XXX]. Both SIS and GCHQ say that working on China *'is a slow burn, slow-return effort'* [XXX].

GCHQ and SIS tasking is set by the Government and, rightly, they cannot work outside the Government's priorities. Nevertheless, the fact that China was such a relatively low priority in 2018 – the same year in which China approved the removal of term limits on the Presidency, allowing President Xi Jinping to remain in office as long as he wished – is concerning. Work must continue to be prioritised now to make up for this slow start and there must be clear measurement and evaluation of effort.

Almost following MI5's lead in describing the challenges posed by the Chinese, SIS set out in some detail the obstacles that had to be overcome:

Prior to the pandemic, the UK's relationship with China was based on an approach that sought to balance prosperity with national security issues – unlike Russia, which is seen unambiguously as a threat. Although that balance appears to have shifted since, with the push to protect the UK's domestic economic security, HMG acknowledges that China's economic might cannot be ignored.

This has an impact when planning action. For example, exposure of intelligence work may damage bilateral relations to the extent that UK trade and investment interests are affected. Similarly, when HMS *Albion* performed a Freedom of Navigation Operation in the South China Sea in 2018, China appeared to reduce economic engagement with the UK. In 2019, the Senior Responsible Owner told us that HMG [XXX] had discussed how to re-engage the Chinese:

[it] *was re-established after [XXX] diplomacy and engagement, there were some decisions that the Treasury had to take about how they were approaching that dialogue, [XXX]. Because of the cross-cutting nature of that, that wasn't a decision that the Treasury could just take alone. So we worked through the coordinating process to get a clear set of choices and decisions* [XXX]

Surveillance
China is often referred to as a surveillance state, using a range of methods from state-of-the-art technology to neighbourhood watch schemes to monitor its citizens and residents. There is near-comprehensive CCTV coverage in Beijing as well as in most other major cities.

The rapid pace of technological development is only increasing this challenge. China is in the process of integrating its world-leading technologies, such as face recognition and artificial intelligence (AI), in order to allow state authorities to track and follow all residents around its cities. Further development and integration of AI would allow monitoring and automated flagging of unusual behaviour or activities.

When, in July 2019, we asked the Intelligence Community about this, China was described as a *'totally censored environment . . . censors everywhere and computers making sense of those feeds for individuals to spot* [an] *anomaly '* [XXX]. It was expected that such an environment would *'increasingly become the norm* [XXX] *because this technology is cheap and will be exported '*. [XXX]

[XXX] Surveillance of Chinese citizens with access to secret information is particularly acute: individuals working on sensitive areas are subject to travel bans and cannot leave the country without express permission. The Chinese intelligence system is both hugely capable and uncompromising: those convicted of espionage can face the death penalty.[XXX].

Surveillance in China has also extended to the virtual world. China's well-established domestic technology sector poses a significant challenge in terms of SIGINT collection. The blocking of Western web services and applications, and the dominance of Chinese apps [XXX]

Even without the challenges of Chinese surveillance, the sheer size of the Chinese state presents a significant challenge when it comes to gaining coverage. It can be extremely difficult to keep track of the vast host of Chinese ministries and party organs, the status of which within the Chinese Communist Party and government is constantly evolving. [XXX]

It is clear that both GCHQ and SIS face a formidable challenge in relation to China. What we were unable to assess – without the specific requirements set for the Agencies or any idea of the prioritisation of the 'outcomes' within the Intelligence Outcomes Prioritisation Plan – is how effective either Agency is at tackling that challenge.[14]

Although it is hard to navigate through the heavily-redacted ISC report, the content reads as a serious warning about a perceived economic offensive that has resulted, by not much stealth, of a huge Chinese investment in the UK's nuclear energy industry, its telecommunications infrastructure and even its all too vulnerable political system. Whereas there have been dozens of instances of technology transfer in the United States, and theft of intellectual property, the emphasis in the UK has been more subtle, partly because of the lack of equivalent legislation. While the American intelligence community endured wholesale penetration, London seems to have embraced Chinese real estate investors and placed no obstacle in the path of senior civil servants taking lucrative appointments with supporters of President Xi's increasingly authoritarian regime.

* * *

If, as the evidence suggests, Xi's regime goes far beyond casting a Nelsonic eye over the activities of technology theft from Western companies and institutions by non-state actors, it is hard not to reach the conclusion that cyber-attacks and the illicit acquisition of potentially valuable commercial information have become part of Beijing's unacknowledged foreign policy. The behaviour of Chinese hackers has become more brazen, perhaps encouraged by a perceptible political reluctance to tackle the problem robustly, This may also be a reflection of the growing confidence of the state-sponsored hackers active in Chinese time zones, and perhaps an adoption of the tactics and tradecraft to be found at the lower end of the cyber warfare spectrum where supposedly independent criminals practise their skills and engage in nuisance strategies that could escalate instantly if so required. There is good reason to suppose that there is a direct link connecting the CCP to the unavowed hackers who, at the flick of a switch, can be deployed in support of the Party's foreign policy objectives.

In July 2019, Chinese hackers from the group designated APT10 targeted three US utility companies with a spear-phishing campaign to gain access to computer networks. Allegedly APT10 had been active since 2012, and was assessed as having been affiliated with another, previously unidentified Chinese espionage group, known as APT41, which had gathered data from firms in telecommunications, healthcare, semiconductor manufacturing, and machine learning. The group was also thought to be active in the theft of virtual currencies. In 2016 a large APD10 attack, designated CLOUD HOPPER, was detected by GCHQ and was assessed to have 'facilitated economic and strategic espionage'. It then re-re-emerged in December 2018 and was publicly named by the British government as being a Chinese instrument. This was the very first time the UK had attributed a specific attack to the Chinese regime, and the statement was made at a time of deteriorating relations with Beijing, following the deployment of the amphibious warship HMS *Albion* to the Pacific on a mission to exercise international navigation rights in the South China Sea, close to the disputed Paracel Islands. China protested about the *Albion*, which was buzzed by PLAAF jets, and observers suggested it was no coincidence, and that CLOUD HOPPER had been deployed to demonstrate Beijing's displeasure. Since it is both politically and culturally unlikely that the hackers would have taken the initiative to meddle in issues reserved to the leadership, the inescapable conclusion is that Beijing has created a powerful global reach for the MSS, and equipped the PLA with the ability to engage in disruption and sabotage on a hitherto unimagined scale.

NOTES

Introduction

1   FBI Office of Public Affairs, 16 November 2012.
2   *China* (Parliamentary Intelligence and Security Committee Report, 13 July 2023).

Chapter I: HONEY BADGER

1   'China: The Forgotten Nuclear Power' by Ronald N. Montaperto (*Foreign Affairs*, July/August 2000).
2   FBI Office of Public Affairs, 21 January 2011.
3   Ibid., 22 November 2019.
4   Ibid., 17 May 2019.
5   Ibid., 24 September 2019.
6   Ibid., 9 July 2019.
7   Ibid., 17 August 2020.
8   Ibid., 20 January 2017.
9   Ibid., 8 October 2020.

Chapter II: Political Influence

1   *Report on the Investigation of Peter Lee* (Senate Committee on the Judiciary, 20 December 2001).
2   House Ethics Committee Report, 23 June 2023.
3   *Executive Summary of the Investigation of the Independent Special Committee Established by the Interim Board of Directors of The Pierre Elliott Trudeau Foundation*, 2 February 2024.
4   MI5 Security Alert, 13 January 2022.
5   Joint address at Thames House by Christopher Wray and Ken McCallum, 5 July 2022.
6   *110 Overseas; China's Overseas Policing Gone Mad* (Safeguard Defenders, 12 September 2022; Patrol and Persuade, 13 December 2022).
7   Ibid.
8   Ibid.

Chapter III: Compromise

1   FBI Criminal Complaint, 4 March 2013.
2   Ibid.
3   Ibid.

Chapter IV: The PLA

1   Department of Justice Office of Public Affairs, 10 February 2020.
2   Ibid.
3   Ibid., 28 January 2020.
4   *Information about the Department of Justice's China Initiative and a Compilation of China-related Prosecutions since 2018*, 29 July 2021.

Chapter V: Military Unit Cover Designator 61398

1   See www.Project2049.net
2   *APT1: Exposing One of China's Cyber Espionage Units* (Mandiant, 2013).
3   Ibid.

Chapter VI: One Thousand Talents.

1   *The China Threat* (www.FBI.gov).
2   House Armed Services Committee, 29 May 2008.
3   FBI Office of Public Affairs, 14 May 2021. See also Defense Counterintelligence and Security Agency's Center for Development of Security Excellence.
4   Department of Justice Office of Public Affairs, 28 January 2020.
5   Ibid., 24 August 2020.
6   Ibid., 7 April 2022.
7   Ibid., 9 September 2022.
8   Ibid., 11 May 2020.
9   Ibid., 14 May 2020.

Chapter VII: Huawei

1   Department of Justice Office of Public Affairs, 29 August 2012.
2   *US National Security Issues Posed by Chinese Telecommunications Companies Huawei and ZTE* (HPSCI, October 2012).
3   Ibid.
4   Ibid.
5   FBI Office of Public Affairs, 28 January 2018.
6   Parliamentary Intelligence Security Committee *Annual Report 2012-2013*.
7   Ibid.
8   Ibid.
9   HCSEC Annual Report, March 2015.
10   Ibid.
11   Ibid.
12   HCSEC Annual Report, September 2020.

Chapter VIII: Signals Intelligence

1   Ted Price retired from the CIA as DDO in 1996, having previously served as Director of Counterintelligence.
2   *Defense News*, 22 March 2024.
3   *Newsweek*, 23 February 2024.
4   *No Place to Hide* by Clayton Swope Center for Strategic Intelligence Studies, 19 January 2024.

Chapter IX: Commercial Espionage

1   *Moscow 1911-33* by Allan Monkhouse (London: Gollancz, 1933).
2   Ibid.
3   Ibid.
4   *The Circumstances Surrounding My Work As A Soviet Agent* by Sam Semyonov.
5   FBI/DoJ Office of Public Affairs, 2 July 2013.
6   Ibid., 17 December 2016
7   Ibid.
8   Ibid.
9   FBI/DoJ Office of Public Affairs, 2 July 2013.
10   Ibid., 26 September 2016.
11   Ibid., 5 September 2014.
12   Ibid.,1 9 September 2018.
13   Ibid., 9 May 2019.
14   Ibid.
15   Ibid., 1 July 2019.
16   Ibid.
17   Ibid., 1 October 2015.
18   Ibid., 8 May 2015.
19   Ibid., 1 September 2020.
20   Ibid., 10 October 2019.
21   Ibid., 18 October 2019.
22   Ibid., 19 October 2016.
23   Ibid., 23 November 2017.
24   Ibid., 29 July 2019.
25   Ibid., 21 October 2017.
26   Ibid., 12 June 2018.
27   Ibid., 22 July 2021.
28   Ibid., 3 January 2023.
29   Ibid., 17 July 2018.
30   Ibid., 28 October 2020.
31   Ibid., 9 May 2022.
32   Ibid., 27 May 2020.
33   Ibid., 30 January 2019.
34   Ibid., 1 June 2023.
35   Ibid., 18 September 2019.
36   Ibid., 17 March 2020.
37   Ibid., 21 January 2022.
38   Ibid., 29 October 2020.
39   Ibid., 18 November 2020.
40   Ibid., 20 April 2021.
41   Ibid., 29 January 2021.
42   Ibid., 2 April 2022.
43   Ibid., 6 May 2022.
44   Ibid., 21 June 2018.
45   Ibid., 28 October 2020.
46   Ibid., 30 October 2018.
47   Ibid., 16 November 2022.
48   Ibid., 25 January 2023.
49   Ibid., 11 February 2020.
50   Ibid., 4 April 2018.
51   Ibid., 18 January 2015.

52 Ibid., 8 February 2012.
53 Ibid., 9 June 2016.
54 Ibid., 12 July 2018.
55 Ibid., 22 March 2016.
56 Ibid., 20 June 2016.
57 Ibid., 2 January 2020.
58 Ibid., 25 April 2012.
59 Ibid., 7 May 2012.
60 Ibid., 23 May 2012.
61 Ibid., 28 June 2012.
62 Ibid., 8 October 2019.
63 Ibid., 18 October 2010.
64 Ibid.,10 August 2014.
65 Ibid., 10 December 2013.
66 Ibid., 12 August 2015.
67 Ibid., 30 May 2013.
68 Ibid., 28 September 2017.
69 Ibid., 2 August 2012.
70 Ibid., 25 March 2013.
71 Ibid., 25 January 2013.
72 Ibid., 17 January 2017.
73 Ibid., 18 December 2012.
74 Ibid., 31 October 2012
75 Ibid., 15 September 2010
76 Ibid., 19 September 2012.
77 Ibid., 29 August 2012.
78 Ibid., 19 September 2012.
79 Ibid., 9 August 2013.
80 Ibid., 7 February 2011.
81 Ibid., 24 September 2009.
82 Ibid., 21 December 2011.
83 Ibid., 9 December 2007.
84 Ibid., 4 April 2011.
85 Ibid., 23 September 2014.
86 Ibid., 9 December 2007.
87 Ibid., 12 August 2011.
88 Ibid., 27 March 2007.
89 Ibid., 25 January 2011.
90 Ibid., 8 December 2010.
91 Ibid., 21 October 2010.
92 Ibid., 29 October 2010.
93 Ibid., 31 December 2008.
94 Ibid., 8 February 2010.
95 Ibid., 23 July 2014.
96 Ibid., 1 September 2015.
97 Ibid., 13 April 2016.
98 Ibid., 2 March 2018.
99 Ibid., 21 July 2015.
100 Ibid., 4 February 2011.

Chapter X: Taiwan

1   Since the ceasefire in Korea in July 1953 the PLA has not been tested in any significant or prolonged conflict, apart from the Sino-Vietnamese War of 1979 in which the PLA performed poorly. Similarly the PLA engaged in numerous border incursions against along the frontier with India, but the troops invariably lost ground, maybe because of the PLA's traditional defensive doctrine of training against a foreign invader.
2   PLANESMAN was the CIA code name for the MSS defector Yu Qiangshen who in 1985 exposed the CIA mole Larry Wu-Tai Chin and the French spy Bernard Boursicot.
3   See *Fires of the Dragon* by David E. Kaplan (New York: Atheneum, 1992).
4   *Taipei Times*, 17 March 2017.
5   Admiral Ho Chin-chiang in BBC News, 17 March 2023.
6   Radio Free Asia, 11 January 2023.
7   *Bangkok Post*, 22 February 2014
8   *Taipei Times*, 11 May 2017.
9   Ibid., 28 April 2016.
10 Ibid., 22 July 2016.
11 *Hong Kong Free Press*, 15 September 2017.
12 *Taipei Times*, 29 April 2011.
13 Intel News, 1 December 2015.
14 *Historical Dictionary of Chinese Intelligence* by I.C. Smith (New York: Rowman & Littlefield, 2021).
15 Ibid.
16 *Taipei Times*, 19 January 2014.
17 *China's Espionage Against Taiwan* by Peter Mattis (Jamestown Foundation, 7 November 2014).
18 *Taipei Times*, 20 March 2014.
19 Radio Free Asia, 11 January 2023.

Chapter XI: The China Threat

1   *China* (Parliamentary Intelligence and Security Committee Report, 13 July 2023).
2   Ibid.
3   Ibid.
4   Ibid.
5   Ibid.
6   Ibid.
7   Ken McCallum, 14 October 2020.
8   *China*.
9   Ibid.
10 Ibid.
11 Ibid.
12 Ibid.
13 Ibid.
14 Ibid.

INDEX